Advancing Race and Ethnicity in Education

Advancing Race and Ethnicity in Education

Edited by

Richard Race
School of Education, University of Roehampton, UK

and

Vini Lander
Faculty of Education, Edge Hill University, UK

First published 2014 by
PALGRAVE MACMILLAN

Palgrave Macmillan in the UK is an imprint of Macmillan Publishers Limited,
registered in England, company number 785998, of Houndmills, Basingstoke,
Hampshire RG21 6XS.

Palgrave Macmillan in the US is a division of St Martin's Press LLC,
175 Fifth Avenue, New York, NY 10010.

Palgrave Macmillan is the global academic imprint of the above companies
and has companies and representatives throughout the world.

Palgrave® and Macmillan® are registered trademarks in the United States,
the United Kingdom, Europe and other countries

ISBN: 978–1–137–27475–5

This book is printed on paper suitable for recycling and made from fully
managed and sustained forest sources. Logging, pulping and manufacturing
processes are expected to conform to the environmental regulations of the
country of origin.

A catalogue record for this book is available from the British Library.

A catalog record for this book is available from the Library of Congress.

Contents

List of Illustrations

Figure

Tables

Foreword

There is an overriding view that 'race' and related issues are currently off the political and policy agenda. Race has been subsumed into 'equalities' and 'social justice'; at its most prominent, race is referred to as 'diversity', although this has become a fairly meaningless term. Following this, the fight against racism has been diverted and undermined. The struggle against racism is a protracted one, and in any given historical moment can appear hopeless and as though nothing has changed for the better. Looking back 20 or more years we can see that this is not entirely the case; however, as we see in this volume, the reference to underachievement, dysconscious racism and the failure of initial teacher education to address and adequately prepare teachers to work in schools in a diverse, multi-ethnic 21st-century Britain, are just some of the dishearteningly ever-recurring themes. In this context, this book therefore makes an important contribution to foregrounding the importance of race and ethnicity. In doing so the collection of topics and themes demonstrates the complexity and diversity of race and ethnicity issues, particularly in relation to education.

As some of the authors have indicated, the socio-economic and political contexts impact on the development and manifestations of racism which in turn require on-going analyses and strategies. During the past 15 or so years, the nature of migration to Britain and Europe has changed, with an increase in skilled workers, asylum seekers, refugees, and Europeans particularly from Eastern and Central Europe, as well as Roma, predictably resulting in moral panics and the concomitant tightening of immigration laws and regulations. These are uncertain times, with many global societies facing social unrest and a challenge to the status quo. In Britain, as well as demographic shifts, we are facing the effects of a financial crisis and subsequent recession which have led to a significant reduction in social benefits; these are clearly exacerbating poverty and deprivation. Such austerity, contributing to pressure on housing and the rise in unemployment, has in turn given rise to right-wing extremists, such as the English Defence League and also the apparently more acceptable face of the United Kingdom Independence Party (UKIP), which erroneously seek to blame immigration and minority ethnic groups for these problems. Their White supremacist ideologies exploit anxieties of uncertainty about the future and crises of place, of status and of identity.

A further but equally great challenge to addressing racism in education is the effect of the creeping impact of neo-liberal policies resulting in a fragmentation of the education system with the introduction of Free Schools and Academies and increasing privatisation of services. Although, in this volume, Free Schools are discussed as a positive good for some minority ethnic communities, I believe there is a wider and more problematic issue here that needs to be recognised. In particular we know that neo-liberal policies are predicated on individual self-interest which promotes individualistic competitiveness and undermines collective approaches and action for the common good. Moreover, with the changes to the organisation and management of schools there are less-obvious forms of accountability and opportunities for parents and communities to raise or direct their concerns.

In such contested and indeterminate times, sociological analysis needs to be particularly robust and coherent in order to inform a united struggle against racist organisations and practices. That is not to say that we will, or should, agree on everything, but race and education debates have tended to be polarised between various theoretical positions, notably: multicultural and anti-racist education; colour and cultural racism; and colour, social class and gender locations and identities. Such polarisations give rise to the notion of hierarchies of oppression, which is counterproductive. It is in this regard that the intersectionalities framework is relevant and useful. Kathy Davies (2008, p. 67) describes intersectionality as 'the interaction of multiple identities and experiences of exclusion and subordination'. Intersectionality is based on the conceptualisation/ construction of the subject as fluid and becoming – and therefore, not fixed or essentialised – and embodying multiple identities, of which 'race'/ethnicity, gender and class are but three. However, at the same time, whilst essentialism has been used to oppress and discriminate against marginalised and disempowered people, there are times when we need to deploy strategic essentialism (Spivak, 1988). The central issue here is the relationship between the individual with her/his multiple identities and positionalities (differences) and structuralism: the forces of domination that serve to fix the subaltern in certain ways.

One of the constant sources of disagreement in race and ethnicity/ education studies is around culture and colour racism, with the argument that one or the other is the more significant or prevalent. The attributes of culture – such as language, religion, dress and ways of being – are all sources of discriminatory practice if these do not fit the dominant culture. This is part of 'race', racialised practice and racist discrimination. However, all people of colour do not necessarily display cultural attributes different from those that are dominant in society. An outstanding question in this regard is whether White people whose 'culture' does not match the dominant culture, such as Chechen Muslims or Roma and Gypsies and Travellers, experience racism.

The concept of culture is nebulous and elusive. It can be, and often is, used in different ways as a mechanism of racial attack and discrimination. Clear examples of this include the rise of Islamophobia and targeting of Muslims in an essentialist homogenising and derogatory way, such as in terms of accusations of patriarchal attitudes towards women and alleged fanaticism. Culture has often been used as a diversion against challenging racism. It has been used as an excuse to lay blame on, for example, the young minority ethnic people themselves who are underachieving in school. As Sally Tomlinson (2008) pointed out, under New Labour, the reification of Indian and Chinese heritage children's academic successes as the 'model minority' was used as a stick to beat other Black and Minority Ethnic young people, implying a deficit in their very being. Or, a further example, Black and Minority Ethnic parents are accused of not attending parent-teacher meetings or are not involved in school activities because of 'cultural issues' – what I have termed 'the cultural interference model' (Crozier and Davies, 2007). In these ways 'Other cultures' are used as scapegoats to obfuscate responsibility by White society for discriminatory practices.

Furthermore. colour often gets transposed as 'culture'. Consider the largest growing demographic group: 'mixed race' young people. These young people are as likely as not to have been born and brought up in a family that displays dominant cultural traits and by the same token this applies to many second and subsequent generation Black and Minority Ethnic people. Nevertheless, they will still experience racism.

On the other hand, the focus on colour raises the issue of which groups can be defined in this sense. Recent migration from Central and Eastern Europe has led to people being castigated by the British press accusing them of, on the one hand, taking 'British' jobs or, on the other, of coming to Britain merely to claim welfare benefits. These people have been described by Sivanandan (2002) as the 'new Black'; they are people who have come to Britain in search of a better future but have subsequently faced poverty and discrimination and overwhelming prejudice. 'White supremacy' is a powerful concept; it is challenging, and it also implicitly and explicitly confronts the dangerous assimilationist policies which underpinned the Community Cohesion agenda. However,

Whiteness, or rather the privileging of Whiteness, is not equally distributed. There are shades of Whiteness; some are either too White or not White enough. Jean Charles de Menezes, the Brazilian young man shot dead by London Metropolitan police officers in July 2005, is a clear example of 'not being White enough', as is the case with the Eastern Europeans, both Roma and non-Roma, who are exploited in factories and fields and trafficked and herded like cattle in trucks and squalid living conditions. We need more work on Whiteness in order to problematise it, to explore the shades of Whiteness (Crozier, 2012). The issue of what Sivanandan (2002) has referred to as *xenoracism* is becoming, and will become, increasingly important with the changing patterns of migration we have experienced since European expansion. In addition Gypsy, Roma and Traveller people are much neglected by research and policy. Repeated Department of Education statistics identify the Gypsy, Roma and Traveller children as the lowest achieving of any ethnic group on normative assessment measures.

As already indicated, social class issues are central to understanding race and combating racism in all of its complexity. 'Social class versus race' is, however, another example of divisiveness and polarisation in the struggle against oppression. This can be seen in the arguments around the construction of White working class boys as, in Gillborn's (2008) terms, 'the new race victims'. White boys from low socio-economic groups are underachieving academically; this is hardly a new revelation but their underachievement has been juxtaposed against the successes of the 'model minority'. We need to avoid an 'either–or' approach, playing off one against the other. There are different manifestations of racism: state, institutional, popular. Of course they are all interrelated and perpetrated through ideological devices. I believe we need to develop analytical tools and practice that can support a process of unity and solidarity against oppressive and discriminatory laws, policies and practice. We know from historical experience that polarisation of oppressed groups leads to 'divide and rule'. There are times when we need to foreground particular oppressions, but we should not confuse this with privileging one over the other. By the same token I am not suggesting that all forms of oppression have the same, equal impact. They all hurt, they are all undermining, but they may result differentially.

Social polarisations and neo-liberal competitiveness referred to above are counterproductive in achieving equitable educational opportunities. Fraser's (2007) analysis of the relationship between 'redistribution and recognition' is useful to explain the implications of this. Fraser highlights the problems of 'redistribution' counter-positioned with 'recognition'/

identity politics, as well as the shift in sociological research in empha-sising 'recognition' alone. She points out how the focus on 'recogni-tion' can actually undermine the struggle for 'redistribution'. Hence, she argues for a 'two-dimensional analysis' which brings these together. At the same time this process involves, on the one hand, the need to develop understanding of the division of labour and the gendered, classed and racialised nature of this division and, on the other, the danger of decon-textualizing identity, potentially leading to essentialist and stereotypical constructions.

Similar to Fraser, Iris Marion Young (1990) has also argued for the combination of a theory of distribution and relational factors attributed to social injustice. She argues that the concept of justice should refer to the institutional conditions necessary for the development and exer-cise of individual capacities and collective communication and coopera-tion. The distributional dimension – the principles by which material resources and power-related resources are distributed in society – is linked to the stratification of society; this in turn is based on social class, racial and gender differences and hierarchies. So, for example, if we look at an individual child and at why she or he is underachieving in school there will no doubt be a range of factors that could account for this; some or all of these factors may be to blame depending on the individual, on specific circumstances and the contexts, and on a combination of race, class, gender and other identities. These must, therefore, be addressed through a structural analysis.

In this foreword I have identified some of the issues facing the advancement of race and education. The contributions to this volume do a much broader job of analysing these and other concerns. They will also serve to generate the debate facing race, ethnicity and education on the policy front and in practice. Such debate is essential in order to galvanize a commitment to foreground policy failures and move towards more equitable opportunities and experiences.

Gill Crozier
Professor of Education
University of Roehampton, UK

References

Crozier, G. (2011) 'The politics of education: challenging racial discrimination and disadvantage in education in the British context', in Vronyides, M. and Kassimeris, C. (eds), *The Politics of Education: Challenging Multiculturalism*, London and New York, Routledge, 17–30.

Crozier, G. and Davies, J. (2007) 'Hard to reach parents or hard to reach schools? a discussion of home-school relations, with particular reference to Bangladeshi and Pakistani parents', *British Educational Research Journal*, 33 (3), 295–313.

Gillborn, D. (2008) *Racism and Education: Coincidence or Conspiracy*, London, Routledge.

Fraser, N. (2007) 'Feminist politics in an age of recognition: a two dimensional approach to gender justice', *Studies in Social Justice*, 1 (1), 23–35.

Sivanandan, A. (2002) *The Death of Multiculturalism*. Available at www.irr.org.uk/2002/april/ak00000.1.html. [Accessed on 26 October 2010]

Spivak, G. (1988) *In Other Worlds: Essays in Cultural Politics*, London, Methuen.

Tomlinson, S. (2008) *Race and Education*, Berks, Open University-McGraw Hill.

Young, I. M. (1990) *Justice and the Politics of Difference*, Princeton, NJ, Princeton University Press.

Notes on Contributors

Alice Bradbury is a member of the Centre for Critical Education Policy Studies at the Institute of Education, University of London. Her research explores the relationship between education policy and inequalities in terms of class, gender and, particularly, 'race'. Alice's work examines the impact of policy in primary and early years education with a focus on issues of social justice, using poststructural theoretical frameworks and Critical Race Theory to examine both individual and structural inequalities in education. Email: A.Bradbury@ioe.ac.uk

Damian Breen is a lecturer in Education at Keele University. As a sociologist, Damian has a longstanding interest in researching issues around 'race' and ethnicity and marginalised communities in the UK. Specifically, his most recent work has been on the state funding of Muslim schools, although he also has interests in education and the labour market, graduate entrepreneurialism and Critical Race Theory. Damian has taught at the universities of Warwick and Leicester, and has held research posts at the University of Sheffield and London Metropolitan University in addition to the National Institute of Adult Continuing Education (NIACE). Email: d.breen@keele.ac.uk

Sandra Craig is an academic learning adviser at the University of Roehampton. As an educationalist she has a background in issues relating to the student experience in schools and in higher education. In her career she has worked at the Department for Education, contributing to education polices, and worked closely with government ministers. Sandra has conducted research for a nationally funded project from the Higher Education Academy (HEA) looking at Black and minority ethic student achievement. Her current research focuses on initiatives that enhance the achievement of Black students in higher education.

Gill Crozier is Professor of Education and Director of the Centre for Educational Research in Equalities, Policy and Pedagogy in the School of Education, University of Roehampton, London. She is a sociologist of education. Her work is underpinned by a deep concern for equalities and social justice and is informed by the analysis of race, class and gender and the ways these social locations and identities intersect and impact on life chances. She has researched and written extensively about these issues. Specific areas of her work include: parents/families and school relationships; issues relating to young people; access to and participation in higher education; education policy; and the socio-cultural influences upon identity formation and learner experiences. Her books include *Parents and Schools: Partners or Protagonists?* (2000), *Activating Participation: Mothers, Fathers and Teachers Working Towards Partnership* (2005, co-edited with Diane Reay); co-author of: *Widening Participation Through Improving Learning* (2009, M. David, ed.); *White Middle Class Identities and Urban Schooling* (2011, with D. Reay and D. James:). Email: g.crozier@roehampton.ac.uk

Kate D' Arcy is Senior Lecturer in Applied Social Sciences at the University of Bedfordshire. Having worked in education for many years, her practice was mainly situated on the margins of education, supporting a variety of vulnerable and often disengaged young people. Between 2003 and 2010, Kate worked as part of a Traveller Education service to improve educational access and achievement for Gypsy, Roma and Traveller pupils and their families. Consequently, her research interests are centred on Gypsy, Roma and Travellers communities' educational positions as well as: race, equality and education; practitioner-led research; and digital technologies and learning. Email: lemmie9@hotmail.com

Geneva Gay is Professor of Education at the University of Washington, Seattle, Washington, where she teaches courses in General Curriculum Theory and Multicultural Education. Her special interests and areas of scholarship and teaching are the intersectionality and effects of race, culture, ethnicity, teaching and learning as they relate to underachieving students of colour (sometimes referred to as academically at-risk racial minorities) in urban schools. Geneva's interests and advocacies are codified as Culturally Responsive Teaching. In addition to teaching and advising graduate students at the University of Washington, she consults frequently with national and international educational agencies on improving the school achievement of minority students. Email: ggay@uw.edu

Julie Hall is Director of Learning and Teaching Enhancement at the University of Roehampton. She was originally a sociologist teaching in the areas of social justice and equality. Julie's research now focuses on pedagogic practices, the HE student experience and professional development. Julie is co-chair of SEDA (Staff and Educational Development Association) and has contributed to nationally funded projects on assessment, gender and pedagogic relations, widening participation and Black and minority ethnic student attainment. Julie was awarded the National Teaching Fellowship by the Higher Education Academy in 2013. Email: Julie.Hall@roehampton.ac.uk

Vini Lander is Head of Research in the Faculty of Education at Edgehill University which has a dedicated focus on inclusion. Her research focuses on preparing teachers to teach in a multi-ethnic society. She was formally Head of primary Education at the University of Chichester with overall responsibility for primary initial teacher education. From 2004 to 2010 Vini was deputy director of Multiverse, a Training and Development Agency (TDA) funded national professional resource network on achievement and diversity which had a significant impact on teacher education provision with respect to equality and diversity. Vini has an international research profile, including being a keynote speaker on equality and diversity in the United Kingdom and Germany, working in Oman and is part of the Diverse Teachers for Diverse Learners national and international network of teacher educators working with colleagues in Norway, Canada and the United Kingdom. E mail: landerv@edgehill.ac.uk

Ada Mau is an educational researcher who recently completed her PhD at the University of Roehampton. Her research interests are: identities and inequalities of 'race', gender and social class within educational contexts, education and social policies; multilingualism; complementary/supplementary education; and equality and diversity in museums/galleries Ada's research is focused on British Chinese pupils' identities and experiences in mainstream and complementary education. She recently worked on the Academies Commission project, which examined the implications of the academies programme for the English school system. Ada is also a member of the Emerging Scholars Forum at the Runnymede Trust. Email: ada.mau@kcl.ac.uk

Stephen May is Professor of Education in Te Puna Wananga, and Deputy Dean of Research in the Faculty of Education, The University of Auckland, New Zealand. He is also an honorary research fellow in the Centre for the Study of Ethnicity and Citizenship, University of Bristol. Stephen has written widely on language rights, language policy, and language education, including bilingual education, indigenous language education and multicultural education. He is the author of eight books and over 80 academic articles and book chapters in these areas. He is a founding editor of the interdisciplinary journal, *Ethnicities*, and associate editor of *Language Policy*. His homepage is http://www.education.auckland.ac.nz/uoa/stephen-may.

Tariq Modood is Professor of Sociology, Politics and Public Policy at the University of Bristol and is also the founding director of the Centre for the Study of Ethnicity and Citizenship. He was awarded an MBE for services to social sciences and ethnic relations in 2001 and elected a member of the Academy of Social Sciences in 2004. Tariq's latest books include: *Multiculturalism: A Civic Idea* (2nd edition, 2013) and *Still Not Easy Being British* (2010); and, as co-editor, *Secularism, Religion and Multicultural Citizenship* (2009), *Global Migration, Ethnicity and Britishness* (2011), *European Multiculturalism's* (2012), *Tolerance, Intolerance and Respect* (2013) and *Religion in a Liberal State* (2013). His website is <tariqmodood.com>

Greg Noble is Professor at the Institute for Culture and Society, University of Western Sydney. Greg's research focuses on: youth, ethnicity and gender; intercultural relations and cosmopolitanism; embodiment and material culture; and multicultural education. His books include: *Disposed to Learn: Ethnicity, Schooling and the Scholarly Habitus* (2013), *On Being Lebanese in Australia* (2010), *Lines in the Sand* (2009), *Bin Laden in the Suburbs* (2004), *Kebabs, Kids, Cops and Crime* (2000) and *Cultures of Schooling* (1990/2012). Email: g.noble@uws.edu.au

Oscar Odena is Reader at the School of Education, University of Glasgow. Prior to this he was the Doctorate in Education Director at the University of Hertfordshire. Previously he held academic and research posts at the universities of Barcelona, Brighton and Queen's University, Belfast, where Oscar completed a study on the potential of music education projects to diminish ethnic tensions. His areas of expertise include qualitative research approaches, inclusion and music education. Oscar is the co-chair of the Research Commission of the International Society for Music Education and serves in the Review College of the Irish Research Council. Email: Oscar.Odena@glasgow.ac.uk

Jo Peat is a senior lecturer in Learning and Teaching in Higher Education and works in the Learning and Teaching Enhancement Unit and the School of Education at the University of Roehampton. Jo was originally a modern linguist, teaching in a variety of schools in south-west London. Her research now focuses on: pedagogic practices, the HE student experience, retention and success in HE and professional development. Jo is a member of the SEDA Executive (The Staff and Educational Development Association) and has contributed to nationally funded projects on Black and minority ethnic students and attainment and gender and pedagogic relations. Email: j.peat@roehampton.ac.uk

Andrew Pilkington is Professor of Sociology at the University of Northampton. He is currently associate director of the Centre for Children and Youth, and director of the Equality and Diversity Research Group. His research has especially focused on issues relating to race and ethnicity, and he has published widely in this area, including *Racial Disadvantage and Ethnic Diversity in Britain* (2003) and, with Shirin Housee and Kevin Hylton, an edited collection: *Race(ing) Forward: Transitions in Theorising Race in Education* (2009). His most recent book is *Institutional Racism in the Academy: A Case Study* (2011). Andrew is also a fellow of the Royal Society of Arts. Furthermore, Professor Pilkington is also a member of the editorial board of Enhancing Learning in the Social Sciences (ELiSS) and Ethnicity and Race in a Changing World. Email: Andrew.Pilkington@northampton.ac.uk

Richard Race is Senior Lecturer in Education in the School of Education at Roehampton University. Since 2009, he has been MA Education Programme Convener, which delivers on-site and off-site in both domestic and international locations. Moreover, Richard is the author of *Multiculturalism and Education* (2011), which was part of a seven-book series, *Contemporary Issues in Education*, which he co-edited for Continuum/Bloomsbury with Simon Pratt-Adams. This book's second edition is forthcoming with Bloomsbury in 2014. Furthermore, Richard is currently working on another monograph, *Integration and Education Policy-Making*, which is part of another book series, *Policy and Practice in the Classroom*, which he is co-editing for Palgrave Macmillan with Alaster Douglas and Barbara Read. Email: r.race@roehampton.ac.uk

Jasmine Rhamie is Senior Lecturer in Teaching and Learning and assistant programme convenor for the Primary PGCE in the School of Education at the University of Roehampton. She is the author of the monograph: *Eagles who Soar: How Black learners find paths to success*. She has a background as a primary teacher in a range of primary schools in the United Kingdom and in secondary and tertiary education in the Caribbean. Jasmine is a member of the British Psychological Society (BPsS), British Educational Research Association and a fellow of the Higher Education Academy. She holds Chartered Scientist status with the BPsS. Jasmine has research interests in 'race' and ethnicity in education, pupils' understandings of identity, BME male trainee teachers' experiences and African Caribbean academic success factors. Email: Jasmine.Rhamie@roehampton.ac.uk

Megan Watkins is Senior Lecturer in the School of Education and a member of the Institute for Culture and Society at the University of Western Sydney. Megan's research interests lie in the cultural analysis of education, exploring the impact of cultural diversity on schooling and the ways in which different cultural practices can engender divergent habits and dispositions to learning. Recent publications include *Discipline and Learn: Bodies, Pedagogy and Writing* (2011), and a forthcoming book with Greg Noble, *Disposed to Learn: Ethnicity, Schooling and the Scholarly Habitus* (Bloomsbury, 2013). Email: m.watkins@uws.edu.au

Introduction

Richard Race

The idea for this collection of research articles on race and ethnicity within education came out of our work as co-conveners of the British Education Research Association's (BERA) Race, Ethnicity and Education Special Interest Group (SIG). Our predecessors (Bhopal and Preston, 2012) also produced an edited collection, so we build on their good work and example by continuing to bring colleagues together who are researching and writing on educational issues concerning race and ethnicity. Between 2010 and 2013, the editors of the present book, through the support of BERA and other BERA SIGs, helped organise and create, and also participated in, a number of events that positively promoted and analysed issues of race and ethnicity within education. These included 'Enhancing teaching and learning: researching issues within race and ethnicity' (Roehampton University, September 2011); 'Children, schools and teachers: do race and ethnicity still matter?' (University of Chichester, October 2011); 'BME Conference 3, The future of education: new environments and new challenges for black and minority ethnic researchers and academics' (Birmingham University, June 2012); and, 'What are fundamental British values' (University of Chichester, October 2012).

The SIG events, including the annual BERA conferences, have provided us with opportunities to listen to colleagues who are researching and addressing ongoing issues that concern race and ethnicity in education. We feel these areas are buoyant in both domestic and international contexts – for example, the launch of the Centre for Research in Race and Education at Birmingham University in February 2013, and the launch of James Banks's (2012) *Encyclopaedia of Diversity in Education* at the Institute of Education in London University in March 2013. However, many areas still need our attention because issues surrounding race and ethnicity are simply too important to pass over. Moreover, there are contemporary issues, some addressed in this collection, which relate to race inequality rather than to wider race equality or to significantly addressing the non-recognition of some specific ethnicities. The book's aim is to bring together an eclectic variety of current research from education and the wider social sciences, and its objective is to provide a theoretical, empirical and methodological informed discussion of a complex number of issues relating to, and advancing, race and ethnicity within education. The challenge for the reader of this edited collection is not only to increase understandings of race and ethnicity issues but to contribute to ongoing debates which the authors of the following chapters have set out (e.g., Wang, 2012; Vincent et al., 2012; Adjei and Gill, 2013).

Race in education

Walters (2012) gives a very good examination of how both race and ethnicity have been applied within education. She examines how the term 'race' was shown to be scientifically incorrect and to have no intellectual credibility. The term was created to highlight difference based on perceived ability and temperament. As Tomlinson (2008: 5) argues, within an education context, race 'concerns the inequitable way in which the children and grandchildren of migrants from former colonial countries, and then later migrants, have been incorporated into what was initially an education system biased by social class, but which also become racially biased, exacerbated by a post-1988 market orientation based on "choice" and competition' (Ball, 2003). The market orientation still has racial consequences for minority communities (Ball, 2013). Moreover, the term 'race' is still being used politically and socially (Ramji, 2009) as a construct and popular term. However, as Walters (2012: 8) argues, the term 'race' needs to be understood as, 'meanings that people attach to colour or physical characteristics as they go about their everyday lives'. These meanings are social and situational and will change over time and place. However, it is important to highlight, as Gillborn (2008: 3) underlines, that race is still a problematic term and, 'it is necessary to make this point very clearly because there are still powerful voices that repeat the falsehood of separate, fixed and deterministic human races'. Gillborn (2008: 22–23) advocates the use and application of Critical Race Theory (CRT). He argues that CRT 'uses stories and other unusual approaches' to challenge the notion that race is relatively fixed, but decisions made politically about race are about *power*. Chapters in this book also apply CRT to education contexts, as it offers a persuasive explanation for persistent social and educational disadvantage concerning underachievement (Craig et al., 2012). Two further conceptual issues which are also applied to race and education within this book are *whiteness* and *intersectionality*. Leonardo (2009: 6–7) sees the need for a critical study of race caused by the central problem of whiteness, which he calls a *critical social theory of race and education*. He argues that, 'race in education is a complex issue that requires a critical framework that testifies to this very complexity'. That criticality and complexity can theoretically be addressed by intersectionality. As Bhopal and Preston (2012) argue: 'Intersectionality becomes a defining feature of "otherness".... Otherness is related to the notion that identity is fragmented, fragile even, yet constantly evolving through multiple engagements and relationships in society.' Intersectionality refers to race and other social concepts such as class, gender and ethnicity, but it is a way of increasing understanding, not only of outsiders or 'strangers', but of how race is entwined with other social concepts and constructions. Understanding the falsehood of race and the potential of CRT, being critical of the practices in racial identification (Taylor, 2013), being critical of the power behind whiteness and also the application of addressing the complexity of intersectionality, are issues addressed in the chapters of this book and elsewhere (e.g. Chakrabarty et al., 2012; Anthias, 2013).

Ethnicity in education

Walters (2012: 9) underlines how 'ethnicity has emerged as a way of talking about social groupings of people that are based on a notion of difference .... Ethnicity can incorporate notions of belonging to a particular group of people, a belief in a shared ancestry, a shared language or ways of dressing, or customs or religion' (Ansell, 2013). Within school education research, one of the more topical issues within education research is achievement concerning different groups or ethnicities within school education. Several of the chapters in this collection focus directly and indirectly on this issue. A common theme is the limitations of statistical studies that examine the underachievement of ethnic minority groups. Walters (2012: 33–34) summarises the issues concerning these limitations under the following headings: poor sampling; a failure to consider socio-economic factors and class; a failure to consider gender; inconsistent data collection and analysis; and the categorisation and homogenisation of ethnic groups. The issue of education underachievement concerning different ethnicities has been challenged with the question of achievement and how different ethnic groups in education have actually improved achievement statistics (Archer and Francis, 2007). The issue of ethnic and racial diversity and attainment, rather than underperformance, interestingly and importantly changes the focus of government and media analysis on these issues. As Gillborn and Rollock (2010: 140–141) persuasively argue: 'First, it is important to note that *every* ethnic group is capable of the highest achievement.... A second point to remember is that the definitions and assumptions that shape official statistics also influence the terms of debate and determine policy priorities.' The authors also highlight that key information relating to intersectionality, that is, gender and social class, is not visible when looking at official statistics relating to education performance and attainment. The intersectionality of ethnicity with race in education also highlights the importance not only of the two concepts being examined in this book, but other educational and sociological ideas, for example, the notion of interculturalism (Cantle, 2012). Williams and Johnson (2010: 2) also demonstrate how difference and diversity are marked out as membership of one of the minority ethnicities is (or is significantly not) accommodated in welfare delivery. It is worth highlighting Walters's (2012: 152–154) assertion that both race and ethnicity do make a difference to our experiences of education, and that race and ethnicity do make a difference to achievement in schools and in all sectors of education. It is perhaps how the reader defines not only race and ethnicity, but how the bigger picture or wider understanding that intersectionality offers will determine the sophistication of the analysis of the race and ethnicity issues being researched. The authors in this collection continue to question and challenge the assumptions of, amongst many issues, the (under)performance in education of certain minority ethnic groupings – assumptions made by earlier and current official statistics which can reinforce ethnic stereotypes. This continued questioning underlines the need to keep advancing empirical examples of the complex and multiple realities of education, but also the accuracy of statistics concerning performance and attainment of ethnic groups within education (e.g. Basit, 2012; Jawitt, 2012; Rhamie, 2012). Hence, the following chapters in this collection aim not only to advance issues concerning race and ethnicity in education, but to increase our understandings of intersectionality and how race and ethnicity research can also assist when examining wider educational issues (Bhopal and Preston, 2012).

Advancing race and ethnicity in education

Alice Bradbury underlines how Critical Race Theory (CRT) can be used as a essential theoretical framework to increase understandings of race and ethnicity issues. She asks us to reflect on how people are discriminated against within education and how these processes can be addressed and changed. Bradbury importantly highlights that CRT can help us examine debates surrounding institutional racism. She develops an applied method of storytelling, focusing on groups of pupils with low attainment as well as highlighting how moderation can control assessment results and thus impact on underachievement. A counter story can be created which underlines racist outcomes. Bradbury applies CRT work within the legal profession on discrimination in the workplace and a focus on 'identity performance' whereby students and teachers are making decisions through 'discursive agency'. Bradbury, through her own education research, focuses on one student, whose Black identity performance and its mis-reading is shown through the student's behaviour as a 'diva' rather than as a 'good learner'. CRT is a theoretical tool that can challenge the social construct of race and examine processes of racism within education.

Damian Breen uses life history interview methodology to highlight the experiences of a head teacher who moved two Muslim schools from independent to voluntary aided status. The author examines processes of change and the sacrifices schools make when accepting state funding, resulting in the partial disenfranchisement and displacement of, in this instance, Muslim communities. Breen applies a typology of institutional isomorphism which underlines how social pressures and expectations, changes to staff, and conditions at work can contextualise the narratives of both schools involved in the research. Carrying out interviews over a two-year period, the author argues for more research to be carried out *on* and *inside* (the author's italics) Muslim schools. Breen also underlines a fascinating case study concerning the head teacher, who was working within communities and schools rather than being a head teacher at one institution. The head teacher's skills at leading are prominent in the development of *School B*, but the author makes clear that the school could only survive with state funding. Increased parental interest without having to pay tuition fees is an important factor highlighted within *School A*, an application of mimetic isomorphism. Financial sustainability was the objective for both schools, but Breen underlines how complex the narratives actually are when focusing on these processes of change, and how important an experienced Muslim female head teacher was when instigating these changes.

Kate D'Arcy's focus is to examine how Travellers experience education and specifically schooling, and how their experiences remain outside the remit of education policy. Like Bradbury, D'Arcy applies CRT to examine issues of inequality, in her case related to Travellers' inequality. If, as the author suggests from evidence, there are approximately 250,000 Travellers in England and Wales (Willers, 2012), then this is an issue for both the state and Traveller communities. The issue of recognition is raised concerning which Traveller communities are recognised and which are not. D'Arcy applies CRT to Travellers' stories of education to create counter-stories against the dominant discourse which challenges the notion that Travellers are not interested in mainstream education. Significantly, the author suggests that this dominant discourse reveals the overt and covert racism which Traveller communities continue to experience.

Geneva Gay examines the complexity of race and ethnicity narratives within the United States. For Gay, these narratives revolve around the ethnic and racial demography of students and teachers and how ethnicity and race are both conceived and perceived. The former narrative highlights the problem, and the latter offers greater understanding and the road to potential solutions. With changing demographic patterns and regional distributions within the United States, Gay underlines evidence that minority populations are growing faster than the majority White population. The Latino student population is growing in all areas of the country. The author highlights that Asian Americans and European Americans are still outperforming African Americans in scholastic achievement tests. This term refers to SAT tests for high scholars to assess their preparedness for college. It if formally called the SAT Reasoning Test. Gay highlights the notion of 're-segregation', with disparities concerning value orientations, behavioural styles and referential frameworks that result from these differences have profound effects on the dynamics and outcomes of teaching and learning. Gay also highlights a small increase concerning the diversity of the teaching workforce in the United States, although the education profession still remains overwhelmingly European American. A worrying trend, as the author underlines, is the fall in the proportion of African American teachers from 12 per cent of the overall education workforce in 1980 to 7 per cent in 2011. The author argues that racism, prejudice, racial stereotyping and discrimination are visible in all aspects of American society, with some teachers simply ignoring issues of race and ethnicity. Gay highlights research evidence demonstrating teacher colour-blindness, with teachers bringing little cross-cultural knowledge into the classroom.

Moreover, Gay also highlights teaching and learning programmes which are addressing race and ethnicity issues, of which the author highlights five of these interventions. It is not, as Gay concludes, that the majority of students of colour are taught by White, European American teachers, rather it is the response (or lack of it) by these teachers to issues of race and ethnicity. Education curricula that focus on cultural diversity increase knowledge and confidence, which can help deal more coherently with race and ethnicity issues.

Julie Hall, Jo Peat and Sandra Craig examine positive factors and experiences raised by Black and minority ethnic (BME) students when studying in a post-1992 English University. Hall and colleagues use 'Appreciative Inquiry' as their methodology to focus on positive aspirations and outcomes in relation to teaching, learning and assessment processes. The project, managed by a successful Black, mature female undergraduate student, who has moved on to her doctorate, acknowledged the student as a co-producer of knowledge. Using focus groups, interviews and surveys as research tools, Hall and colleagues developed four overarching themes in their findings. Firstly, student care equates to visible and motivated staff, but care is also based around encouragement. Secondly, passion and conviction are important for students when considering teaching styles. The extras that staff were prepared to do for their students were also significant. Thirdly, information on how to improve is also crucial for students, as is the availability of staff to provide this help and encouragement. Fourthly, having the opportunity to be reflective and using personal experiences on the undergraduate courses as an evidence base was raised by the authors as a practical benefit for students to increase understanding of their own histories and backgrounds. Interestingly, some students wanted to construct and develop an identity within the university rather than around their course. Hall and colleagues conclude that it is important that universities keep reflecting upon how they interact and communicate with their students to make them feel more valued.

Vini Lander looks at where race-equality issues reside within initial teacher training. By examining the theoretical framework of *whiteness*, Lander highlights the reluctance of educators to understand their own positions as racialised beings, whereby the 'Other' is marginalised to maintain an unspoken White power structure. A development of racial literacy to counter racism is an early suggestion by Lander, and the classroom is the arena in which race equality needs to be developed for the benefit of all students. Lander provides a context for teacher education, examining past and present policy documents, to show how little has actually changed from the multicultural education initiatives in England of the 1980s. She also shows a dual absence in, first, how the Stephen Lawrence murder precipitated a public and media response relating to race equality and social justice in the 2000s, but little more; a second absence is that of references to ethnic diversity in teacher training, despite the important work of Multiverse. In fact, the author talks about the assimilationist approach when discussing the 2012 Teachers' Standards, which seem to overlook the identity of ethnic minority students. The notion of whiteness as a central organising concept is then analysed. Through a 'hegemonic European-identified racialised Whiteness', a norm has been established, but whiteness allows a refocus from the 'Other' to those who exercise power through structural or institutional racism. The operations of privilege and domination have to be acknowledged, with colour-blind practice being acknowledged and addressed. From the American literature, practitioners deflecting these issues is perceived as a means of protecting whiteness. The author also highlights colour blindness through her own research of secondary trainee teachers, with the 'politically correct shield' being used as a metaphor highlighting the whiteness norm applied earlier in the chapter. Lander highlights the difficulties some course tutors had with ethnic diversity issues in professional practice. One way forward, she argues, is addressing these issues within teams, thereby having an increased focus on race equality.

Stephen May examines the 'paradigm wars' to see what implications 'singular' paradigm analysis has on race, ethnicity and education. Taking the anti-racism/multiculturalism paradigm wars of the 1980s as an evidence base, May underlines the bifurcation and marginalisation of both ideas. Highlighting the emergence of Critical Race Theory as the new education paradigm to contest racism, debates in the United States and Europe concern whether race or ethnicity studies are more beneficial as an analytical tool in research. May proposes Critical Multiculturalism as a possible alternative, which combines identity formation and the multiplicity of racisms. He underlines the key failure of all paradigms to examine the role of language in racism and discrimination. Debates concerning bilingual education for Latinos are examined in the United States and the wider English-only movement, which has its origins in the early 1980s. Care, caution and the complexity of passing constitutional amendments have kept this policy and movement at bay, although the interest to have US English as a national language continues. Thirty states (up until 2010) have adopted English as their state language, and this has implications for bilingualism and multicultural education in the United States. A 'discourse of disinformation' has been created with the fear of second-class citizenship for non-English speakers. Political and public opinion have moved against minority communities with No Child Left Behind (2001) revoking legislation from the 1960s concerning bilingual education. This has changed American education, with English now being seen as advantageous in instruction and assessment. May continues by drawing an interesting comparison of the Americanisation movements of the nineteenth century with anti-immigration groups of today (described in the literature as Hispanophobia) in the light of demographic expansion of the Latino population in the United States. However, the complexity of the contemporary English-only movement can be witnessed in its appeal to Latinos, who politically vote for it as 'good aliens', which encompasses success stories of immigrants within the 'American dream'. May shows how the English-only movement works by inverting the immigration/language axis by focusing on language rather than immigration, which he describes as 'a convenient proxy for a more overtly racialized politics'. The 'threat' of Spanish becomes the new, or another, racism. May then focuses on key exemplars within political theory, highlighting 'linguistic diversity as an obstacle to equality and participation'. He is critical of evidence from the literature which shows stereotypical points between Latino and White American communities in a California school with a preferred solution of offering English instruction for all, which is advocated as a 'cosmopolitan alternative'. The teaching of English is endorsed by several other authors who exhibit the same kinds of highly racialised paternalism, which is similar to that of the English-only movement. May, in his conclusions, calls for a renunciation of singularities, not only in education research concerning languages, but also in continued analysis and examination of subject boundaries.

Ada Mau explores the evolving and emergent identity of British Chinese young people. Drawing on her successful doctoral research and the previous research projects she has been involved in, the author highlights the education performance and perceptions of British Chinese communities. This involves the visibility and invisibility of the British Chinese, the latter condition caused by racism and discrimination. The 'hidden' problems experienced in education are underlined, but emerging identities within second- and third-generation (terms later questioned in the chapter) British Chinese alongside levels of integration, racialisation and racism are examined. Mau describes her sample for data collection and then explores whether the British Chinese youth have successfully integrated into the mainstream. Mau argues that respondents in her research are highly integrated through extra-curriculum activities involving sport and music. This challenges the assumption made in previous research that British Chinese children go home to work in the family business after school which, through Mau's empirical evidence, is shown not now to be the norm. Perceptions of Chinese culture and responses within the education system are critically questioned. Young British Chinese people have friendship groups which are drawn from different races. As the author implies, the stereotype of a homogenous 'Chinese' approach, with families keeping themselves to themselves, is challenged. Mau also addresses the cultural issue of language, highlighting that speaking English did not prevent racial abuse based on appearance. Her sample felt comfortable with living in the United Kingdom as well as with their Chinese heritage, which leads the author to analysis of the complexity of British/Chinese identities. Mau also underlines how individuals in her sample were reminded of their Otherness and asked to perform Chineseness in school, which highlights the negative effects of subtle marginalisation. The need for professional practitioners to recognise issues of racialistion and cultural exoticisation is underlined. Mau concludes that despite apparent success at integrating into school life, British Chinese pupils continue to achieve educationally but encounter overt racism and covert marginalisation.

Tariq Modood analyses how more than one form of multiculturalism can relate to integration in different ways. For Modood, 'discourses of integration and multiculturalism are exercises in conceptualising post-immigration difference and as such operate at three distinct levels: as an (implicit) sociology; as a political response; and as a vision of what is the whole in which difference is to be integrated. For the author, integration is based on opportunities to participate which are context-specific and need to be secured through policy and law. Modood, acknowledging individual opportunities, is interested in how these are viewed through groups and society. A sense of belonging is dependent upon how people are perceived and treated, and upon a general social understanding shaped by political ideas and policy. Within this macro-symbolic level, Modood develops four models of integration: assimilation; individualist integration; multiculturalism; and cosmopolitanism. Assimilation is seen by the author as a one-way process of change which theoretically eliminates difference which is dangerous and needs to be critically inspected. Individualist integration is seen as two-way, by which citizens have to engage with institutions. Multiculturalism is when processes of integration are seen as two-way, which involves individuals and groups with issues working differently for both parties. Each group is different and unique, with the cornerstone of multiculturalism being equality.

Cosmopolitanism accepts the concept of difference while being critical of dissolving the concept of groups. Groups should be recognised within multiculturalism, but recognised differently within cosmopolitanism, which acknowledges processes of globalisation and 'super-diversity'. Modood highlights the 'Big Society' idea of free schools which are community-based, non-state schools. In conclusion, Modood recognises that integration and multiculturalism are continuous exercises in conceptualising difference and which operate on sociological levels and political responses.

Greg Noble and Megan Watkins examine a series of projects reassessing multicultural education to ensure that school practice can underline and develop cultural inclusion and social justice. Within an Australian context, a range of multicultural education programmes are in competition with each other for limited resources. A benign form of multiculturalism of reduced identity politics was a result. Noble and Watkins argue that more effective multicultural education has to consider 'official' multicultural discourse with popular understandings of culture, ethnicity and multiculturalism. The authors apply their own New South Wales contexts and the complexity of different angles on forms of diversity in schools. The important factor for the authors is how teachers see and respond to diversity. Drawing on two of their own research projects, one important finding was how teachers self-identified themselves, which displayed the complexity of cultural diversity in Australia, but this did not extend to how the teachers saw their students. The authors highlight that teachers need the space to reflect on the difficult concept of cultural difference. Understanding needs to move far beyond cultural awareness through 'multicultural days' and professional schemas of difference. Diverse schooled identities are narrow, and schools produce and reproduce ethicised categories they service. Noble and Watkins highlight students with 'Pasifika' backgrounds – who are categorised as a group with pre-determined performance – and the approach to teaching the group should receive. This highlights a bureaucratic essentialism of multiculturalism. Within education policy, ethnicity is seen as an unproblematic category based on boundaries around race and culture. So what is the new contemporary multiculturalism project for Australia? The authors call for a 'reflexive civility', which refers to a cultural engagement that moves beyond respect to increase understandings of living in a multicultural society. This has to be achieved through teacher training and the professional development of teachers.

Oscar Odena examines how Computer Assisted Qualitative Data Analysis (CAQDAS) is used to substantiate researchers' claims in the wider contexts of race and ethnicity. By paraphrasing reflective authors, Odena develops this idea of reflection-in-analysis and reflection-on-analysis when developing theoretical frameworks and data analysis. The use of Information and Computer Technologies (ICTs), and in particular CAQDAS, has changed the way links are made within research data and how emerging ideas are mapped. Odena challenges us to focus on the use of ICTs within research writing and publication. By examining his own ethnic-inclusion research on bringing the main communities together in Northern Ireland with musical activities, semi-structured interviews were digitally recorded, transcribed and then analysed using NVivo software. This enabled the grouping of quotations under categories and subcategories. One of the most important findings of the project was the acknowledgement of integrating educational settings which appeared to be influenced by socio-economic environment. It was a different story for children in economically deprived areas at the time of data collection with segregation of Protestant and Catholic communities. Cross-community music projects remain one of many ways for attempting to overcome segregation. The author also highlights negative stereotypes linked with music traditions of both communities. Odena reiterates, in conclusion, that researchers should be encouraged to disclose the amount of data collected and steps taken when analysing research data.

Andrew Pilkington, drawing on the MacPherson's Report into the death of Stephen Lawrence in 1999 and the consequent acknowledgement of Institutional Racism characterising organisations, examines higher education and how this sector responded to the charge of Institutional Racism. Pilkington highlights research that showed how British Black and minority ethnic (BME) staff and students were both at a disadvantage. The author examines how race-equality policies of widening participation and human resources within higher education have been shaped by the state, both policies being colour blind. By comparing post-1999 Higher Education Funding Coucil for England (HEFCE) funding letters, race and ethnicity are not mentioned as issues, whereas equal opportunities are. Pilkington also suggests that state policy is focused on class not colour, with no focus on BME. The author also presents evidence that equal opportunities policies are perceived sceptically by staff in higher education, with deficiencies in monitoring and target setting, the implication being that these policies need to be taken more seriously when reflecting on race. Pilkington discusses the Race Relations Amendment Act (RRAA) of 2000 by which all public authorities were to focus on racial equality, eliminate racial discrimination, promote good race relations and facilitate equal opportunities.

Highlighting the specific duties which were set out for higher education institutions (HEIs), Pilkington underlines that these duties were colour blind. Furthermore, the Equality Challenge Unit found in 2002 that 45 HEIs had major work to do, or did not align themselves with RRAA requirements. Reassessment of these requirements took place in 2003 and 2004, but the author underlines research carried out in 1999 that found only a handful of universities had race-equality policies in place. The author uses a university race-equality programme as an evidence base in the 1990s, a programme which had been quickly forgotten and had received the lowest grade from the Equality Challenge Unit in 2002. Two university equality and diversity officers gave race a higher profile within higher education from 2004, but the consequent disappearance of these positions entailed a reversal of the progress made. Pilkington highlights 'the sheer weight of Whiteness' in his research case study.

Richard Race analyses the ideas of the 'multicultural dilemma' (Williams, 2013) and the 'integrationist consensus' (Katwala, 2013) and the consequences these notions have for advancing race and ethnicity in education. The main point of the chapter is that continuing debates on multiculturalism and integration need to focus on more than immigration to address how research findings, applied to policy and professional practice, can increase understanding of issues that concern education relating to race and ethnicity. The multicultural dilemma is introduced alongside the notion of multicultural backlash (Vertovec and Wessendoff, 2010) which suggests that multiculturalism is far from dead – which runs counter to the speeches made by David Cameron and Angela Merkel in 2010 and 2011. Race suggests through the literature that multiculturalism is a starting point when examining race relations in the United Kingdom and how the state's education policy has controlled how education performance has shaped ideal social constructions of ethnic majority and minority communities. Integration is also being used by the coalition government from 2010, as it was being used by the previous Labour governments, to shape social and education policy debate. The idea of integrationist consensus is used by Katwala (2013) to show how people from all ethnicities are using their values, for example. obeying the law, speaking English and contributing positively to society, and applying these values educationally within the policy conditions set down by the state. As the author has argued elsewhere (Race, 2011), integration is not only about the conditional relationship set down by the state through policy, it is how the individual and community responds to these conditions. When examining citizenship and the citizenship curriculum, Race highlights a positive promotion of citizenship ideas in primary and secondary schools which, in theory, promotes an integrationist consensus. Both of the main ideas of the chapter are applied to race and ethnicity in education with issues such as achievement and home education being analysed. Race concludes by stating that both integrationist and multicultural ideas are useful when increasing understanding of race and ethnicity issueswhen reflecting on not only which subjects should be taught in schools and universities but on how much training should be provided for all professional practitioners to encourage a more equitable focus on diversity training.

Jasmine Rhamie examines the challenges Black parents face when finding ways to support their children's educational achievement. By using whiteness studies and CRT as theoretical frameworks, Rhamie underlines the need to examine structural racisms and their role in the creation of education policy to further establish White supremacy and Black subordination. Within these contexts, the aim of the chapter is to critically examine current coalition government education policy. The author argues that in an age of austerity, parental choice is being pursued at the cost of inclusive values, the ability to make a choice being dictated by class and colour. Drawing on the Education Act of 2011 in England, schools having greater powers to exclude children has significant consequences on Black communities. Rhamie, like Pilkington, draws on post-MacPherson Report evidence from OFSTED on raising the attainment of children from Black and other ethnic minority groups. She also highlights that whilst racism is being reported in schools, evidence shows that teachers are not prepared to deal with these issues. The move away from specific policy on race and ethnicity is worrying for the author, and she questions current policy of free schools and academies whose admissions criteria have the potential to include or exclude any children they wish without being called to account. The author draws on her own research and the notion of resilience which needs to be applied to protect children from the risks associated with institutional racism within education, the major protective factor being support received within the home. In conclusion, Rhamie highlights how recent education policy is failing to meet the racial and ethnic needs and requirements of Black children. The social construction of Black boys in particular is highlighted and needs to be continually challenged for its implications for Black communities in schools. Rhamie's belief is that Black parents need to be more aware and vigilant in order to keep children's self-esteem and confidence intact, and that current government education policy needs to be challenged to provide greater equity for Black and minority ethnic children.

References

Adjei, P.B., Gill, J.K. (2013) 'What has Barack Obama's election victory got to do with race? A closer look at the post-racial rhetoric and its implication for antiracism education', *Race, Ethnicity and Education*, 16 (1), 134–153.

Ansell, A.E. (2013) *Race and Ethnicity: The Key Concepts*, Abingdon, Routledge.

Anthias, F. (2013) 'Intersectional what? Social divisions, intersectionality and levels of analysis', *Ethnicities*, 13 (1), 3–19.

Archer, L., Francis, B. (2007) *Understanding Minority Ethnic Achievement in Schools: Race, Gender, Class and 'Success'*, London, RoutledgeFalmer.

Ball, S. (2003) *Class Strategies and the Education Market: The Middle Classes and Social Advantage*, London, RoutledgeFalmer.

Ball, S. (2013) (2nd ed.) *The Education Debate*, Bristol, Policy Press.

Banks, J. (ed.) (2012) *Encyclopedia of Diversity in Education*, Thousand Oaks, Sage.

Basit, T.N. (2012) 'But that's just the stereotype: gender and ethnicity in transition to adulthood', *Race, Ethnicity and Education*, 15 (3), 405–423.

Bhopal, K., Preston, J. (eds) (2012) 'Introduction. Intersectionality and "race" in education: theorising difference', in Bhopal, K., Preston, J. (eds), *Intersectionality and 'Race' in Education*, Abingdon, Routledge, 1–10.

Cantle, T. (2012) *Interculturalism*, Houndsmills, Palgrave Macmillan.

Chakrabarty, N., Roberts, L., Preston, J. (2012) 'Critical race theory in England', *Race, Ethnicity and Education*, 15 (1), 1–3.

Craig, G., Atkin, K, Chatoo, S., Flynn, R. (eds) (2012) *Understanding 'Race' and Ethnicity: Theory, History, Policy, Practice*, Bristol, Policy Press.

Gillborn, D. (2008) *Racism and Education: Coincidence or Conspiracy?* London, Routledge.

Gillborn, D., Rollock, N. (2010) 'Education', in Bloch, A., Solomos, J (eds), *Race and Ethnicity in the 21st Century*, Houndsmills, Palgrave Macmillan, 138–165.

Jawitt, J. (2012) 'Race and assessment practice in South Africa: understanding black academic experience', *Race, Ethnicity and Education*, 15 (4), 545–559.

Katwala, S. (2013) *The Integration Consensus. 1993–2013: How Britain changed since Stephen Lawrence*, London, British Future.

Leonardo, Z. (2009) *Race, Whiteness, and Education*, London, Routledge.

Race, R. (2011) *Multiculturalism and Education*, London, Continuum.

Ramji, H. (2009) *Researching Race. Theory, Methods and Analysis*, Maidenhead, McGraw-Hill Education.

Rhamie, J. (2012) 'Achievement and underachievement: the experiences of African Caribbeans', *Race, Ethnicity and Education*, 15 (3) 405–423.

Taylor, P.C. (2013) *Race: A Philosophical Introduction*, Cambridge, Polity Press.

Tomlinson, S. (2008) *Race and Education*, Maidenhead, McGraw-Hill Education.

Vertovec, S., Wessendorf, S. (2010) 'Introduction: assessing the backlash against multiculturalism', in Vertovec, S., Wessendorf, S. (eds), The Multiculturalism Backlash. European discourses, policies and practices, New York, Routledge, 1–31.

Vincent, C., Rollock, N., Ball, S., Gillborn, D. (2012) 'Intersectional work and precarious positionings: black middle-class parents and their encounters with schools in England', *International Studies of Sociology of Education*, 22 (3), 259–276.

Walters, S. (2012) *Ethnicity, Race and Education: An Introduction*, London, Continuum.

Wang, L. (2012) 'Social exclusion and education inequality: towards an integrated, analytical framework for the urban-rural divide in China, *British Journal of Sociology of Education*, 35 (2), 409–430.

Willers, M. (2012) Tackling inequalities suffered by Gypsies and Travellers, *Travellers Advice Team (TAT) news*, Newsletter Spring 2012, Traveller Advice Team part of Community Law Partnership.

Williams, C., Johnson, M.R.D. (2010) *Race and Ethnicity in a Welfare Society*, Maidenhead, McGraw Hill Education.

Williams, M.H. (2013) 'Introduction: the multicultural dilemma', in Williams, M.H. (ed.), *The Multicultural Dilemma*, Abingdon, Routledge, 1–11.

1

Identity Performance and Race: The Use of Critical Race Theory in Understanding Institutional Racism and Discrimination in Schools

Alice Bradbury

Introduction

In this chapter, I explain two ways in which Critical Race Theory (CRT) offers useful contributions to the field of race and education and, more specifically, to discussions of institutional racism and classroom discrimination. I begin with some background on CRT and its use in education, both in the United States and increasingly, in the United Kingdom. I then set out the first illustration of the use of CRT in education, which focuses on the use of storytelling or chronicles in CRT scholarship and their use in examining the operation of processes of institutional racism at a national, local or school level. The second illustration concerns the use of theories of 'identity performance' from the work of CRT legal scholars Devon Carbado and Gulati to interrogate practices of discrimination at the micro-level of the classroom. By no means do I mean to suggest that these are the only productive uses of CRT, only that these appear to be two examples of the use of the theoretical and methodological tools offered by CRT.

A wider aim here is to make a claim as to the use of theoretical tools, both those offered by CRT and other theoretical frameworks, in studies of race and education. The issue of discrimination in schools based on race has long been a concern for those working in the sociology of education, and a range of research – dating back decades – in domestic and international contexts, has focused on the ways in which teachers' attitudes, education policy and classroom practices have worked to create and maintain disparities in educational attainment at all levels of the education system (see, for example, Coard, 1971; Wright, 1992;

Gillborn, 1995; Connolly, 1998). As a researcher, my concern has been to contribute to the increased understandings of this picture, by considering practices in primary and early years education which effectively discriminate on the grounds of race (and other axes of identity, which are not my concern here; see for example, Bradbury, 2011, 2013). This research aims to add to a complex picture of how race works in schools which, although long-established, seems to evolve and remake itself as the political and social picture changes over time. My wider claim in this chapter is that in order to make sense of the various forms of data provided by research, in all their complexity and yet relative familiarity (at least in terms of the overall effects of racism), we need the insights offered by critical theoretical perspectives, such as Critical Race Theory. These perspectives provide ways of thinking about how children and young people are discriminated against in schools and, in turn, provide ways to think about how this can be challenged and resisted.

Critical Race Theory

Critical Race Theory (CRT) is a broad range of ideas concerning race inequality, a theory which originated in legal scholarship in the United States. Increasingly, CRT is used in many social-science disciplines, including education, both in the United Kingdom and worldwide (Ladson-Billings and Tate, 1995; Ladson-Billings, 2004; Dixson and Rousseau, 2006; Gillborn, 2006a, 2006b). CRT emerged as response to Critical Legal Studies (CLS), a legal movement which rejected traditional legal scholarship 'in favor of a form of law that spoke to the specificity of individuals and groups in social and cultural contexts' (Ladson-Billings, 2004, p. 52). Although CLS focused on the impact of legal discourses relating to inequalities, there was a relative neglect of race and racism, so CRT provided an alternative theorisation which centred on race and its role in society (Crenshaw et al., 1995). In this section I consider the basic tenets of CRT and how these have been applied to the field of education.

A fundamental tenet of CRT is a description of racism as endemic, 'deeply ingrained legally, culturally, and even psychologically' (Tate, 1997, p. 234). Within CRT, racism is not considered as limited to isolated episodes of individual prejudice or violence, but as 'normal, not aberrant' (Delgado, 1995) in every-day life. There is a focus on lived experience, the micro-practices of discrimination and disadvantage that people from minoritised groups experience on a daily basis, and their cumulative effects. These are what Delgado (1995) calls 'business as usual' forms of racism, established, unseen and unchallenged.

The language of CRT reflects this focus on the operation of power in relation to race; the term 'White supremacy' is used not in relation to extremist groups but as a description of 'the operation of forces that saturate the everyday mundane actions and policies that shape the world in the interests of white people' (Gillborn, 2008, p. 35). Research and scholarship thus focuses on the ways in which institutions and practices work to maintain and reproduce White supremacy in all fields of life. This links to a concurrent focus on White privilege – the benefits of Whiteness in all aspects of everyday existence – which McIntosh describes as an 'invisible package of unearned interests' (McIntosh, 1992).

Within CRT, 'race' is consider to be a social construct: there is no such thing 'ontologically prior to its production and instantiation in discourses' (Carbado, 2002, p. 181). 'Race' is a construct applied to human bodies, and acted upon as such. This conception of race rejects the idea of fundamental physical differences, but accepts the importance of visual racial markers in affecting individuals' lived experiences. Some literature influenced by CRT reflects on the flexibility of racial terms over time and in different contexts (Allen, 2009; Gillborn, 2010; Rampersand, 2011); and links can be made to work outside CRT focused on the political motives of changing racial categories and hierarchies in terms of the continuation of White dominance (such as Ignatiev, 1995; Nayak, 2009).

As I demonstrate further in my first illustration, some CRT literature also employs non-conventional formats, such as the use of chronicles and story-telling, in order to examine the 'myths, presuppositions, and received wisdoms that make up the common culture about race' (Delgado, 1995, p. 14) through a focus on experience (see, for example, Bell, 1992; Ladson-Billings, 2006; Gillborn, 2008). The aim is to provide a counter to supposedly-scientific notions of neutrality within research, to 'add necessary contextual contours to the seeming "objectivity" of positivist perspectives' (Ladson-Billings, 2004, p. 53).

In the United Kingdom, the main proponent of the use of CRT in education has been Gillborn (2008), who uses a CRT framework to explore the issue of institutional racism in the United Kingdom's school system (see also Gillborn, 2006c). This work follows a body of literature in the United States from a wide range of CRT scholars focused on education (Tate, 1997; Ladson-Billings, 2004; Dixson and Rousseau, 2006; Taylor et al., 2009), and forms part of a wider adoption of CRT within the field of education worldwide (Ladson-Billings, 2004; Gillborn and Youdell, 2009). Gillborn's work, and specifically his use of counterstories, is central to my first illustration of the use of CRT in education.

Using stories to examine institutional racism

Over the last two decades, discussions of racism in schools have moved away from the idea of individual acts of racism – what Gillborn (2002) calls the 'rotten apple' notion of racism – to more nuanced analyses of practices and systems which unintentionally discriminated against children and young people from minoritised[1] communities. This has been aided by the definition of 'institutional racism' provided for the Macpherson Inquiry into the police investigation of the death of the Black teenager Stephen Lawrence – a definition which has been used widely by academics and commentators since:

> [T]he collective failure of an organisation to provide an appropriate and professional service to people because of their colour, culture or ethnic origin. It can be seen or detected in processes, attitudes and behaviour which amount to discrimination through unwitting prejudice, ignorance, thoughtlessness and racist stereotyping which disadvantage minority ethnic people. (Macpherson et al., 1999, p. 28)

This shift in focus towards unwitting acts which nonetheless result in outcomes which disadvantage minoritised communities has affected research into discrimination in schools, and the analysis of this research. For a time at least, this definition reinvigorated interest in this issue (Blair et al., 1999; Gillborn, 2006b). However, attempting to research unintentional actions and their outcomes brings with it problems of interpretation, as was seen in methodological debates of the 1990s (Connolly and Troyna, 1998; Foster, 1990, 1991; Gillborn, 1990; Wright, 1990). There has also been resistance to accusations of institutional racism in the education system and, since the late 2000s, there has been a shift in public and political concern away from the issue of race in education, with an alternative focus on the 'White working class' as the victims of the education system (Sveinsson, 2009; Gillborn, 2011; Reay, 2009). The success of some groups of minoritised students from the 'model minority' Indian and Chinese communities has also been used simplistically to argue that there is no institutional racism in education (an issue discussed in more detail below). Yet, disparities in attainment have continued from early years to higher education (DfE, 2010a, 2010b; DfE, 2012), and contemporary research continues to suggest that discriminatory practices occur in complex ways which conform with with Macpherson's definition of institutional racism (Bradbury, 2011, 2013).

The continued resistance against claims of institutional racism is based on both the misreading of the term as indicating specific acts of crude racist behaviour and, simultaneously, a reluctance of individuals to acknowledge how their 'unwitting' acts might combine to create systemic processes which discriminate. This is where, I would argue, an approach taken by CRT scholars can help in illuminating our thinking about intentionality in discussions of institutional racism. The concept of institutional racism has expanded the popular conception of how racism can operate even when 'not in the minds of those involved' (Gillborn and Youdell, 2000). CRT scholars take this further by asking educators to consider how racism can operate within the 'normal workings' of the education system – in everyday practices and systems in schools. One way to explore this is through the use of counter-stories to illustrate how racist outcomes can result from apparently innocuous practices or reforms. Gillborn (2006c) used a story about an imaginary, explicitly racist society to consider changes made to the assessment of children in the first year of school. In this story, a 'despised group' are doing well in a test, and so the government changes the test so that they no longer have a higher level of attainment.

> In my story, the despised group is excelling at a test that every pupil must take. ... But if the dominant group cannot restrict entry to the test, it seems that only one course of action remains; change the test. The test must be redesigned so that the despised group no longer succeed.
> Simple.
> But, of course, such a crass and obviously racist set of events could never occur in the real world. There would be an outcry. Wouldn't there? (Gillborn, 2006c, pp. 324–326)

Gillborn used this story – which I have truncated here – to discuss the results from the Foundation Stage Profile, which was an assessment used in Reception (children aged 4–5) in England from 2003. These results showed a pattern of attainment by an ethnic group that was similar to that at older key stages, including lower attainment by Black ethnic groups (to use the Department of Children Schools and Families (DCSF's) terminology). However, some of the data collected through local systems of assessment *before* 2003 indicated that Black pupils had high levels of attainment at age five. But, just like in the imaginary racist society Gillborn describes, there was no outcry about the new pattern of results. This does not suggest, he argues, that the change was done deliberately, but it is significant that the results are the same:

But there is no evidence of conscious intent: there is no conspiracy. It is more frightening than that. Rather than being generated by a deliberate strategy (one that is readily open to exposure and reversal) these changes appear to have resulted from the *normal* workings of the education system – a system that places race equality at the very margins of debate and takes no action when Black students are judged to be failing. (Gillborn, 2006c, p. 334)

Gillborn uses a simple technique of telling an imaginary story to illustrate the seriousness of the outcomes that can and do result from systemic reforms for minoritised young people. I took up Gillborn's story in my discussion of an ethnographic research project examining the same assessment for five-year-olds (which was renamed the Early Years Foundation Stage Profile in 2008) and the classroom practices it produced (Bradbury, 2011, 2013). I used the story to analyse the creation of a system in which low results could be maintained over a period of time. This story was informed by the findings from long-term ethnographic studies of two Reception classrooms in inner London, but was again based on an imaginary racist society:

A new test is introduced; the despised group do badly, and the status quo is preserved. But, the new test is for very young children, and so has to be based entirely on teachers' judgements and observations. There is a risk that the despised group might start to get better scores. How to control the teachers, and ensure the scores are kept down? (Bradbury, 2011, p. 671)

I used this story to consider the impact of the practices identified in the data collected in real schools. I focused on two processes, both of which I identified in the data from the Reception classrooms I studied. First, the discourse of inevitable low attainment was reinforced through policies which singled out particular groups of pupils and whole clusters of schools as needing additional help. As the assessment was based on teacher's judgements alone, these low expectations were obscured, and even expected. A second process, in the language of the story 'ensures that if the teachers do start to give children from the despised group high scores, this can be monitored and prevented' (Bradbury, 2011, p. 671). Moderation systems conducted by the local authority deemed results from one inner city school to be 'too high' and therefore inaccurate enough so as to require readjustment, which meant removing marks from some pupils to lower their attainment. I concluded the story on an imaginary society thus:

> Through these two processes, the group gets low scores. The results are published each year, and this backs up the idea that it is only commonsense that the despised group do badly, and no one is to blame. Everyone is quietly pleased with the wonderfully circular, self-perpetuating way in which the group stays lower than the other groups in this test, especially since it provides the benchmark for all of the children's further progress. As long as the advisors keep checking, the teachers keep feeling that they need to get it 'right', and the idea that the group will inevitably do badly keeps circulating, the despised group will get poor scores and keep getting poor scores. (Bradbury, 2011, p. 672)

This use of a counter-story illuminates the ways in which familiar, seemingly 'normal' practices in education, such as moderation, the identification of areas of 'underachievement' and, indeed, teacher assessment, can work in ways which produce racist outcomes. *Society does not need to be overtly and explicitly racist, as in the counter-story, for the same outcomes to result.* As Gillborn (2006c) says, it is 'more frightening than that'. By relocating the analysis to an imaginary context, we can learn something about the real-life context in which the education system operates; a context in which racist outcomes are not a concern if they are not intentional. This can perhaps lead to more productive discussions about intentions and responsibility, and about the continuing presence of institutional racism within the education system.

Using theories of 'identity performance' to explore discrimination in classrooms

Concepts from CRT scholarship are also useful in the analysis of discrimination at the level of an individual classroom and, in particular, in thinking about the complexity of differential expectations in schools with different groups of minoritised pupils. There is an argument which supposes that if discrimination exists it must apply equally to all pupils in that context, and therefore the low attainment of one minoritised group or one individual cannot be attributed to discrimination if other minoritised students have high attainment. This is the deployment of a 'model minority' argument – which uses the high attainment of Chinese and Indian pupils to dismiss claims of institutional racism in the education system as a whole – on a smaller scale. This 'racist to all or none' defence is sometimes used in relation to schools with high proportions of minoritised pupils, where it is claimed that racism does not exist because some minoritised pupils are the high attainers, but it can also be applied in schools with few minoritised pupils, only some of whom suffer from low expectations. What CRT offers, I would argue, is a critique of these arguments, based on concepts from legal scholarship, specifically the work of Carbado and Gulati on 'identity performance' (Carbado and Gulati, 2000a, 2000b, 2001).

Carbado and Gulati's work offers tools for what I regard as a more nuanced analysis of classroom interactions, an analysis which attempts to examine the constitutions of students as different types of learners based on their minoritised status. This (precarious and temporary) constitution on a spectrum of 'good' and 'bad' learners, an area on which Youdell (2006a, 2006b) has written extensively (and my work has attempted to contribute to its development), is based not only on teachers' assumptions, but takes into account the pupils' own agency in making choices about how to 'perform' their identities. 'Identity performance' is the term Carbado and Gulati use to describe these choices about appearance, behaviour, association and many other elements that adults in a workplace make on a daily basis. This CRT analysis owes much to Butler's (1997, 1995, p. 46) discussion of performatives and 'discursive agency' (a scholar located quite separately from CRT) which they acknowledge.[2] Butler explains that 'to claim the subject is constituted is not to claim that it is determined; on the contrary, the constituted character of the subject is the very precondition of its agency'. This emphasis on 'discursive agency' can be applied to discussions of students as well as adults, I would argue. This agency may be limited by context, but is nonetheless important, as Youdell (2006b, p. 519) explains:

> Discourse and its effects ultimately exceed the intent or free will of an agent, but, like Foucault's practices of self, the performatively constituted subject can still deploy discursive performatives that have the potential to be constitutive.

It is this deployment of discursive performatives that I am concerned with here, which I discuss using the language from these CRT scholars of 'identity performance'.

Carbado and Gulati (2001, p. 701) are legal scholars, focusing on issues of discrimination in the workplace. They describe identity performance theory thus:

> In a nutshell, the theory of identity performance is that a person's experiences with and vulnerability to discrimination are based not just on a status marker of difference (call this a person's status identity) but also on the choices that person makes about how to present her difference (call this a person's performance identity).

Carbado and Gulati (2000b, p. 1265) argue (in accordance with Butler) that gender is a series of performances and that individuals 'cannot decide *whether* they want to bring gender into being' (emphasis in original), but they emphasise that 'they do have some choices about *how* to bring gender into being'. Using an example of two male employees, they comment that the variety of 'options' about how to 'wear' gender mean that the men can engage in 'very different performances and still be intelligible as gendered subjects'. I have some concerns that that this idea of how to 'wear' gender perhaps overstates the capacity of the subject to question established discourses through performatives, and it underestimates the regulatory functions of discourse; there are, after all, only a limited number of ways in which these hypothetical employees may 'give meaning' to their gender and remain intelligible, and these are organised hierarchically and always subject to positioning in relation to binaries of Norm/Other, desirable/abject, and so on. Nonetheless, what is useful about Carbado and Gulati's analysis of identity performance in thinking about discrimination in a classroom and a 'racist to all or none' denial of racism (discussed above) is the argument that the interaction between a person's identity and a person's *performance* of this identity can be a site where discrimination can occur.

Within this framework, two individuals from the same minoritised group (and with the same other identity markers also) may perform these identities differently, and this may result in only one being discriminated against within the context of a particular institution. Carbado and Gulati (2001) argue that elements of identity performance – such as behaviour, appearance and choice of associations – can work to distance minoritised individuals from acceptable identities, even when other individuals from the same group are seen as successful. The authors use this analysis to discuss a situation in which one Black woman is not promoted but another four Black women in the same workplace are, and where the company's defence is that if they were racist, they would not have promoted any of the women. Furthermore, Carbado and Gulati (2001) argue that discrimination based on identity performance – in this case the dress, actions and associations of the fifth Black woman which constituted her as unacceptable within this workplace – *is still discrimination*. By this logic, the suggestion that just because some pupils within a minoritised group have high attainment, no discrimination in any classroom can be dismissed. Discrimination does not have to be all or nothing, and discrimination based on identity performance is one powerful way in which pupils can be disadvantaged based on their minoritised identity, even when other pupils succeed.

To illustrate this contribution of CRT further, I focus here on an example based on some data collected during the ethnographic study mentioned earlier, which was based in a Reception classroom of four- and five-year-old children in a school in inner London. In this research I was particularly interested in how models of a 'good learner' in this first year of school could work to exclude some children from positions of educational success, and in the links to the assessment discussed above (see also Bradbury, 2013). The data relate to one pupil – Abeje – and the importance of her identity performance in the constitution of her learner identity.

As a female, African-Caribbean pupil in a class where the majority of pupils were from minoritised communities, there was some 'intelligible space' for Abeje to be constituted as a 'good learner'. She spoke two languages – English and French – and was enthusiastic about her learning and keen to answer questions. She often helped out in the classroom and was eager to please the teacher. In many ways her behaviour and conduct in the classroom was entirely in keeping with the models of 'good learning' that operated in this Reception classroom: she was hardworking, vocal and keen to engage with the range of activities on offer. She was also described at times as being of 'high ability'. However, it was her identity perform- ance in particular that constituted her as being outside of intelligible good- learner status. Abeje behaved in ways which, although helpful, challenged the rules of the classroom. The following field notes illustrate moments of transgression which were interpreted as bad behaviour:

> Abeje is missing from storytime. Someone asks, 'Where's Abeje?'; Paul [class teacher] says, 'Probably faffing around somewhere' and carries on. A few minutes into the story, Abeje arrives with dustpan and brush and puts them neatly away.
>
> The class is sitting on the carpet: Paul sings the 'Everybody sitting down' song. Afterwards Abeje sings it again, and is told to leave the

circle. Paul explains to the others: 'She's not listening so she's sitting out.' Later the same day, Abeje comes to Paul for a hug; on the way back she dances and is sent away from the carpet. (Field notes)

The teacher's reaction to Abeje cleaning up and singing the song at the wrong time illustrates how her behaviour was interpreted, not as enthusiasm, but as resistance to the rules of the classroom. Furthermore, by Abeje dancing and singing when she should not, she failed to display the kind of bodily control required to be a 'good' learner in Reception. These performative practices also resonate with discourses of Black musicality and physicality (Sewell, 1997). Abeje was also a very confident child, and was willing to argue with the teacher when she thought he was wrong; on occasion this led to her being reprimanded and being made to sit away from the rest of the class, even when she was trying to be helpful. As has been found previously in relation to inner-city, working-class girls (Archer et al., 2007), Abeje's assertiveness was understood as deviant and aggressive, particularly for minoritised girls. Thus, Abeje was constituted negatively through discourses of a feisty Black woman, a 'diva' who did not adhere to the model of the enthusiastic, but obedient, 'good learner'. Her mother was also willing to come into the classroom and comment on Abeje's learning, and this was interpreted by the staff, not as a keen interest in her progress, but as challenging the school's authority. In Reception, where parents' identities are key in the production of children's identities as learners, Abeje's mother's behaviour further constituted her as being 'difficult'.

Abeje's negative learner identity was compounded by the fact that through her physical appearance she did not engage in the 'identity work' that Carbado and Gulati (2001) argue is required to succeed as a minoritised person, whereby minoritised individuals engage in 'racial comfort' for White people by de-emphasising their racial status (also Carbado, 2002). Abeje often wore her hair in a large Afro with a 'Rasta hat' woollen cap in green, red and yellow stripes, and she often talked about her home country of Nigeria. These physical manifestations were the opposite of 'identity work' in that they emphasised her Black identity in the classroom; they were part of an 'identity performance' which was incompatible with models of success in this classroom. Following Carbado and Gulati's (2001) argument, the negative constitution of Abeje as a learner is still discrimination; it may not be obvious or easy to identify, but in this classroom this pupil was understood, and treated, in ways which systematically disadvantaged her, which were inextricably linked to her minoritised status.

This analysis of the data relating to Abeje's negative learner identity, despite her high standard of academic work and her enthusiasm in the classroom, is aided by the tools offered by Carbado and Gulati's work on adults in a workplace and additionally by wider insights from CRT. The idea that racism is endemic and 'business as usual' is helpful in considering how the normal workings of a classroom – the practices, dominant discourses and the models of good learning – can exclude some children from positions of educational success. On an individual level, the concept of identity performance as the basis of discrimination is useful in considering how Abeje came to be constituted negatively, although another child in her intersectional position might not be if they engaged in an alternative identity performance. Furthermore, this kind of detailed analysis is in keeping with the emphasis in CRT on the lived experiences and micro-aggressions suffered by minoritised people on a daily basis; indeed, it would be greatly improved by the inclusion of the voices of the pupils themselves.[3]

Concluding comments

This chapter has sought to illustrate the potential use of CRT in under-standing race and education at a variety of levels, and to emphasise the importance of theory in the field of race and education. But theory is only useful in helping to make sense of what happens in classrooms and in the education system as a whole, not as an end in itself. Critical theoretical tools, such as those offered by CRT, are essential in any analysis of the operation of the social construct of race in education, and in any attempt to deconstruct and challenge its pernicious effects. Racism is inherently complex, evolving, and is historically and geographically contingent; at the same time, education is an increasingly complex arena, with shifting values, structures and systems of measurement. The complexity of this terrain, in a time where 'race' is often at the margins of debates in educa-tion, requires theoretically informed critical approaches.

Notes

1. I used the term 'minoritised' to refer to those not from the group who are the majority population, which in the case of the UK, is a White British group. This term is used in recognition of the fact that there is nothing inherently 'minority' about the other groups present in the UK, and that the very idea of 'ethnic groups' is itself a social construct. That some groups are 'minoritised', a position which suggests different and inherent 'otherness', is a phenom-enon which is historically and geographically contingent.

2. I use both the terms 'discursive agency' (Butler, 1997) and 'identity performance' (Carbado and Gulati, 2000a) because, although Butler's phrase describes
   the role of the individual in resisting particular types of subjectivation through
   discourse, Carbado's and Gulati's work applies her ideas to real-life situations
   involving racial discrimination, and thus bridges the gap between theory and
   lived experience that some have seen as limiting the use of Butler in education
   (Hey, 2006).
3. As a White researcher I am aware of and wish to emphasise the limitations I
   face in the analysis of these and other data relating to the lived experiences of
   minoritised children and young people.

References

Allen, R.L. (2009) 'What about poor White people?', in Ayers, W., Quinn, T. and
Stovall, D. (eds), *Handbook of Social Justice in Education*, New York, Routledge,
209–230.

Archer, L. et al. (2007) 'Inner-femininities and education: 'race', class, gender and
schooling in young women's lives', *Gender and Education*, 19 (5), 549–567.

Bell, D. (1992) *Faces at the Bottom of the Well: The Permanence of Racism*, New York,
BasicBooks.

Bradbury, A. (2011) 'Rethinking assessment and inequality: the production of
disparities in attainment in early years education', *Journal of Education Policy*,
26 (5), 655–676.

Bradbury, A. (2013) *Understanding Early Years Inequality: Policy, Assessment and
Young Children's Identities*, London, Routledge.

Butler, J.P. (1995) 'For a careful reading', in Benhabib, S., Butler, J.P., Cornell,
D. and Fraser, N., *Feminist Contentions: A Philosophical Exchange*, New York,
Routledge, 127–143.

Butler, J.P. (1997) *Excitable Speech: A Politics of the Performative*, New York,
Routledge.

Carbado, D. (2002) 'Afterword: (E)racing education', *Equity and Excellence in
Education*, 35 (2), 181–194.

Carbado, D. and M. Gulati (2000a) 'Conversations at work', *Oregon Law Review*,
79, 103–145.

Carbado, D. and M. Gulati (2000b) 'Working identity', *Cornell Law Review*, 85,
1259–1308.

Carbado, D. and M. Gulati (2001) 'The fifth black woman'. *Journal of Contemporary
Legal Issues*, 11, 701–729.

Coard, B. (1971) *How the West Indian Child is Made Educationally Subnormal in
the British School System: The Scandal of the Black Child in Schools in Britain*,
London, New Beacon for the Caribbean Education and Community Workers'
Association.

Connolly, P. (1998) *Racism, Gender Identities and Young Children: Social Relations in
a Multi-ethnic, Inner-city Primary School*, London, Routledge.

Connolly, P. and Troyna, B. (1998) *Researching Racism in Education: Politics, Theory
and Practice*, Buckingham: Open University Press.

Crenshaw, K., Gotanda, N., Peller, G. and Thomas, K. (1995) *Critical Race Theory:
The Key Writings that Formed the Movement*, New York, New York Press.

Delgado, R. (1995) *Critical Race Theory: The Cutting Edge*, Philadelphia, Temple University Press.

DfE (2010a) 'Early Years Foundation Stage Profile Attainment by Pupil Characteristics in England, 2009/10'. Retrieved 21 January 2011, from http://www.education.gov.uk/rsgateway/DB/SFR/s000979/index.shtml.

DfE (2010b) 'GCSE and Equivalent Attainment by Pupil Characteristics in England, 2009/10'. Retrieved 21 January 2011, from http://www.education.gov.uk/rsgateway/DB/SFR/s000977/index.shtml.

DfE (2012) 'Early Years Foundation Stage Profile Attainment by Pupil Characteristics, England 2010/11. Retrieved 20 January 2012, from http://media.education.gov.uk/assets/files/pdf/m/main%20text%20sfr292011.pdf.

Dixson, A. and C. Rousseau (2006) *Critical Race Theory in Education: All God's Children Got a Song*, New York, Taylor and Francis.

Foster, P. (1990) 'Cases not proven: an evaluation of two studies of teacher racism', *British Educational Research Journal*, 16 (4), 335–349.

Foster, P. (1991) 'Case still not proven: a reply to Cecile Wright', *British Educational Research Journal*, 17 (2), 165–170.

Gillborn, D. (1990) *'Race', Ethnicity and Education: Teaching and Learning in Multiethnic Schools*, London: Unwin Hyman.

Gillborn, D. (1995) *Racism and Antiracism in Real Schools: Theory, Policy, Practice*, Buckingham, Open University Press.

Gillborn, D. (2002) *Education and Institutional Racism*, London: Institute of Education University of London.

Gillborn, D. (2006a) 'Critical race theory and education: Racism and anti-racism in educational theory and praxis', *Discourse: Studies in the Cultural Politics of Education*, 27 (1), 11–32.

Gillborn, D. (2006b) 'Critical race theory beyond North America: towards a transatlantic dialogue on racism and antiracism in educational theory and praxis', *Critical Race Theory in Education: All God's Children Got a Song*, eds A.D. Dixson and C.K. Rousseau, New York, London, Routledge, 241–265.

Gillborn, D. (2006c) 'Rethinking white supremacy: who counts in "Whiteworld"', *Ethnicities*, 6 (3), 318–340.

Gillborn, D. (2008) *Racism and Education: Coincidence or Conspiracy?* London, Routledge.

Gillborn, D. (2010) 'The White working class, racism and respectability: victims, degenerates and interest-convergence', *British Journal of Educational Studies*, 58 (1), 3–25.

Gillborn, D. (2011) 'The White working class, racism and respectability: victims, degenerates and interest-convergence', in Bhopal, K. and Preston, J. (eds), *Intersectionality and 'Race' in Education*, London, Routledge, 24–56.

Gillborn, D. and D. Youdell (2000) *Rationing Education: Policy, Practice, Reform and Equity*, Buckingham, Open University Press.

Gillborn, D. and D. Youdell (2009) 'Critical perspectives on race and schooling', in Banks, J. A. *The Routledge International Companion to Multicultural Education*, New York, Routledge, 173–185.

Hey, V. (2006) 'The politics of performative resignification: translating Judith Butler's theoretical discourse and its potential for a sociology of education', *British Journal of Sociology of Education*, 27 (4), 439–457.

Ignatiev, N. (1995) *How the Irish Became White*, New York, Routledge.

Ladson-Billings, G. (2004) 'Just what is critical race theory and what's it doing in a *nice* field like education?', in Ladson-Billings, G. and Gillborn, D. (eds), *The RoutledgeFalmer Reader in Multicultural Education: Critical Perspectives on Race, Racism and Education*, London, RoutledgeFalmer, 49–68.

Ladson-Billings, G. (2006) Foreword: 'They're trying to wash us away – the adolescence of Critical Race Theory in education', in Dixson, A. and Rousseau, C. (eds), *Critical Race Theory in Education: All God's Children Got a Song*, New York, Taylor and Francis, v–xiii.

Ladson-Billings, G. and W. Tate (1995) 'Toward a critical race theory of education', *Teachers College Record*, 97 (1), 47–68.

Macpherson, W. et al. (1999). *The Stephen Lawrence Inquiry*, London, Stationery Office.

McIntosh, P. (1992) 'White privilege and male privilege: a personal account of coming to see correspondances through work in women's studies', in Delgado, R. and Stefanic, J. (eds), *Critical White Studies: Looking Behind the Mirror*, Philadelphia, Temple University Press, 291–299.

Nayak, A. (2009) 'Beyond the pale: chavs, youth and social class', in Sveinsson, K.P. (ed.), *Who Cares About the White Working Class?* London, Runnymede Trust, 28–35.

Rampersand, R. (2011) 'Interrogating pigmentocracy: the intersections of race and social class in the primary education of Afro-Trinidadian boys', in Bhopal, K. and Preston, J. (eds), *Intersectionality and 'Race' in Education*, London, Routledge, 57–75.

Reay, D. (2009) 'Making sense of White working class educational underachievement', in K. Sveinsson (ed.), *Who Cares About the White Working Class?* London, Runnymede Trust, 22–28.

Sewell, T. (1997) *Black Masculinities and Schooling: How Black Boys Survive Modern Schooling*, Stoke-on-Trent, Trentham Books.

Sveinsson, K. (ed.) (2009) *Who Cares About the White Working Class?* London, Runnymede Trust.

Tate, W. F. (1997) 'Critical Race Theory and Education: history, theory and implications', in Apple, M.W. (ed.), *Review of Research in Education*, Washington, D.C., American Educational Research Association, 234–235.

Taylor, E. et al. (2009) *Foundations of Critical Race Theory in Education*, New York and London, Routledge.

Wright, C. (1990) Comments in Reply to the Article by P. Foster, 'Cases not proven: an evaluation of two studies of teacher racism', *British Educational Research Journal*, 16 (4), 351–335.

Wright, C. (1992) *Race Relations in the Primary School*, London, Fulton.

Youdell, D.C. (2006a) *Impossible Bodies, Impossible Selves: Exclusions and Student Subjectivities*, Dordrecht, Springer.

Youdell, D.C. (2006b) 'Subjectivation and performative politics – Butler thinking Althusser and Foucault: intelligibility, agency and the raced-nationed-religioned subjects of education', *British Journal of Sociology of Education*, 27 (4), 511–528.

2
British Muslim Schools: Institutional Isomorphism and the Transition from Independent to Voluntary-Aided Status

Damian Breen

Introduction

This chapter draws on first-hand qualitative research carried out inside Muslim schools in the United Kingdom. In particular, insights are drawn from life-history interviews conducted with a key informant, 'Nasira', who led two Muslim primary schools through the transition from independent to voluntary-aided (VA) status. These narratives will demonstrate how making the transition from being independent to voluntary-aided Muslim schools necessarily resulted in processes of institutional isomorphism. These processes arise in response to commonly held perceptions and expectations associated with institutions operating within a given sector. As summarised by Dacin (1997, p.4), conformity to institutional norms creates structural similarities, or isomorphism, across organisations. These processes of change primarily affect the profile of staff, parents and pupils for independent Muslim schools which enter the maintained sector. To simplify discussions, the terms 'School A' and 'School B' will be used to refer to the first and second schools that Nasira, as head teacher in each case, saw through the transition from independent to voluntary-aided status. Whereas School A had already been in the state sector for four years at the time of the research, School B was studied during its final months as an independent school prior to becoming a state-funded Muslim primary school.

This chapter will argue that processes of change, consistent with institutional isomorphism, have dramatic implications for Muslim schools which undertake the transition into the state sector. These changes include the replacement of staff, changes in admissions policies and the removal of fees and subsequent changes in the profile of parents. Meer (2007, pp. 67–68) argues that the development of voluntary-aided Muslim schools represents a step forward in the relationship between Muslim communities and the state. Whilst this is an important point, the argument presented in this chapter is that the transformative requirements for entering the state sector mean that, in exchange for the financial security offered with voluntary-aided status, independent Muslim schools are obliged to sacrifice specific ways in which they function as independent schools. In short, the fact that the vast majority of Muslim schools are independent means that large proportions of the Muslim community are not included in these partnerships. Furthermore, when a given independent Muslim school enters the voluntary-aided sector, proportions of staff, parents and children who previously contributed to the character of the school become displaced (see Breen 2009), left to find another independent school to suit their needs. Thus, partnerships between community and the state manifested through voluntary-aided Muslim schools do not uniformly enfranchise Muslim communities.

The purpose of this chapter is not to present an argument that is critical of voluntary-aided Muslim schools. The arguments posed by Meer (2007) are important in that they highlight processes whereby important steps are made in developing partnerships between Muslim communities and the state. However, the advantages of these partnerships (i.e., free Islamic education and increased access to resources) have masked processes of displacement which occur as a result of independent Muslim schools entering the voluntary-aided sector.

Faith schools in the context of England and Wales

Faith schools in England and Wales take two forms: those that are independent, and those which receive some degree of state funding. The latter include voluntary-aided and voluntary-controlled schools plus some Foundation schools and Academies. Independent schools, some of which embody a religious character, are entirely privately funded through charitable status and receive no financial support from local or central government. The School Standards and Framework Act introduced the concept of a 'religious character' in 1998 thus modifying the range of state-funded faith schools (DfEE, 1998). Whilst not permitted for community, foundation, and voluntary-controlled schools, voluntary-aided schools are free to have denominational religious education (RE). Currently, voluntary-aided schools with a religious character are funded up to 90 per cent by local authorities, with outstanding costs being covered by a relevant religious organisation (DfES, 2002). Prior to 1998, the 1993 Education Act provided an opportunity for independent religious schools to apply directly to the Department for Education for state funding through 'grant-maintained' status (DfE, 1993). Schools successful in the application process would be answerable to central government rather than to the then 'local education authorities', although strict financial and demand-led criteria imposed at the time made it difficult for evangelical Christian schools and Muslim schools to enter the state system (Walford, 2003, p. 165). From 2003 the Department for Education and Skills offered independent schools the opportunity to apply to be designated as a school with religious character under the Designation of Schools Having a Religious Character (Independent Schools, England) Order 2003. Furthermore, in 2005, the White Paper, *Higher Standards, Better Schools for All*, invited independent schools to enter the state sector, with a particular emphasis on encouraging Muslim schools to apply for voluntary-aided status (DfES, 2005).

Following from the above, in September 2007 the government, along with representatives of major faith groups, released the document, *Faith in the System*. The paper 'unveiled a joint declaration and shared vision of schools with a religious character in twenty-first century England', stating that the government recognises the aspirations of faith communities to secure more schools to offer education in accordance with the tenets of their faith (DCSF, 2007, p. 4). With reference to the Muslim community, the paper states that nearly 15,000 Muslim children attend independent schools with a particular religious character and, therefore, availability of places in the state sector could provide an important contribution to integration and empowerment of these communities (DCSF, 2007, p. 18). It is worth noting here that the arrival of the Coalition government in 2010 led to some confusion over the level of support that faith communities will continue to receive. In particular, recent cuts in public spending and David Cameron's statement that multiculturalism has failed (Helm et al., 2011) bring into question the issue of whether or not the state will continue to encourage faith schooling for minority communities.

Here, the focus on the voluntary-aided sector above is of central relevance, as 12 of the 14 Muslim schools in England which currently receive state funding are voluntary-aided schools, with the outstanding two operating as free schools (AMS, 2014). The discussion above also demonstrates that there has been a sustained political rhetoric focused on encouraging independent faith schools in general, and Muslim independent schools specifically, to enter the state education system. However, in reality only a very small number of independent Muslim schools have made this transition. There are currently around 7,000 voluntary-aided faith schools in England, the vast majority being Church of England or Roman Catholic (Tinker, 2009, p. 540). There are 53 voluntary-aided schools with a religious character other than Church of England or Roman Catholic. These 53 comprise 37 Jewish, 2 Sikh, 1 Greek Orthodox, 1 Seventh Day Adventist (Tinker, 2009, p. 540) and 12 Muslim schools (AMS, 2014). However, there are approximately 120 independent Muslim schools in England and Wales (AMS, 2014). As can be seen, in proportion to the wider number of voluntary-aided schools and in comparison to the number of Muslim schools overall, only a small number of Muslim schools have entered the state sector as voluntary-aided schools. The rise of academies since 2010 (and 'free schools') may very well result in a significantly increased number of state Muslim schools if the practical application of legislative frameworks allows more freedom than that afforded in the voluntary-aided sector. One particularly pertinent example is the recent proposal for teachers to no longer be required to have formal teaching qualifications to work in the academy sector (Harrison, 2012). This point will be discussed in detail later in the chapter.

In light of the contextual framework within which Muslim schools currently function in England and Wales, the term 'Muslim school(s)' will be used to refer to those faith schools which offer Islamic provision in line with their distinctive religious character and are affiliated to an Islamic religious organisation. In light of the above definitions the term 'state-funded Muslim school' will be used to refer to voluntary-aided Muslim schools which receive state funding within the context of the education policy of England and Wales. Having contextualised the position of Muslim schools in the education system in England and Wales, in the next subsection I will briefly outline theories of institutional isomorphism as a backdrop against which School A's and School B's transitions from independent to state-funded Muslim schools will be analysed.

A typology of institutional isomorphism

As outlined above, independent Muslim schools have traditionally entered the state sector as voluntary aided schools. The narratives of this transition at School A and School B indicate that acquiring voluntary-aided status both required and resulted in observable processes of institutional isomorphism. DiMaggio and Powell (1983, 1991) offer a typology comprising three forms of institutional isomorphism: *coercive*, *mimetic* and *normative* (DiMaggio and Powell, 1983, p. 150). Coercive isomorphism results from both formal and informal pressures exerted on organisations by other organisations upon which they are dependent and by expectations in the society within which the organisations function (ibid.). With coercive isomorphism, pressures may be felt as force, as persuasion, or as invitations to join in collusion (DiMaggio and Powell, 1991, p. 67).

In addition to coercive pressures, DiMaggio and Powell also identify processes of mimetic isomorphism resulting from standard responses to uncertainty within and between organisations (DiMaggio and Powell, 1983, p. 151). Uncertainty leads unstable organisations to model themselves on other organisations which appear to be successful (DiMaggio and Powell, 1991, p. 69). The modelled organisation serves as a convenient source of practices which the borrowing organisation may use (DiMaggio and Powell, 1983, p. 151). Models may be diffused unintentionally and indirectly through employee transfer or staff turnover (DiMaggio and Powell, 1983, p. 151). Modelling through the transfer of staff has been of central relevance in the historical narratives of School A and School B. For example, prior to taking the role of head at School A (and later School B), Nasira had previously had an instrumental role as a trustee at another Muslim school which had successfully become voluntary-aided. Furthermore, following School B's successful transition into the state sector, Nasira moved on to work with another voluntary-aided Muslim school. Typically, the schools she has worked with have benefited from her expertise during the process of applying for voluntary-aided status. The tendency for Nasira to occupy a transitory role in Muslim schools represents an example of mimetic isomorphic modelling in practice.

Finally, DiMaggio and Powell identify normative isomorphism as being inherently derived from 'professionalisation'. For DiMaggio and Powell, professionalisation is the collective struggle of members of an occupation to define the conditions and methods of their work, establishing a cognitive base and legitimation for their occupational autonomy (DiMaggio and Powell, 1991, p. 70). One important example of normative isomorphism is the filtering of personnel in relation to skill-level requirements for particular occupations (DiMaggio and Powell, 1991, p. 71). Normative isomorphism is of specific relevance for Muslim schools entering the voluntary-aided sector because the process necessitates the filtering of teaching staff, with only formally qualified teachers retaining their jobs. Thus, within the voluntary-aided sector, the title 'teacher' means an individual with Qualified Teacher Status (QTS) who has undergone a prescribed scheme of training. Although having the same occupation, an individual who has taught in independent Muslim schools without QTS will not be employed as a teacher within the voluntary-aided sector should their school make the transition into the state. Having identified DiMaggio and Powell's typology of institutional isomorphism, I will now move on to introduce the narratives of School A and School B as a means of demonstrating how processes of isomorphism were manifested in each school's transition from independent to voluntary-aided status.

Outlining the study: the narratives of School A and School B in context

This chapter draws on interviews conducted with Nasira at School A and School B to contextualise findings from a larger comparative ethnographic case study of two Muslim primary schools, one independent and one voluntary-aided. Interviews with Nasira were carried out intermittently on-site at School A, from 2006 to mid 2007, and further interviews were carried out on-site at School B during the academic year 2007–2008. Given the nature of the political and media attention concerning faith schools generally during the research period, and on Muslims in particular following the terrorist attacks in New York on 11 September 2001 and the London bombings on 7 July 2005, careful consideration was given to appropriate approaches to interviews. The approach was consistent with that of empathetic interviewing as defined by Fontana and Frey (2005). In the past, according to Fontana and Frey, attitudes to interviewing have centred on ideas of the interview as a neutral tool, while more recent trends in qualitative methodology suggest that the interview is historically, politically and contextually bound. Thus the interview is more than an exchange that consists of asking questions and giving answers – it is a collaborative effort involving two or more people, called 'the interview' (Fontana and Frey, 2005, p. 696).

The rationale for the research was based on an argument, best articulated by Tinker (2009, p. 550), that contrasting viewpoints about the effects of Muslim schools are largely based on assumptions or anecdotal evidence. Tinker concludes that there is a clear need for further empirical research to inform any future debate (ibid.). To be more specific, there is a need for not only more research *on* Muslim schools, but for more ethnographic sociological research which has been conducted *inside* Muslim schools in England and Wales. Although this chapter primarily draws on semi-structured interviews to outline the historical narratives of School A and School B, interviews were conducted on-site and, consequently, observation data also informs the narrative of each school.

Background: the origins of School A and School B

School A had been an independent Muslim primary school for between 10 and 12 years before making the transition into the state sector for the beginning of the academic year 2004–2005. At the time of the research the school was in its fourth academic year as a voluntary-aided school. School A had started out with eight children from three families in a small room in a mosque, then grew steadily, moving its location several times. Growth had been gradual over a period of five to six years as word of the school spread between parents and prospective families. After growing to around 120 pupils, the school's intake stabilised for a time, mainly due to limitations on space. The school then moved to a different building to accommodate the children more effectively, which allowed further growth, from around 120 to approximately 240 pupils, School A's largest intake as an independent Muslim primary school. On entering the state system as a voluntary-aided school, the intake dramatically grew in size again over a three-year period, to around 420 pupils, with 60 new pupils joining each year as a two-form entry school which subsequently grew from the bottom up. Following the move into the state sector, the school was able to relocate to a new purpose-built premises as School A's current home.

At the time of the research School B had been an independent Muslim primary school for 12 years and was in the process of applying for voluntary-aided status. The school was initially founded on-site at a mosque close to the school's current building, initially providing for a small number of children from around six families. Nasira became involved with School B in July of 2007, following contact from the trustees, who wanted to consider a future in the state system. Nasira was pursued based on her experience of having successfully led School A into the state sector, and she joined School B as acting head for a six-week period to assist and to offer guidance with the application process. In addition to having headed School A through the transition to voluntary-aided status, Nasira had also played an instrumental role as a trustee of another school which had acquired state funding, and she had 'led all the negotiations and discussions with the council, though I didn't head that school personally'. Her experience in liaising with the council was an additional factor in School B's pursuit of Nasira's expertise.

Prior to Nasira's involvement, the trustees at School B had consulted the local council to discuss necessary prerequisites for applying for voluntary-aided status. At the point of Nasira's arrival, correspondence between the school and the council had broken down. Thus, negotiations effectively restarted in September of 2007, following Nasira's arrival at School B on 22 July. First priorities were to develop the building so that it represented a school to prospective visitors. Although conditions were poor, Nasira felt that this was a typical trend for many independent Muslim schools. She stated:

> [School B] had not a single penny. Muslim schools, typically, if you go into any of the 120 that don't have state funding, their conditions are pretty dire. They live hand-to-mouth. What they don't realise necessarily is that for a third party the first impression counts, and if the person can't even imagine it being a state school, they can't get beyond that to what you're teaching, what the children are learning, what the school has to offer, what the staff are like, because they cannot even see it.

At the time of the last visit, in June 2008, the intake at School B was approximately 115, and tuition fees were set at £2,500 per year. The school building itself changed dramatically during the year-long period over which the life-history interviews were carried out. Laminate floors had been laid, a large, open office space next to a medical room with a sink and bed had developed, and classrooms previously void of the presence of children were home to colourful displays of pupils' work. Nasira's conviction was that even though developments had been made swiftly over a short period of time, 'this now looks the best it can in this building as a state school'. Prior to the final inspection in the application process, due to take place two weeks following the final on-site interview with Nasira, School B had been informed that the school would indeed be awarded voluntary-aided status. However, their assessment in an inspection would determine whether they received it for the academic year 2008–2009, or for 2009–2010. On anticipating the decision, Nasira explained, acquiring state funding had become a necessity for the school, owing to the time and money which had been invested in meeting the criteria required of applicants. Although she had been assured that the school would be given more time if it failed the assessment in the final inspection, Nasira explained that without funding for the coming academic year the school would most likely have had to close. An extended deadline simply meant an extension of the amount of time spent struggling to survive in the independent sector.

Nature of surrounding communities: School A and School B

The communities surrounding School A and School B had differing characteristics. Following the transition to voluntary-aided status, the intake of School A had changed in several ways. Whereas the local Muslim population had been primarily South Asian, the number of Somali pupils at School A grew steadily over a period of 2–3 years, with around a third of the intake being of Somali descent at the time Nasira moved to School B. This factor actually counters one possible application of isomorphism: the argument that changes to admissions policies on entering the voluntary-aided sector necessarily result in the intake being primarily composed of local Muslim families. Nasira argued the contrary, that Somali families demonstrated a commitment by travelling 'huge distances' to the school on a daily basis. The characteristics of families at School A also changed over time, although these were more directly related to the school's voluntary-aided status. Nasira explained that when, in the independent sector, both the faith-based nature of the school and its often-delicate financial situation had resulted in a dependency on two particular characteristics in parents: they needed to be either committed to the faith, or able to pay fees, or both, if they were to obtain an Islamic education for their children. Reflecting on the limited resources at School A whilst in the independent sector, Nasira stated:

> I used to say they used to pay money to send children to my prison, because that's what I used to compare it to because of the lack of resources and the tiny rooms! But they valued something they got there that they couldn't get anywhere else.

On entering the state sector those characteristics among parents changed. The new increase in parental interest was one of the immediately obvious effects of the removal of tuition fees. The primary implication of this was that many families who could not afford to pay tuition fees would now have access to the school. A secondary implication was that opening up the school in this way resulted in interest from families that might not have considered Islamic education for their children had it required financial investment. Drawing on DiMaggio and Powell's (1991) typology of isomorphism, the above demonstrates how processes of mimetic isomorphism resulted in a change in the nature of parents at School A. As defined by DiMaggio and Powell (1991), mimetic isomorphism arises from fear of instability – in this instance financial instability. In exchange for the financial stability afforded through acquiring voluntary-aided status, the parent body came to be characterised by groups of parents who placed less of an emphasis on Islamic provision than had those parents who had invested economically whilst School A was in the independent sector.

At School B, interviews were carried out as the school was entering the state sector and, thus, it is difficult to conclusively identify the effect this may have had on the parent body. At the time of the research the intake at School A was predominantly South Asian, the majority from Pakistani families with smaller numbers of Gujarati and Bengali families. There were also a number of Somali families, who comprised the school's second-largest ethnic group after children of Pakistani background. However, at School B the majority of the intake, approximately two thirds, was Somali. This trend had been a recent development in the school's history, as it had been founded by a largely revert (Muslim convert) community. According to Nasira, the community of School B had been ethnically diverse, but financial restrictions over the 12-year period of maintaining the school and the local mosque saw the founding community diminish. Nasira described the current profile of the intake at School B as follows:

So here we're two thirds Somali, we have some African-Caribbean, lots of mixed marriages, Algerians, there's quite a mix, and in the families you've got some Irish families, you've got some White families, lots of revert families, got some Chinese families, from all over, the grouping is very different [to School A] here.

The typical desires of parents at School A and School B also differed. Nasira's experience at School A, she stated, was that the focus of South Asian communities was on the reading, recitation and finishing of the *Qur'an*. Families at School B, by contrast:

Focused more on the understanding of faith with a heavy emphasis on the oneness of *Allah*. So you listen to the *dua*s the little children know [which] are more than I know at my age, and that is such a pleasure in the morning listening to them in assembly.

Nasira concluded that the Somali community 'valued their faith immensely', and that 'they, more than most, want to send their children to Muslim schools'. Consistent with this, Nasira, in summarising the Islamic provision at School B, placed an emphasis on understanding the Islamic faith and putting it into practice. She explained that, especially for parents, it was important for children to develop an understanding of the faith. Nasira emphasised that these differences in approaches to faith reflect trends across particular Muslim communities. However, her account of a shift, over time, in parental interest away from Islamic provision at School A, along with the fact that School B was an independent school at the time of the interviews, supports the theory that processes of mimetic isomorphism inherent to entering the voluntary-aided sector necessarily resulted in these changes in the parent body at School A.

Profile of staff at School B

At the time of my final on-site interview at School B, there was a very small number of non-Muslim National Vocational Qualification (NVQ) level-three trainees, and the rest of the class teachers and teaching assistants were Muslim. Nasira's explanation for the prevalence of Muslim teachers was that 'staff here currently are all Muslims because you have to be fairly committed to work in a school for [a limited] salary!' The profile of staff represented a key theme in School A's transition into the voluntary-aided sector, and it was anticipated that this would be the same for School B. The pursuit of voluntary-aided status had resulted in a shift towards hiring qualified teaching staff to replace unqualified teachers. This had also resulted in the appointment of a number of non-Muslim teachers at School A. A long-term objective was for the schools to utilise the Graduate Teacher Programme (GTP) with the aim of training graduates in the local community. Through this mechanism, community members could gain Qualified Teacher Status (QTS) by teaching on-site at School B. A fundamental problem was that independent schools are required to pay to register for the GTP and so, owing to financial restrictions, it could not be utilised at School B prior to acquiring voluntary-aided status. Having a fully qualified teaching staff is a necessary prerequisite for making the transition to voluntary-aided status, so Nasira had 'imported a lot of staff'. The imported staff were predominantly South Asian, and with their arrival the school had three class teachers with QTS and one with a High Level Teaching Assistant (HLTA) qualification, which demonstrated sufficient experience to teach, although it was not QTS. The initial stages of replacing unqualified staff with qualified teachers had also begun in preparation for School B's transition into the state sector.

Adjustment on entering the VA sector

The discussion throughout this chapter indicates that the main benefit of acquiring voluntary-aided status would be financial sustainability for School A and School B. Although planning for expansion at School B had taken place in anticipation of a successful application for voluntary-aided status, Nasira remained cautious about any overly positive reaction to the transition. Teaching staff would be affected by increased paperwork, accountability and workload. On entering the state sector, the school as a whole also became accountable to the local authority. Drawing on experiences at School A, Nasira recalled that, whilst the process of acquiring voluntary-aided status represented a struggle, the following transitional three- to four-year period was also challenging. Although financial restrictions were reduced, a lack of experience – along with staff having become accustomed to processes in the independent sector – had led to a difficult period of adjustment. Nasira also felt that limited strategic planning and support networks in the local authority had caused problems during these early stages.

For School B, meeting the criteria for assessment had become of paramount importance. Nasira outlined the process:

> The main ones they're going to judge [are] the teaching, the learning, the assessment, the planning, the feedback of the assessment into the planning, the pupil tracking systems. The trained teachers have only been here since the 28th of April. I'm going to be judged on *a month's teaching*.

Other priorities included renovation of the school building to meet with health and safety requirements. Although faced with the prospect of achieving the necessary requirements with no remaining financial resources, Nasira remained positive. At my final visit to School B, Nasira's parting words were: 'The impossible we do every day, miracles take a bit longer!' Telephone interviews with Nasira a fortnight later confirmed that School B had been awarded voluntary-aided status as of the start of the academic year 2008–2009.

Concluding analysis of the narratives of School A and School B

Nasira's narratives give important insights into the process of acquiring voluntary-aided status for Muslim schools. Entering the state sector gave financial stability to School A and School B and ensured the sustain-ability of the schools. However, acquiring voluntary-aided status also resulted in multiple examples of processes of institutional isomorphism affecting the infrastructure of both schools. Drawing on DiMaggio and Powell's typology, isomorphic change predominantly took the form of both mimetic and normative processes (DiMaggio and Powell, 1983, 1991). DiMaggio and Powell argue that organisational models emerge as a response to uncertainty, and unstable institutions may knowingly or unknowingly adopt these models in the pursuit of stability (DiMaggio and Powell, 1991, p. 69). A recurring motivational factor in the deci-sion to apply for voluntary-aided status at both School A and School B was economic instability and uncertainty over the sustainability of the schools in the independent sector. Particularly in the case of School B, sustainability was a matter of urgency as financial resources had expired prior to the school's final inspection date. Here, acquiring voluntary-aided status represented a process of mimetic isomorphism in practice, as the key motivation was fear of closure. Furthermore, Nasira's concept of a sustainable model for School B was the voluntary-aided Muslim school towards which she had worked in transforming School A. Nasira, herself, was the conduit for School A and School B to adopt these models.

Processes of mimetic isomorphism initiated a chain reaction which had implications for further normative processes at both schools. Acquiring voluntary-aided status in the case of School A required a change in admis-sions, which had a profound impact on the parent body. The removal of fees opened the school up to Muslim parents who desired an Islamic education for their children but could not afford the fees demanded in the independent sector. However, the change in admissions also opened the school up to fami-lies who would only consider an Islamic education for their children once fees had been removed. With the exception of Somali families, changes in admissions policies also resulted in a large proportion of the intake quickly coming to consist of local families rather than of committed parents travel-ling from various destinations. Siblings also had priority following the shift, whereas economic limitations previously meant that only the financially committed could secure places for all of their children.

Changes in the parent body represented a key process of isomorphic change consistent with normative isomorphism. For DiMaggio and Powell, under processes of normative isomorphism, professionalism is as much assigned by the state as it is created by the activities of the profes-sions (DiMaggio and Powell, 1991, p. 71). Nasira's narratives of acquiring voluntary-aided status for School A and School B represent examples of normative isomorphism, whereby entering the state sector had a direct impact on the infrastructure of both schools. The change in the profile of staff represented a further example of normative isomorphism for both School A and School B. In both cases, state regulations resulted in the importing of trained teaching staff to replace unqualified staff members. In addition to qualified Muslim teaching staff, this subsequently resulted in the appointment of School A's first non-Muslim teachers. Such isomorphic changes in infrastructure – as those documented in the narrative of School A and set in motion for School B – were necessary stages in making the transition from an independent to a voluntary-aided Muslim school.

In conclusion, the structural changes which occurred at School A on entering the state sector, and at School B in preparation for entering the state sector, both represent clear examples of institutional isomorphism inherent to the process of acquiring voluntary-aided status. Applying theories of institutional isomorphism gives grounds for anticipating that independent Muslim schools entering the state sector will experience inherent changes in terms of staff, resources, parental interest and intake as part of a necessary process of becoming voluntary-aided. Obviously, the school then becomes accessible to a wider community demographic. However, the implication here is that proportions of the parent body which previously had actively invested in Islamic education in the independent sector become disenfranchised through various processes of isomorphism. Specifically, these parents are faced with new staff, new resources and a shifting parent body. Although such processes were necessary for sustainability, these parents may ask, 'What has been sustained?' These families, actively engaged with their faith, become displaced from the partnership with the state as manifested in the development of voluntary-aided Muslim schools. Although this only refers to portions of the parent bodies at School A and School B, it is not insignificant. The fact that the number of independent Muslim schools is ten times that of those which have entered the voluntary-aided sector indicates that the vast majority of stakeholders are mobilised outside of these partnerships. The future may reveal the extent to which government initiatives on academies, and possibly on free schools, are utilised within Muslim communities. These new mechanisms could have dramatic implications for the extent to which processes of isomorphic change inherent to acquiring voluntary-aided status may be overcome for Muslim schools entering the state sector.

References

Association of Muslim Schools (AMS) (2014) 'Muslim Schools', in *The Association of Muslim Schools UK*. Available at http://www.ams-uk.org/muslim-schools. [Accessed on 17 February 2014]

Breen, D. (2009) 'A qualitative narrative of the transition from independent to voluntary aided status: a problem for the concept of the Muslim school', in A.A. Veinguer, G. Dietz, D. Jozsa and T. Knauth *Islam in Education in European Countries – Pedagogical Concepts and Empirical Findings*, New York, Waxmann, 95–112.

Dacin, T.M. (1997) 'Isomorphism in context: the power and prescription of institutional norms', *Academy of Management Journal*, 40 (1), 46–81.

Department of Children Schools and Families (DCFS) (2007) *Faith in the System: The Role of Schools with a Religious Character in English Education and Society*, London, Department of Children Schools and Families.

Department for Education (1993) *The Education Act*, London, Her Majesty's Stationery Office.

Department for Education and Employment (DfEE) (1998) *School Standards and Framework Act*, London, Department for Education and Employment.

Department for Education and Skills (DfES) (2002) *Regulatory Reform (Voluntary-aided Schools Liabilities and Funding) (England) Order 2002*, London, DfES.

Department for Education and Skills (2005) *The Schools White Paper: Higher Standards, Better Schools for All*, London, Her Majesty's Stationary Office.

DiMaggio, P.J. and Powell, W.W. (1991) 'The iron cage revisited: institutional isomorphism and collective rationality in organisational fields', in Powell, W.W. and DiMaggio, P.J. (eds), *The New Institutionalism in Organisational Analysis*, Chicago, University of Chicago Press, 63–82.

DiMaggio, P.J. and Powell, W.W. (1983) 'The iron cage revisited: institutional isomorphism and collective rationality in organisational fields', *American Sociological Review*, 48, 147–160.

Fontana, A. and Frey, J.H. (2005) 'The interview: from neutral stance to political involvement', in Denzin, N.K. and Lincoln Y.S. (eds), *The SAGE Handbook of Qualitative Research*, Thousand Oaks, Sage, 695–727.

Harrison, A. (2012) 'Academies told they can hire unqualified teachers', BBC news 27 July 2012. Available at http://www.bbc.co.uk/news/education-19017544. [Accessed on 7 August 2012]

Helm, T., Taylor, M. and Davis, R. (2011) 'David Cameron sparks fury from critics who say attack on multiculturalism has boosted English Defence League', *The Guardian*, 5 February 2011. Available at http://www.guardian.co.uk/politics/2011/feb/05/david-cameron-speech-criticised-edl. [Accessed on 10 May 2011]

Meer, N. (2007) 'Muslim schools in Britain: challenging mobilisations or logical developments?' *Asia Pacific Journal of Education*, 27 (1), 55–71.

Tinker, C. (2009) 'Rights, social cohesion and identity: arguments for and against state funded muslim schools in Britain', *Race, Ethnicity and Education*, 12 (4), 539–553.

Walford, G. (2003) 'Muslim schools in Britain', in Walford, G. (ed.), *British Private Schools: Research on Policy and Practice*, London, Woburn Press, 158–176.

3
Educational Inclusion: Meeting the Needs of All Traveller Pupils

Kate D'Arcy

Introduction

The purpose of this chapter is to provide a critical insight into Travellers' experiences of school, to highlight inequality and press for improvements. The difficulties Gypsies and Travellers experience within the mainstream education system are historic and well-documented in research and reports. As early as 1967, the Plowden Report described Travellers' underachievement as a cause for concern, as their 'educational needs are extreme and largely unmet' (DES, 1967, p. 595). At this time, problems centred mainly on access to school: attendance was irregular, and many Travellers received no schooling at all (Reiss, 1975).

Although access has improved over the last 30 years, Gypsy and Travellers' attendance and attainment remains worryingly low, particularly at secondary school level. Indeed, Gypsies and Travellers are among the only ethnic minority groups[1] in the United Kingdom whose performance in school has deteriorated (Equality and Human Rights Commission, 2010). Thus, the issues for many Traveller pupils are not new, yet they are persistent. Informed by Critical Race Theory, this chapter juxtaposes the literature on Travellers' experiences in school and Travellers' own accounts with current education policy and guidance. The intention is to reveal the inequalities Travellers continue to experience in school and to highlight how this inequality remains invisible in policy, despite a wealth of research on this topic.

The chapter begins with an overview of Travellers and terminology. Critical Race Theory (CRT) is then discussed, as it provides a useful anti-racist framework and critical lens through which to examine Travellers' experiences of mainstream school, and by which to highlight issues of inequality. This is followed by an overview of the literature on Travellers' educational experiences. The next section draws specifically on research which consults with Traveller communities and on the author's own research, to support increased understandings about education and inclusion. This research on Travellers' experiences of inequality is then compared to education reports to illuminate the continuing public invisibility of this inequality. This chapter concludes with a summary of the issues raised and recommendations to improve Travellers' educational inclusion.

Travellers and terminology

The term *Traveller* is a general one which often is used to describe a number of distinct and separate groups, including Romani Gypsies, Irish Travellers, Welsh Travellers, New Age Travellers, fairground or showmen families, circus families and bargees, or boat dwellers. It is difficult to provide an accurate account of these different groups as the records are limited.[2] Nevertheless, it has been estimated that there are between 200,000 and 300,000 Gypsies and Travellers in England alone (Willers, 2012).

Romani Gypsies, Travellers of Irish Heritage and Scottish Travellers are recognised as ethnic minorities in England. Other Traveller groups, such as showmen and circus families are not. Ethnic minority status or no ethnic minority status, it is important to remember that most Traveller groups are marginalised on account of their perceived cultural differences to the settled community. Indeed, overt discrimination toward all Traveller groups remains a common experience (Willers, 2012). For brevity, in this chapter the term Traveller is used when referring to all groups; this is not to suggest that all these communities have common cultures or identities or that they face identical challenges. Reference to specific Traveller groups, such as Romany/Gypsy or showmen, are made as and when required.

Critical Race theory, travellers and education

Roithmayr (1999, p. 1) describes CRT as 'an exciting, revolutionary intellectual movement that puts race at the centre of critical analysis'. Critical Race Theory emerged in the United States in the 1980's from the work of Derek Bell and Alan Freeman, who wanted to advance racial reform. The foundations of CRT are located in the legal movement and critical legal studies (Ladson-Billings, 2009). CRT was transposed from legal studies into education in the mid-1990s (Dixson and Rousseau, 2006). Gloria Ladson-Billings and William Tate were at the forefront

of this movement. Although CRT originated in the United Sta
scholarly approach has now crossed disciplines and continen
growing in the United Kingdom. Gillborn (2006, p. 249) has argueu una.
it is a necessary theory in the United Kingdom to ensure that anti-racist
scholarship retains a radical and critical edge.

CRT is in part about critical thinking. Although there is no one
central definition of the CRT doctrine or methodologies, there are five
key elements that represent a CRT position (Gillborn, 2006). The first is
that racism is endemic in society, thus race and racism are at the centre
of critical analysis. Gillborn (1995, p. 23) proposes that racism is no
longer based on racial superiority versus inferiority – instead, the key
focus is on 'cultural difference'. This development of racism captures the
definition of racism within this chapter. This form of 'cultural' racism
characterises the way in which Traveller communities are continually
discriminated against on account of their cultural 'differences', which
are seen to depart from the 'norm'. Cultural racism resorts to 'essentialised, immutable cultural and religious differences' of minority communities that are seen to be in conflict with 'British values and ways of
life' (Chattoo and Atkin, 2012, p. 28). Although race and racism are
central to CRT, scholars view their intersection with other inequalities
based on gender and class to highlight the full picture of discrimination
(Solorzano and Yosso, 2002).

A further element of CRT is that it challenges and critiques dominant
principles of equal opportunities as, in reality, systems are slow-moving
and limit in actually addressing issues of race and racism. Indeed, they
claim that equal opportunity policy and practice often camouflage the
self-interest, power and privileges of the majority (Solorzano and Yosso,
2002).

A third relevant tenet is the way in which CRT advocates the voices of
marginalised groups, whose accounts are not often heard. CRT scholars
consider this knowledge as essential for a deeper understanding of education (Ladson-Billings, 2009). Hence, CRT scholars assert that the reality
of the true educational context can only be understood by listening to
the experiential knowledge of marginalised groups and individuals and
telling their stories. CRT uses conceptual tools such as storytelling and
counter-stories to do this. CRT is therefore theoretical, yet it is also practical as it advocates critical anti-racist research and practice through the
use of narrative. Solorzano and Yosso (2002, p. 32) emphasise the use
of counter-story as 'a tool for exposing, analysing and challenging the
majoritarian stories of racial privilege'. Hence counter-stories can be used
to turn dominant assumptions on their heads and question myths and

stereotypes (Gillborn, 2006). This chapter recounts Travellers' stories of education, and uses this evidence to build a counter-story against the dominant discourse, which suggests that Travellers are not committed to, or interested in, mainstream education.

The fourth component advocates a commitment to social justice. As Ladson-Billings (2009, p. 33) states, adopting CRT as a framework for educational equity means 'exposing racism in education and offering radical solutions to address it'. Thus, CRT is theoretical yet also very practical and calls for a variety of disciplines and scholars to work together towards social justice. CRT is a relevant theoretical framework for Travellers and education because it reveals the overt and covert nature of racism which Traveller communities continue to experience. Moreover, its call to action is imperative in addressing the ingrained nature of racism that is particularly hard to address as it presents as an everyday occurrence. To reveal and remind readers what the literature already tells us, the next section provides a critical insight into the literature on Gypsy, Roma and Travellers' inequalities in school.

What the literature tells us: Gypsy, Roma and Travellers' experiences of mainstream school education

The aforementioned Plowden Report (DES, 1967) signalled the beginning of many reports and investigations into the educational needs of Traveller children. Although the Swann Report, *Education for All* (DES, 1985), was a report of the Committee of Enquiry into the Education of Children from Ethnic Minority Groups, it dedicated an entire chapter to Traveller children. A decision the authors felt they needed to justify:

> Many people may be surprised to find not only that we have devoted a chapter of our report to considering the educational needs of children from travelling families, but also that we regard the travelling community as an ethnic minority group at all. (DES, 1985, p. 739)

In the 1980s, Traveller communities were not recognised as ethnic minorities; yet the authors state that 'many travellers (sic) regarded themselves as an ethnic minority group and were anxious for this Committee to consider their situation'. The Swann Report includes Travellers' own concerns:

> Unless your Committee is prepared to consider them [i.e., Travellers' children], we feel that there is a very real danger that they will slip through the net of existing provision. (ibid.)

Even when Gypsy, Roma and Irish Travellers became recognised ethnic minority groups, learners continued to slip through the net of educational provision. Indeed, Ofsted (1996) reported on the education of Travelling children and found that, although the situation in primary schools was improving, an estimated 10,000 Traveller children of secondary age may not be registered in any secondary school. The Pupil Level Annual Schools Census (PLASC) began to record data for Gypsy/ Roma and Travellers of Irish Heritage ethnic categories in 2004. Since that time children within these categories have consistently been at the bottom of measures of achievement (DCSF, 2009; Myers et al., 2010). In 2005, the DFES reported that Irish Travellers were the lowest-achieving group and Gypsy/Roma pupils were the lowest-achieving at Key Stages 3 and 4.[3] For example, 23 per cent of Gypsy/Roma pupils achieved 5 = A*– C in 2003 compared to a 51 per cent national average for all children. This report also confirmed that Gypsy/Roma attendance was problematic and that only one third of Gypsy/Roma pupils were registered at KS4 (end of secondary school). Less than half of Irish Travellers were registered by the time they left secondary school.

More recent research shows that little has changed. Traveller children's attendance rates in schools is around 75 per cent, the lowest of any ethnic minority (Equality and Human Rights Commission, 2010). The study of Wilkin et al. (2010) confirms that retention in secondary school remains problematic, and only one in five Traveller pupils complete secondary school. Gypsy, Roma and Traveller pupils are more likely to be identified inappropriately as having Special Education Needs (SEN). Gypsy, Roma and Traveller boys are also four times more likely to be excluded from school as a result of their behaviour (DCSF, 2005; Foster and Norton, 2012).

Scholars in the field of Traveller education (Liegeois, 1998; Kiddle, 1999; Bhopal, 2001; Derrington and Kendal, 2004; Levinson, 2007; Bhopal and Myers, 2008) have consistently drawn attention to the barriers that prevent Travellers' access and achievement in mainstream education. This literature highlights that among the main barriers Traveller children face are racism and bullying, negative teacher attitudes, high mobility and interrupted learning, disproportionate levels of exclusions, inconsistent or inadequate support, inappropriate identification of SEN among Traveller children and irrelevance of the curriculum – particularly at secondary school. Hence, Travellers' inequalities in school are well documented.

For example, the reasons for the high levels of exclusions, especially among Traveller boys, have been found to have parallels with the experiences of African Caribbean boys in school (Foster and Norton, 2012). Both have disproportioned high exclusion rates and are labelled and identified as underachievers (Tomlinson, 1983). Furthermore, the numbers of Traveller students with Special Educational Needs are disproportionately high. In Eastern Europe many Roma continue to be segregated into special schools on account of assumed 'different' learning needs; still, in these schools 'standards of teaching and faculties are poor' (Wilkin et al., 2009, p. 10). Thus, Roma pupils cannot access quality education on account of their race. Although the situation in the United Kingdom is not as extreme, there are concerns about the over-representation of ethnic minority pupils among those identified as having SEN (Cemlyn et al., 2009).

Thus, the difficulties Traveller learners experience in school are well documented. Yet these issues are not commonly cited or debated in public view. There remain unhelpful, widespread assumptions that all Traveller families are highly mobile, whereas, many Travellers today are settled on permanent sites or live in houses. This mobility rhetoric perpetuates a presumption that the problems Traveller pupils experience in school are the result of their mobility. A further example of the focus on Travellers' cultural differences is found across England and Europe; due to the tradition of non-acceptance of Traveller or Roma pupils in school, literacy levels among the adult population are low. Yet, dominant discourse suggests that nomadism is the cause of illiteracy, not school attitudes and structures. This discourse depicts the entire Traveller community as 'deviant' and prevents necessary responses for their children today. As Liegeois (1998, p. 101) suggests, 'where a correlation between two facts (illiteracy and nomadism) is to be found it does not signify a causal relationship between them'. This is not to say that literacy or mobility are not an issue: as with other non-Traveller groups, both have an impact on education. Yet, it is the perception of all Travellers' itinerancy as deviant from the settled society that results in their needs going largely unmet. Derrington and Kendal (2008, p. 127) confirm that 'too much emphasis on cultural explanations can lead to a theory of cultural pathology in which other related factors may be insufficiently considered'.

Critically examining, through a CRT lens, the difficulties Travellers experience in school reveals that racism and prejudice have significant consequences on Travellers' educational opportunities and experiences. Consequently, CRT can play an important role in unmasking and reminding us of the equality issues behind Travellers' difficulties in school. To illuminate racism and rethink pedagogy and practice in accordance with the new knowledge, CRT scholars use narrative to tell the stories of marginalised groups. Following this tradition the next section contemplates what Travellers say, using research work which has consulted with these communities.

What Travellers say

O'Hanlon and Holmes (2004) point out that the majority of research on Travellers' experiences of school systems has concerned itself with Travellers' relationships to education, and the researchers consulted with schools and official bodies to do so. Research which consults with Traveller families is limited, and Travellers' own voices are rarely heard regarding educational matters. It can be argued that this is partly related to the difficulties of accessing the community. A long history of discrimination means that the families may be wary, reluctant to speak to officials, and relationships and trust need to be established before data can be collected. This can be a time-consuming and costly process, and one that needs to be built in from the start.

My own qualitative study twice interviewed 11 Traveller families over the period of six months. My respondents included two showmen families and nine Romany/Gypsy families; these families were from different geographical parts of one particular county in England. Their socio-economic situations were also diverse. Although my research project was focused on Travellers and home education,[4] all families had initially educated their children in school and had much to say about mainstream school systems and spaces. It is this data I will draw upon for the purposes of this chapter.

Obviously, my respondents are those who have withdrawn their children from school, and it might be argued that this data will therefore portray only a negative perception of schooling. I concur that there is also a need for more research on the success stories of individual Traveller pupils in school. Nevertheless, I believe that these accounts are important because they illustrate issues of inequality in schools, and they challenge dominant assumptions about Traveller communities' alleged lack of interest and commitment to their children's education.

Problems in school

An analysis of data from interviews with Traveller families revealed three main problems with school; these are listed below and discussed in turn.

(1) Bullying and discrimination;
(2) Traveller children not being safe in school;

(3) Traveller children learning things that are not in keeping with their culture.

1. Bullying and discrimination

The DfES (2005) reported that school was perceived by many Traveller families as a dangerous space where racist bullying occurs. This was certainly the case for my participants. Seven of my respondents spoke of direct bullying incidents, and at least four families spoke of wider discrimination and of their child's segregation due to being a Traveller. There is a wealth of literature that confirms that the most common reason given by Traveller parents for their reluctance to send their children to school is racism and bullying (Ulreche and Franks, 2007; Lloyd and McClusky, 2008; Cemlyn et al., 2009; Wilkin et al., 2009).

All the Traveller parents I interviewed felt very anxious about bullying in secondary school. One daughter, Vanessa,[5] had had a reasonably positive experience in her first secondary school, but then moved to a new school:

> I was happy at my old school where I was before; I was happy, not really happy, but I was getting on at school, you know? I did not get on at this school. Bullying [was the main problem – KD]. I did not have any friends at this school either and honestly don't think it was a very good school altogether.

Vanessa had experienced bullying first-hand at her new school and reported a lack of response:

> Yes I told teachers – told near enough every teacher in school, but they never said anything about it really, they just said if it happens again come back. Kept going back and back and…nothing.

Foster and Norton (2012), experts in the field of Traveller education, confirm that schools do not always effectively tackle allegations of racist bullying. My research revealed that the fear of racism and bullying could prevent transfer from primary to secondary school:

> I think she would have liked secondary school, but it doesn't come like that does it?…I think she would have enjoyed it but…you got all the bad points…like with being a Traveller haven't you?

Another mother told me how her son was harassed by local young people who told him that he would be bullied when he arrived at secondary school. He did not transfer to secondary school. In addition to racist bullying, I found that there were often several complex intersections of inequality at play that caused problems in school, which included: illiteracy; social class; gender and special educational needs. For example, several Traveller children were bullied on account of their low literacy levels as well as of their ethnicity.

Discrimination by staff and students was a common topic in discussions about school. Many families spoke about feeling different because of their Traveller background and how they did not feel that their children were respected or their educational needs met. The accounts of Traveller families confirmed that issues of racism and discrimination towards Travellers remain endemic. Their accounts also illuminated the layers of subordination Travellers experience on the basis of various inequalities. Racist structures and prejudiced attitudes in society combine to represent a pervasive force that can be difficult to ignore and address (Derrington and Kendal, 2004). Despite rhetoric of equal opportunities, school remains a dangerous space for many Traveller pupils, particularly at secondary level.

Traveller children not being safe in school

Analysis of data revealed that all 11 families were concerned about their children's safety and wellbeing in mainstream schooling; a place where their children are in the minority. The account below highlights how vulnerable Travellers feel in school:

> It's different when you get lots of Traveller children going, but when you only have one or two.... When there is a lot [of Traveller children] it is usually okay. Primary was easy because there was about 50 Traveller children...so they are used to them and they go from when they are small...then they change [schools]. You usually get other children going from other schools to the college [secondary school] what perhaps have not even had any contact with Traveller children.

Derrington and Kendal (2004) found that Traveller parents are very protective of their children, an attribute which is often admired by school staff. Nevertheless, the authors also suggested that Traveller parents' desire to protect their children from physical and emotional harm could limit their educational opportunities. Myers et al. (2010) suggest that the protective Traveller community environment is often about protecting children from the negative influences of the 'outside world', including drugs, alcohol, liberal sexuality and racist bullying. Several parents in Bhopal and Myers's research (2009) also considered the Traveller world as a safe haven compared to the non-Traveller world. One mother in my sample described this situation as living in a 'bubble' and recognised that this protectiveness could also limit educational and social opportunities. Yet, this was a risk she felt was worth taking to keep her daughter safe.

All Traveller families considered their children's education carefully. Most felt that an education in school was ultimately best because of the resources available, but that in practice school was not necessarily good for Travellers on account of the racism they experienced there. These findings provide important counter-stories to the discourse of socialisation within which school attendance is perceived as necessary for healthy child development (Monk, 2004). Raey (2011) confirms that, for many young Travellers, despite the widespread perception that formal education is good, school is not their education system and does not belong to them; hence, they have little sense of belonging to it. I concur with Myers et al. (2010), who recommend that schools should rethink how they engage with Gypsy and Traveller cultures to create spaces in which they can feel safe. Feeling safe is about physical safety from bullying and discrimination, but also about respect for Traveller culture and values, a matter which is discussed next.

Traveller children learning things that are not in keeping with their culture

Many Traveller families still do have concerns about the content and relevance of the curriculum at secondary school (Ivatts, 2006). Difficulties in school were found to be complex. Vanessa's case provides an apt example. Her family wanted her to have a school education, yet their wish for her not to attend sex education lessons was not respected. Vanessa's older sister[6] explained:

> They teach them things that they should not know. I did not go along. ... I wrote on papers that she wasn't allowed to be taught [on sex] but she was still to be taught them. Vanessa told the teachers she was not allowed to be in that lesson, and I had already signed papers, but the teacher ignored and made her sit in.

In addition, Vanessa was bullied, and the school did not address this issue, thus her older sister eventually, reluctantly withdrew her. The difficulties Traveller children experience in education are, therefore, not solely concentrated on accessing and achieving standards and measures of the taught curriculum. Teacher attitudes and expectations also shape unequal educational opportunities (Mayers and Grosvenor, 2001). Vanessa's tale helps build my counter-story, which contradicts the notion that Traveller families do not desire an education for their children; instead it is the discriminatory systems and attitudes that do not support Traveller children in school.

There is certainly a general ignorance of Traveller cultures and an urgent need to address this situation. Suggestions to improve teacher education have been noted in many reports. Yet CRT scholars (Solorzano and Yosso, 2002; Kretovics and Nussel, 1994; Persell, 1977) have criticised teacher training, as it commonly draws on majoritarian stories to explain educational inequality through a cultural deficit model and, in doing so, passes on beliefs that pupils from minority groups are culturally deprived. Thus, in order to improve understandings and respect towards Traveller communities the content and nature of training must reflect an accurate picture of different Traveller cultures by involving Travellers themselves in the delivery and design of training.

Overall, my research found that Traveller parents did want their children to be educated in school but felt compelled to withdraw them because of concerns about their welfare, especially at secondary school level. My findings correlate with those of others who have listened to the voices of Travellers and to other marginalised groups' experiences of education (Derrington and Kendal, 2004; Bhopal and Myers, 2009). Still, the on-going invisibility of reported racism towards Travellers and the consequences on their educational opportunities are deeply concerning. Despite a wealth of research and evidence on the inequalities Traveller children face in school, there is little said on these matters in dominant education policy and practices. The next part of this chapter provides evidence to support this claim.

What policy leaves unsaid

A pertinent example of the invisibility, in policy, of Travellers' inequalities can be found in a very recent Ofsted (2012a) report. This report was called *No Place for Bullying*, and it evaluated the effectiveness of the actions of 56 schools in creating positive school culture and preventing and tackling bullying. This report begins by acknowledging how research evidence shows that there are groups of pupils who are bullied disproportionally. Yet the report only refers to disabled pupils, those who have special educational needs and homosexual pupils (Ofsted, 2012b, p. 5).

The otherwise well-reported issues for Travellers are not mentioned. A further example is found in the new Ofsted (2012b) school inspection framework, in which there is also no reference to Gypsies, Roma or Travellers as vulnerable groups. Indeed, this document is a step backwards from previous inspectors' guidance reports (Ofsted, 2010), which stated that inspectors should acknowledge that if the school is judged to be inadequate in promoting equal opportunity and tackling discrimination, its overall effectiveness is also likely to be judged to be inadequate.

These reports provide a sample of evidence to highlight how policy ignores the academic literature which stresses that issues of racism are central to Travellers' barriers to attending school. Stovall (2006, p. 232) confirms that schools often operate as spaces where realities of race and racism are not talked about, even if understood by students. The fact that race equality is diluted and ignored raises critical questions about the purpose and function of education. Gillborn (2005) notes that education cannot remove racism from society, but educators do have opportunities and responsibilities to address racism as it presents itself in school. Exactly because racism is such an ingrained feature of our landscape, it is essential that it is named in order to address it and work towards social justice.

Conclusion

The purpose of this chapter has been to provide critical insight into Travellers' experiences of school, to highlight inequality and advocate for improvements. Racism and a continuing short-sighted unjustified approach towards Travellers are significant factors in mainstream schooling, and the literature indicates clear issues related to educational equality for Traveller children in school. Yet, dominant rhetoric of cultural difference often hides the real issues Travellers face. They are still perceived as 'different' and 'deviant', and there is no ongoing, firm commitment to address the barriers Travellers face in school. Nevertheless, there should be. Research evidence confirms that when Traveller pupils are given the right learning environments and experiences they can be as successful as any other group (DCSF, 2009). The United Nations Convention on the Rights of the Child (1989, Article 28) 'recognizes the right of the child to education, and with a view to achieving this right progressively and on the basis of equal opportunity'. Yet, for many Traveller children and young people this is still not the case.

This chapter has drawn on CRT to critically analyse the literature and present Travellers' own accounts in order to build a counter-story that challenges the invisibility, in policy and practice, of their disadvantages. Their stories also highlight the reality of the educational situation; widespread racism and prejudiced attitudes towards Travellers in society and education continue to marginalise and exclude Traveller pupils from achieving and staying on in school. Solorzano and Yosso (2002) suggest that substantive discussions of racism are missing from critical discourse in education. I concur and propose that in order to meet the needs of all Traveller pupils; race and ethnicity need to be placed firmly back on the political education agenda. There needs to be a collective resolve to address the educational and social marginalisation of Traveller communities and their children. Educators can play a part in raising critical questions about inclusion in school and creating safe spaces in their own schools and local communities. Researchers and educators should continue to consult and engage with Traveller communities to ensure their voices are heard, and I propose that CRT can provide a useful anti-racist strategy to illuminate issues of inequality and work towards social justice. Furthermore, any critical discourse of racism in education needs to include Traveller communities themselves in order to challenge broad societal perceptions about Travellers – perceptions that play out in policy and practice.

Notes

1. See below for clarification on ethnic minority groupings.
2. Ethnic categories for Gypsy and Irish Travellers were first included in the census in 2011.
3. Key Stages (KS) 1 and 2 represent primary school age children; Key Stages 3 and 4 represent secondary school level.
4. D'Arcy (Forthcoming)
5. This is a pseudonym to protect the identity of this young Traveller.
6. Vanessa's sister was also responsible for her care.

References

Bhopal, K. (2001) 'Gypsy Travellers and education: changing needs and changing perceptions', *British Journal of Education*, 52 (1), 17–61.

Bhopal, K. and Myers, M. (2008) *Insiders, Outsiders and Others; Gypsies and Identity*, Hatfield: University of Hertfordshire Press.

Cemlyn, S., Greenfields, M., Burrett, S., Matthews, Z. and Whitwell, C. (2009) *Inequalities Experienced by Gypsy and Traveller Communities: A Review*, Research Report 12, Equality and Human Rights Commission.

Chattoo, S. and Atkin, K. (2012) 'Race, ethnicity and social policy: theoretical concepts and the limitation of current approaches to welfare', in Craig, G., Atkin., K, Chattoo, S. and Flynn, R. *Understanding Race and 'Ethnicity': Theory, History, Policy and Practice*, Bristol, Polity Press, 19–40.

D'Arcy, K. (Forthcoming) *Why Gypsies and Other Traveller Home Educate: Educational Spaces & Inequality*, London: Trentham & IOE Press.

Department of Education and Science (DES) (1967) *Children and their Primary schools, the Plowden Report*, Central Advisory Council for Education (England), London, HMSO.

Department of Education and Science (DES) (1985) *Education for All: The Report of the Committee of Enquiry into the Education of Children from Ethnic Minority Groups, the Swann Report*, London, HMSO.

Department for Education and Skills (DfES) (2005) *Ethnicity and Education: The Evidence on Minority Ethnic Pupils* (Research Topic Paper RTP01–05) Nottingham, DfEs. Available online at https://www.education.gov.uk/publications/eOrderingDownload/DFES-0208–2006.pdf. [Accessed on June 2012]

Department for Children, Schools and Families (DCSF) (2009) *Moving Forward Together: Raising Gypsy, Roma and Traveller Achievement*, Booklet 1, Introduction, The National Strategies DCSF.

Derrington, C. and Kendall, C. (2004) *Gypsy Traveller Student in Secondary Schools*, Trentham, Trentham Books.

Derrington, C. and Kendall, S. (2008) 'Challenges and Barriers to secondary education: the experiences of young Gypsy Traveller students in English secondary schools', *Social Policy and Society*, 7, Part 1, Cambridge, Cambridge University Press.

Dixson, A.D. and Rousseau, C.K. (2006) *Critical Race Theory in Education: All God's Children Got a Song*, London and New York, Routledge.

Equality and Human Rights Commission (2010) *How Fair Is Britain: The First Triennial Review*, Equality and Human Rights Commission.

Foster, B. and Norton, P. (2012) 'Educational equality for Gypsy, Roma and Traveller children and young people in the UK', *The Equal Rights Review*, 8, 85–112.

Gillborn, D. (1995) *Racism and Anti-Racism in Real Schools*, Milton Keynes, Open University Press.

Gillborn, D. (2005) 'Education policy as an act of white supremacy: whiteness, critical race theory and education reform', *Journal of Education Policy*, 20 (4), 485–505.

Gillborn, D. (2006) 'Critical Race Theory beyond North America: toward a transatlantic dialogue on racism and anti-racism in educational theory and praxis', in Dixson, A.D. and Rousseau, C.K. (eds), *Critical Race Theory in Education: All God's Children Got a Song*, Oxford: Routledge, 243–269.

Ivatts, A. (2006) *Elective Home Education: The Situation Regarding the Current Policy, Provision and Practice in Elective Home Education for Gypsy, Roma and Traveller Children*, Department for Education and Skills.

Kiddle, C. (1999) *A Voice for Themselves*, London, Jessica Kingsley Publishers.

Kretovics, J. and Nussel, E. (eds) (1994) 'Transforming urban education, Boston', *Harvard Educational Review*, 39, 1–123.

Ladson-Billings, G. (2009) 'Just what is CRT and what is it doing in a nice field like education?' in Taylor, E., Gillbourn, D. and Ladson-Billings, G. (eds), *Foundations of Critical Race Theory in Education*, London: Routledge, 17–37

Lloyd, G. and McClusky, G. (2008) 'Education and Gypsy Travellers: contradictions and significant silences', *International Journal of Inclusive Education*, 12 (4), 331–345.

Levinson, M.P. (2007) 'Literacy in English Gypsy Communities: cultural capital manifested as negative assets', *American Educational Research Journal*, 44 (1), 5–39.

Liegeois, J. (1998) *School Provision for Ethnic Minorities: The Gypsy Paradigm*, Gypsy Research Centre, Hertfordshire, University of Hertfordshire Press.

Mayers, K. and Grosvenor, I. (2001) 'Policy, equality and inequality: from the past to the future', in Hill, D. and Cole, M. (eds), *Schooling and Equality: Fact, Concept and Policy*, London, Kogan page, 249–265.

Monk, D. (2004) 'Problematising home-education: challenging "parental rights" and "socialism"', *Legal Studies*, 24 (4), 568–598.

Myers, M., McGee, D. and Bhopal, K. (2010) 'At the crossroads: Gypsy and Traveller parents' perceptions of education, protection and social change', *Race, Ethnicity and Education*, 13 (4), 533–548.

Persell, C. (1977) *Education and Inequality: The Roots and Results of Stratification in America's Schools*, New York, Free Press.

Office for Standards in Education (Ofsted) (1996) *The Education of Travelling Children*, April 1996, Crown Copyright.

Office for Standards in Education (2009) *Inspecting Equalities: Guidance for Section 5 Inspectors*, September 2012, Crown Copyright 2012. Available at URL www.communitycohesionncc.org.uk/docs/484.doc. [Accessed on March 2012]

Office for Standards in Education (2010) *Inspecting Equality: Guidance for Level 5 Inspectors*, September 2010, Crown Copyright 2010.

Office for Standards in Education (2012a) *The FrameWork for School Inspection: Guidance and Grade Descriptors for Inspecting Schools in England under Section 5 of the Education Act 2005*, January 2012, Ref 090019, OFSTED.

Office for Standards in Education (2012b) *No Place for Bullying: How Schools Create a Positive Culture and Prevent and Tackle Bullying*, June 2012, Ref 110179, OFSTED.

O'Hanlon, C. and Holmes, P. (2004). *The Education of Gypsy and Traveller Children: Towards Inclusion and Educational Achievement*. Stoke on Trent: Trentham Books.

Raey, D., Crozier, G. and James, D. (2011) *White Middle Class Identities and Urban Schooling*, Houndsmills, Palgrave Macmillan.

Reiss, C. (1975) *Education of Travelling Children: A Report for the Schools Council*, London, Macmillan.

Roithmayr, D. (1999) 'Introduction to Critical Race Theory in educational research and praxis', in Parker, L., Deyhle, D. and Villenas, S. (eds), *Race is...Race Isn't: Critical Race Theory and Qualitative Studies in Education*, Oxford, Westview, 1–7.

Solorzano, D.G. and Yosso, T.J. (2002) 'Critical Race Methodology: counter-story-telling as an analytical framework for educational research', *Qualitative Inquiry*, 8 (23), 121–136.

Stovall, D. (2006) 'Where the Rubber Hits the Road: CRT goes to high school', in Dixson, A.D. and Rousseau, C.K. (eds), *Critical Race Theory in Education: All God's Children Got a Song*, Oxon, Routledge.

Tomlinson, S. (1983) *Ethnic Minorities in British Schools: A Review of Literature 1960–1982*. London, Heinemann Educational Books.

Ulreche, H. and Franks, M. (2007) *This is Who We Are: A Study of the Views and Identities of Roma, Gypsy and Traveller Young People in England,* London, The Children's Society.

The United Convention on the Rights of the Child (UNCRC) (1989) 'United Nations Convention on the Rights of the Child: The Articles'. Available at http://www.dcsf.gov.uk/everychildmatters/strategy/strategyandgovernance/uncrc/unitednationsarticles/uncrcarticles/ [Accessed on November 2010]

Wilkin, A., Derrington, C. and Foster, B. (2009) *Improving the Outcomes for Gypsy, Roma and Traveller Pupils, Literature Review,* Research Report DCSF-RRO77, DCSF.

Wilkin, A. Derrington, C., White, R., Marton, K., Foster, B., Kinder, K. and Rutt, S. (2010) *Improving the Outcomes for Gypsy, Roma and Traveller Pupils: Final Report,* Department for Education, Research Report DFE-RR043.

Willers, M. (2012) 'Tackling inequalities suffered by Gypsies and Travellers', *Travellers Advice Team (TAT) News,* Newsletter Spring 2012, Traveller Advice Team, part of Community Law Partnership.

4
Race and Ethnicity in US Education

Geneva Gay

Race and ethnicity are definitive features of society and schools in the United States. They are not new phenomena, but historical legacies, and are generative as well as problematic and contentious. As Benjamin Barber (1992, p. 41) explained, the United States has always been a tale of many different peoples 'trying to be a People, a tale of diversity and plurality in search of unity'. This diversity is multifaceted – including age, gender, class, religion, language, and origins – but race and ethnicity are the United States's most compelling and challenging social issues. Hawley and Nieto (2010) noted that, while inconvenient and troubling for many educators and people in general, it is nonetheless true that race and ethnicity matter significantly in the learning opportunities and outcomes of diverse students, now and always in the United States.

Contemporary variations of these legacies and dilemmas are distinguished by their complexity rather than by their novelty. The salience and challenge of race and ethnicity in US society are embodied educationally in two major narratives. One has to do with the changing ethnic and racial demographics of students and teachers, and programmatic and pedagogical implications of them. The other narrative focuses on how race and ethnicity are conceived and perceived. One version tends to emphasise problems primarily, while the other examines challenges along with productivity and positive possibilities. Hawley and Nieto (2010) identify these areas of concern as the effects teachers' attitudes, beliefs, and behaviours regarding race and ethnicity have on students' responses to school curricula and instruction, and teachers' assumptions about how much different students are capable of learning and how they learn. These perspectives are explored in the following discussion, beginning with a summary of the demographic gaps between students and teachers and their implications for teaching and learning. This is followed sequentially by explanations of conventional reactions to race and ethnicity in educational programmes and practices, and then by some alternative possibilities for achieving more effective efforts and outcomes.

Race and ethnicity demographics among students and teachers

One of the most graphic indicators of the prominence of race and ethnicity in US schools is the physical, social, and cultural diversity of students and teachers. Student populations in kindergarten through secondary (K-12) schools are becoming more ethnically, racially, linguistically, culturally, and socially pluralistic, but teachers continue to be overwhelmingly mono-racial, mono-ethnic, mono-cultural, and monolingual. These patterns are confirmed by various reports produced by different local, state, and national private and governmental agencies and individual researchers. The conclusions across these sources are similar – the demographic dominance of US society and schools that people of European ancestry have maintained for so long is dissolving.

According to the Centre for Public Education (2012), already one in ten US states has a population that is more than 50 per cent non-White. Furthermore, *ethnically and racially diverse populations are growing more quickly than the nation's population as a whole. This is especially true of Latinos.* Between 2000 and 2010, the total US population increased by 9.7 per cent. The Latino and Asian populations each grew by 43 per cent, and the African ancestry population by 12.3 per cent. The European ancestry population grew by only 4.9 per cent for that time period. The US Census Bureau (2010) reports that from 2000 to 2010, the multiracial population grew by 32 per cent, for a total of 9 million. This rate represented a 0.5 per cent gain, from 2.4 to 2.9 per cent of the total US population. These trends are evident throughout the country and are reflected in the demographics of both elementary and secondary schools. However, they are more pronounced in some regions, states, cities, and schools than in others, and the specifics of particular ethnic and racial population patterns vary similarly.

National shifting population trends in US society and schools are documented and reported annually by the National Centre for Educational Statistics (NCES). The most recent detailed information available is for 2010, although some of it is based on data compiled as early as the 2007–2008 school year. Therefore, since the data are not completely current, some discrepancies may occur between what is reported and what actually exists. Yet, the patterns prevail across generations. For example, between 1990 and 2010 the European American (e.g., Whites) student population in US schools decreased 13 per cent from 67 per cent to 54 per cent. During the same period African Americans also decreased, from 17 per cent to 15 per cent, as did Native Americans, from 0.9 per cent to 0.7 per cent. However, Latino Americans and Asian Americans/ Pacific Islanders increased, from 11.7 per cent to 23 per cent and from 3 per cent to 4 per cent, respectively. In 2010 NCES began providing information on multiracial student populations as well. Those with two or more ethnic and racial identities comprised 2.9 per cent in 2010 (National Centre for Educational Statistics, 2010).

NCES also provides other valuable information about: the ethnic and racial distribution of student populations across regions of the country, school levels and locations, and educational programming. For example, African American, Latino, and Asian American/Pacific Islander students are concentrated in cities and suburbs, European Americans in suburbs and rural areas, and Native Americans in rural areas. More African, Latino, and Native Americans attend high-poverty schools than do European and Asian Americans. And, higher percentages of Native American and native Alaskans than any other ethnic groups are served under the Individuals with Disabilities Act (National Centre for Education Statistics, 2010). In 2007 (the most recent year for which data are available) there were 49 million students in elementary and secondary public schools in the United States, with another 5.5 million attending private schools. The 20 largest school districts enrolled five million students, or 11 per cent of that total. In 18 of those districts the majority populations are students of colour, ranging from 55 per cent to 95 per cent. Across all districts, those in which European Americans comprise half or more of the student population enrolled 87 per cent of European American students, 51 per cent of Native Americans and Alaskans, 40 per cent of Asian/Pacific Islanders, 26 per cent of African Americans, and 23 per cent of Latino Americans. Schools in which half of the total student population is African American enrolled 48 per cent of all African Americans, and those with half or more of Latinos enrolled 57 per cent of that ethnic group (National Centre for Education Statistics, 2010).

The racial and ethnic distribution of public school students also differed by regions (North, Midwest, South, and West) of the United States from 1990 to 2010. The National Centre for Education Statistics (2012a) reported that over this 20-year period the number and percentage enrolment of European Americans decreased in all regions, with the exception of the South, where their enrolment fluctuated but the overall percentage decreased during this period. The number of African Americans fluctuated in all four regions, and their percentage declined in the West and South. The number and percentage of Latino students increased in all four regions. The number and percentage of Asian American students increased in all regions except the West, where their number and percentage of enrolment fluctuated. Native Hawaiian/Pacific Islander and American Indian/Alaska Native students each represented 1 per cent or less of student enrolment in all regions of the United States in 2010. Students of two or more races made up 4 per cent of enrolment in the West, 3 per cent in the Midwest, and 2 per cent each in the Northeast and South. In 2010, White students comprised 50 per cent or less of school enrolment in 12 states and the District of Columbia; African American students had the largest percentage of public school enrolment in Mississippi and the District of Columbia; Latinos in Arizona, California, New Mexico, and Texas; and Asian Americans and students of two or more races in Hawaii (National Centre for Education Statistics, 2012a).

Ethnic and racial student population distributions are even more compelling in urban schools. A report on the characteristics of the 100 largest school districts by the National Centre for Education Statistics (2010) indicated that, together, Latinos and African Americans account for 63 per cent of their student populations. These districts range in size from 47,000 to 982,000, and serve 22 per cent of the more than 49 million total students in the United States, even though they account for only 10 per cent of all school districts in the country. In 70 of the districts, Latinos, African Americans, Asian/Pacific Islanders, Native Americans and Alaskans, and bi-racial or multi-racial students comprise more than 50 per cent of the total population and, in 35 of the 100 largest districts, that representation is 75 per cent or more.

Although African and Latino Americans, especially males, are still over-represented in special education, some better news is apparent on the other ends of the educational spectrum. National data on course-taking for 2008–2009 indicate that all racial groups are taking more high-level mathematics and science classes and advanced placement (AP) exams. Yet, the good news is not without qualification. The patterns of performance in these courses and exams are consistent with long-established patterns in other performance areas, such as on national and state tests, the graduate records exam (GRE), and the Scholastic Achievement Tests (SAT). Asian and European Americans consistently perform the highest in subjects tested (reading, mathematics, science, United States history, geography, and civics), and African Americans the lowest on these measures of achievement across all grade levels assessed. Scores on the 2008 AP tests are illustrative of these trends. The average score across all ethnic groups was 2.83 of a highest possible of 5.0, with 3.0 required to receive credit. The average scores by specific ethnic groups were 3.08 for Asian Americans, 2.96 for European Americans, 2.42 for Latino Americans, 2.39 for Native Americans and Alaskans, and 1.91 for African Americans. While 64 per cent of Asian Americans received a score of 3.0 or higher, only 26 per cent of African Americans did so (National Centre for Education Statistics, 2012b).

Other measures and indicators of school achievement, such as attendance, graduation rates, and disciplinary referrals follow similar patterns, with the dubious distinction of having the lowest positive performance records being shared or traded among African Americans, Latinos, and Native/Alaskan Americans. For instance, even through high school graduation rates are improving for all ethnic groups, they are still significantly lower for Latinos (64 per cent in 2011) compared to 84, 87, and 88 per cent for African Americans, Asian Americans, and European Americans, respectively (Centre for Public Education, 2012).

These composite data indicate that what some scholars call 'school resegregation' (Boger and Orfield, 2005; Tatum, 2007; Orfield, Kucsera and Siegal-Hawley, 2012) and disparities in educational achievement by race and ethnicity of students continue to occur unabated. That is, students in US schools are concentrated by ethnic and racial groups, and they are not receiving comparable quality educations. These tendencies are particularly striking for poor African and Latino students in large urban districts. Their concentrations are at the lowest end of the education, economic, and achievement spectrums. The same is true for Native Americans and Native Alaskans, but their dire circumstances are disguised somewhat by their small numbers, although this is an inexcusable oversight. Orfield, Kucsera and Siegel-Hawley (2012, pp. 7–8) summarised some of the negative consequences of school segregation for diverse student populations, accordingly:

> The consensus of nearly sixty years of social science research on the harms of school segregation is clear; separation remains extremely unequal. Schools of concentrated poverty and segregated minority schools are strongly related to an array of factors that limit educational opportunities and outcomes. These include less experienced and less qualified teachers, high levels of teacher turnover, less successful peer groups, and inadequate facilities and learning materials. There is also

a mounting body of evidence indicating that desegregated schools are linked to important benefits for all children, including prejudice reduction, heightened civic engagement, more complex thinking, and better learning outcomes in general.

Ethnic and racial disparities in the educational enrolment and perform-ance of students do not end with high school. Although the data for colleges and universities are not as systematic and readily available as those for pre-collegiate education, they indicate that the patterns are similar. Latino, African, and Native American students have lower college admission test scores than European and Asian Americans; they are under-represented in college enrolments and degree completion, take longer to complete degrees, and have lower grade-point averages. They also report feeling more isolated and neglected by professors who do not spend much quality time interacting with and mentoring them. For example, two 2010 documents (Lynch and Engle, 2010a, 2010b) released by the Education Trust indicate that, while 60 per cent of European Americans completed their college degrees in six years, only 49 per cent of Latino Americans and 40 per cent of African Americans did so. No information was provided for Native and Asian Americans; nor were the data disaggregated by areas of study. In many colleges and universities Asian Americans are proportionally over-represented, espe-cially in those regions where they comprise a significant percentage of the general population, such as in California and Washington.

In some ways the ethnic and racial ratio trends among teachers in the United States tends to be similar, yet very different from the student populations. The established patterns of their respective demographics are persistent across time, but the specific details of these trends are reversed. Both student and teacher populations are becoming more ethnically and racially diverse, but the increase among teachers is too minuscule to be significant overall. Furthermore, the decline in the representation of one ethnic group (African Americans) of teachers is barely compensated by the increase in other ethnic groups (Latino and Asian Americans). Consequently, the overall ratios of ethnic and racial distribution of US teachers have remained largely the same for many years. Despite the fact that the number and percentage of European American teachers has declined recently, the teaching profession is still overwhelmingly European American. This is true at all levels of educa-tion, including elementary and secondary schools, colleges and universi-ties, and teacher education programmes, as well as for public and private institutions. The exception is historically Black colleges and universities

(HBCUs), where the majority of students and instructors traditionally have been African Americans.

The most recent profile of US teachers released by the National Centre for Education Statistics (Feistritzer, 2011) revealed that 84 per cent of all public school teachers are European American (down from 91 per cent in the late 1980s). Only 7 per cent are African American, 7 per cent are Latino American, and 2 per cent are from other ethnic groups, including Asian/Pacific Islanders and Native American/Alaskans. These numbers represent a significant decline among African Americans, who comprised as much as 12 per cent of the national teaching force at their peak in the 1980s. In addition to the disproportional representation of Latino and African American teachers compared to the representation of Latino and African American students, other troubling disparities are apparent as well. For instance, teachers who work in schools with high populations of ethnically and racially diverse students (as well as of students in poverty) are less experienced and qualified than the national averages; their turnover rates are much higher; funding is significantly lower; and physical facilities are often outdated and/or dilapidated.

Race and ethnic demographics of college and university faculties are not reported by areas of study. For the institutions as a whole, the distributions are similar to those of K-12 teachers. In 2009 approximately 79 per cent of college- and university-wide faculties were European American, 7 per cent African American, 6 per cent Asian/Pacific Islander, 4 per cent Latino, and 1 per cent Native American/Alaskan (National Centre of Educational Statistics, 2011). It is likely that the race and ethnic distribution in faculties of colleges of education is not notably different.

These student and teacher demographic statistics attest to the fact that race and ethnicity matter in significant ways in teaching and learning, and that US teachers and students often come from different socialised, identity, and experiential backgrounds. The value orientations, behavioural styles, and referential frameworks that result from these differences have profound effects on the dynamics and outcomes of teaching and learning. The wider the demographic gaps between students and teachers the most detrimental the circumstances are for achievement. While teachers' membership in the same ethnic and racial group as their students does not ensure instructional effectiveness, some ancillary positive benefits do result, such as the psycho-emotional value of students being exposed to people from their own ethnic groups engaged in classroom teaching and other functions throughout the educational enterprise. More powerful effects derive from teachers being knowledgeable, accepting, and positively responsive to ethnic, racial, and cultural differences in their instructional strategies and other interactions with students. All of these types of benefits need to be identified and employed in transforming educational opportunities for students of colour.

Challenges of race and ethnicity in teaching and learning

Given the prominence and pervasiveness of racial and ethnic diversity in US society and schools, one would think that educators have long since come to terms with these realities, resolved any conflicts they may have initiated originally, and accepted them as so normative as to no longer command any particular attention. But this is not the case. Race and ethnicity continue to be sources of much conflict and contention in all levels of society and schooling, from personal relationships to institutional practices to governmental and legal regulations of various kinds of opportunities, resources, and achievement outcomes. There also is much unrecognised and underused productivity, promise, and possibility in ethnic and racial diversity.

More often than not, prospective, novice, and experienced teachers are sceptical about or resist explicitly engaging race and ethnicity in the content of their instruction and other classroom interactions with students. Or, they view race and ethnicity in only negative, pathological, and problematic terms. For instance, many teachers continue to assume that discussions and actions that focus on race-based and ethnic-based group and community differences are analogous to discrimination, preferential treatment (as in affirmative action), or inviting division and hostility (Howard, 2010; McLean Donaldson, 2001). Yet, educators (and people at large) in the United States make strong and consistent ideological claims about valuing individual worth and maximising individual potential. At the level of action, though, individuality is de-contextualised from race, ethnicity, and culture in spite of the fact that all individuals have these attributes.

Why is this so? Several explanations are possible. First, attitudes and actions such as these may be cultivated by, and reflect the racial climate prevalent in, US society, especially the negativism and pathology. Unfortunately, racism is still pervasive in every aspect of society, and ethnically and racially different people are stereotypically portrayed as being dependent, unproductive, hostile, violent, strange, and always 'the other' (for Latino and Asian Americans this translates into always being considered as foreigners). Asian Americans are the exception to many of the negative perceptions. They are considered instead as 'model minorities' by being complacent, conformist, non-aggressive, and productive in ways that are acceptable to mainstream society. Of course this is not true for all Asian Americans, but the stereotype does not allow for intragroup variability. Therefore, these images may be implanted in teachers' sub-consciousness and influence how they react to ethnic and racial diversity in their schools and classrooms.

Second, because negative connotations are attached to race, and it is frequently conflated with racism, some teachers associate being explicit about and responsive to race and ethnicity in their instructional thinking and actions as analogous to being prejudicial and racist. Their knowledge of the historical record of intergroup and interpersonal tensions and acts of violence provoked by discrimination and racism may lead them to try to avoid these provocations at all cost, even when these desires are instinctual instead of resulting from deliberate forethought. These teachers consider the best course of action is to ignore race and ethnicity, or deny their existence. In an antiracist curriculum and instruction project that included 512 teachers who were mostly European Americans, McLean Donaldson (2001) found that: most of the teachers did not believe racism existed in their schools and communities; thought racism was too painful and embarrassing to examine directly; considered the claims of under-represented groups about being victimised by racism as exaggerations; and assumed that working in schools with predominately students of colour indicated their non-racist status. These may be some of the reasons why declarations of colour-blindness are still so common among teachers at all levels of professional experience. The thoughts of Hawley and Nieto (2010, pp. 67–68) are worth noting here. They suggest that:

> Although colour-blindness is a good thing when it means that people do not discriminate on the basis of race, it can have negative consequences when educators refuse to see their students' racial, ethnic, cultural, and linguistic differences. Instead, teachers need to respect and build on differences to foster student learning.

A third reason why teachers are reluctant to deliberately engage race and ethnicity in their teaching may be lack of pedagogical competence and confidence. They may not feel adequately prepared with the knowledge, skills, and personal experiences needed to deal adequately with race and ethnicity in curriculum, instruction, and relationships with students. If this is the case, it is understandable how doubts, coupled with anxiety about the assumed volatile nature of race, can cause teachers to respond with avoidance, diffidence, and/or denial. So, they reason to the effect that, 'I would if I could but, since I don't know how, it's best that I don't try'; or, 'race is not the issue of importance, but something else, probably class'; and, 'it's really the individuality of students that counts, not their race'. Ethnicity may be less threatening, but since it is often co-mingled with race that when one is feared and avoided, so is the other.

These possibilities are confirmed by the research findings and practical experiences of many scholars from different ethnic backgrounds and involved in various levels of the educational enterprise, from classroom teachers to teacher educators, policy makers, and administrative leaders. Some of them are summarised by Tatum (2007), Howard (2010), Gay and Jackson (2006), Cochran-Smith (2004) and McLean Donaldson (2001). The information they provide concerns primarily European American prospective and practicing teachers. Based on her summary of research conducted in the 1990s with European American pre-service teachers, Sleeter (2001, p. xi) concluded:

> Studies...in varied geographic areas of the United States have found consistently that although a large proportion [of pre-service teachers] anticipate working with children of another cultural background, as a whole they bring very little cross-cultural background, knowledge and experience. [They are] fairly naïve and hold stereotypical beliefs about urban children, believing that culture does not affect education, and also that urban children bring attitudes that interfere with education.... White teachers...have little awareness of discrimination inside or outside schools.... Further, white teachers often question whether they can actually teach students of colour [and] tend to be ignorant of or resistant to using strategies and programs that work for culturally diverse student populations.

In reflecting on their experiences as teacher educators with how prospective teachers resist or refuse to accept the significance of ethnic, racial, and cultural diversity in teaching and learning, Gay and Jackson (2006, p. 203) noted:

> Most of these were subtle and probably not consciously intentional. Certainly they were most often not coded as deliberate resistance but the effects were, in that the attitudes and behaviours exhibited interfered with the effective progression of teaching and learning about racial, ethnic, and cultural differences. We often have to divert our energies from teaching to defending the credentials of [ethnically diverse] scholars, justifying the ideological beliefs of multicultural

education, soothing personal hurt feelings of European American students, and convincing them that their fragile egos and identities will not be ignored or crucified in the process of examining the cultures, lives, and experiences of groups of colour.

Little research has been done on the attitudes and actions of prospective and practicing teachers of colour with regard to race and ethnicity. That research which does exist indicates that they generally are less resistant to engaging with race and ethnicity, even though they do not necessarily have any more formal preparation in their professional development than their European American counterparts (McLean Donaldson, 2001; Howard, 2010; Bennett, Cole and Thompson, 2000; Bennett, 2002). However, some have doubts about the salience of race and ethnicity – doubts that are similar to those of their European American peers. For example, in a project that she directed – designed specifically for preparing African and Latino American teacher candidates – Bennett (2002) found that some felt concerns about racism were inflated, that considerations of race and ethnicity fostered stereotyping, and that talking about discrimination encourages people of colour to view themselves as victims.

The failure of so many teachers and other educators to deal explicitly with race and ethnicity has immediate and long-range consequences. The immediate consequences are limiting and ineffective educational experiences, while the long range consequences are detrimental effects on society at large. As Tatum (2007, p. xvi) explains, in the near and distant future it is.

> the rising generation of students of colour and those [who] follow them [who] will be our national supply of talent. We have to talk about how the way our socialisation about race prevents us from fully recognising that talent, and the way that the dynamics of race in our society have kept us from fully educating youth of colour. If we don't fully engage in dialogue about what we can do differently, and bring an understanding of the legacy of race and racism in our society into that conversation, we will not be successful in addressing this and other national challenges

Marilyn Cochran-Smith (2004) advises teachers to unlearn both unintentional and deliberate racism, and cautions them that this a difficult and discomforting, although necessary, task for improving the education of ethnically, racially, and culturally diverse students. She counsels teachers to realise that

this is a slow and stumbling journey and that along the way difficulty, pain, self-exposure, and disappointment are inevitable. To teach
lessons about race and racism ... is to ... interrogate the assumptions that
are deeply embedded in the curriculum, to own our own complicity
in maintaining existing systems of privilege and oppression, and to
grapple with our own failure. (Cochran-Smith 2004, p. 101)

This, alone, is enough to persuade some teachers to avoid or circum-
vent the journey for both themselves and for the students under their
tutelage.

Even when teachers overcome their hesitancy and pathological
perceptions enough to attempt to include positive attributes of race and
ethnicity in their curriculum and instruction, the results are often less
than desirable. There is a tendency to focus on 'safe topics and techniques', and to de-contextualize ethnic experiences and traditions. These
techniques include: memorising facts about historical issues and events
and the accomplishments of select ethnic individuals (particularly those
who have already gained entry into mainstream narratives); highlighting
contributions to mainstream society of ethnic groups and individuals,
to the virtual exclusion of contributions to their own communities;
and emphasising stylised and superficial aspects of cultural differences,
such as cuisine, traditional clothing, and ceremonial customs. Thorough
analyses of issues such as oppression, exploitation, racism, power, privilege, inequities, and social justice in contemporary society and across
ethnic and racial groups are frequently absent (Gay and Jackson, 2006).

Race and ethnicity matter in teaching and learning

Despite these prevailing tendencies, there are some alternative efforts
that tell very different stories about dealing effectively with race and
ethnicity in teaching and learning. More often than not they are derived
from special intervention programmes and practices instead of being
part of routine school curricula and instruction. It is likely that efforts
similar to those of these special initiatives are occurring daily in some
classrooms, but they are not readily accessible to outsiders because they
are not widely disseminated to the education profession at large.

Results from these special programmes demonstrate that many of the
doubts and anxieties teachers have about race and ethnicity in education are unfounded. Instead, deliberately addressing them is a means
of solving the achievement problems of ethnically and racially diverse
students, as well as preparing both minority and majority students to

become effective advocates for social justice, equity, and antiracism. This evidence is being produced by initiatives designed separately for African, Asian/Pacific Islanders, Latino, Native and Alaskan American students, as well as for poor European Americans in both urban and rural school environments, and in preparing teachers for ethnic and cultural diversity. Some of these programmes and practices are described by scholars such as Wigginton (1985, 1991), Boggs, Watson-Gegeo and McMillen (1985), Tharp and Gallimore (1988), Lipka (1998), Lipka, Andrew-Ihrke and Yanez (2011), McCarty (2002), Lee (2001, 2007, 2009), Cochran-Smith (1995, 2000, 2004), Gay (2010) and Ladson-Billings (2001). They usually fall under the conceptual categories of culturally relevant teaching, culturally responsive teaching, ethnic and race responsive teaching, antiracist education, multicultural education, and various kinds of ethnic-centred teaching (such as Afro-centrism and Latino-centrism). A brief summary of five of these interventions illustrate their techniques, audiences, and effects.

Wigginton (1985, 1991) created a project called Foxfire to help poor, underachieving, rural European American students improve their skills in academic literacy, communication, ethnic and cultural pride, journalism, and self-efficacy by having them conduct ethnographic studies of the histories, customs, beliefs, values, and traditions of their own communities. The results were positive in all measures of achievement, including improved standardised test scores, ethnic identity and cultural affiliation, school persistence, journalism and literacy skills (such as writing essays and poetry, editing, and publishing), and feelings of personal confidence. The project began in the late 1960s with high school students in rural Georgia and expanded to over 200 education sites throughout the United States and was culminated in some other countries. At its peak, Foxfire included the publication of a student-produced magazine and several books that were compilations of the ethnographic studies conducted by students; the construction of a replica of the villages where the students lived; a national network for training teachers in the Foxfire technique; a Broadway play in New York City; and a commercial film based on the teaching technique and the students' learning experiences. Thus, Foxfire was a phenomenal success – academically, culturally, and emotionally – for its targeted audience of poor White rural students, and it gained international fame. Some remnants of it still exist today

Over several years, McCarty (2002) studied the bilingual elementary and secondary programmes instituted by the Navajo nation to improve its students' mastery of English and the Navajo language and to integrate indigenous knowledge into areas of school learning such as mathematics, literacy, science, and social studies. The children who were taught in both languages performed better on academic, cultural, linguistic, and personal empowerment measures than their counterparts who were taught in English only. Lipka (1998) and his colleagues (Lipka, Andrew-Ihkre and Panez, 2011) found similar results from more than 25 years of working with Yup'iks in Alaska, using their indigenous knowledge and cultural practices to teach academic skills, and by collaborating with community elders in designing culturally relevant instructional programmes. The interventions have been particularly noteworthy in improving the students' achievement in math and science.

Lee (2001, 2007, 2009) used resources she called 'cultural data sets' (contemporary novels, visual art images, and popular music lyrics produced by African Americans) and a technique termed 'cultural modelling' to successfully teach high-order literary reasoning and narrative-writing skills to underachieving secondary and elementary African Americans in urban schools. Her strategies included contrastive analyses, in which students were taught how to analyse the social and cultural discourse styles they used in their daily social lives to identify similarities in literary works produced by highly successful African American authors, and to recognise parallels between these cultural styles and the formal literary concepts and techniques typically taught in schools through the use of the mainstream Eurocentric literary canons. Thus, their cultural practices, or what Gonzáles, Moll and Amanti (2005) described as 'funds of knowledge', became effective tools for learning important, but not all, academic content. Some literacy skills (such as literary interpretation, use of good narrative writing techniques, longer written texts) and efficacy skills (such as interest, motivation, participation, personal confidence, time on task) improved significantly, but some basic writing abilities (such as punctuation, spelling, and paragraph formation) did not. However, these basic writing skills were not part of the interventions.

The Kamehameha Early Education Program (KEEP) was designed to improve the reading performance of Native Hawaiian children in the early grades, as well as to increase their investment, ownership, pride, and engagement in schooling generally (Boggs, Watson-Gegeo and McMillen, 1985). KEEP focused more on using instructional techniques that were compatible with Polynesian-based cultural values, beliefs, discourse styles and participation structures than on modifying curriculum content. The KEEP classes used small cooperative learning groups, high-level interactive discussions, and co-narrations and oral 'talk stories' in which students worked together to create meaning and construct performances in learning situations. Over more than 20 years, teams of researchers and scholars worked closely with classroom teachers to track and record the progression and effects of the project. Consequently, there is a large body of evidence on KEEP complied across the years of its existence. The results indicate that the programme had profound effects in improving the reading performance of the participating students as well as their engaged time on academic tasks and overall classroom behaviours (Tharp and Gallimore, 1988; Au and Kawakami, 1994).

Although teacher candidates are often reluctant to deal with race and ethnicity, these attitudes and behaviours can be reversed with deliberate and direct efforts. Some (but not enough) teacher educators are doing so and achieving positive results. Illustrative of these efforts are projects and/or courses conducted by Ladson-Billings (2001), Howard (2010), McLean Donaldson (2001), Bennett (2002), Bennett, Cole and Thompson (2000) and Cochran-Smith (2004). Most of the information available on projects and practices that develop skills for teaching race and ethnicity focus on prospective teachers. However, practicing teachers need this education as well.

These initiatives operate independently, but there are some common features among them. First, participating teacher educators agree that while the intended audiences are primarily European Americans, prospective and practicing teachers of colour also are benefactors. While underachieving African Americans and Latino Americans command more attention, Native Americans and Asian/Pacific Islanders need to be addressed as well. Furthermore, teachers need more knowledge of, and ways to, respond to racial and ethnic issues affecting academically achieving students of colour. Second, better and more sustaining results are possible when preparation programmes in race and ethnicity include different layers and styles of learning. Essential among these are: teachers' acquiring self-consciousness and critical analytical skills regarding their own ethnicities and raciality, and their beliefs, attitudes, and behaviours toward the race and ethnicity of diverse students; comprehensive profiles of the salience of race and ethnicity in American society, schools, and classrooms; knowledge about the histories, heritages, cultures, and contributions of different ethnic and racial groups – knowledge that dispels common stereotypes and prejudices; exposure to, and experiences with, diverse racial and ethnic groups in their own communities and daily activities; and pedagogical skills for modifying and transforming curriculum content and instructional strategies to be more ethnically, racially, and culturally inclusive. Third, opportunities for teachers to participate in various levels and kinds of supervised practicum experiences that illuminate both negative and constructive approaches to race and ethnicity in regular classroom interactions and procedures instead of only at special times and in programmes and events.

Teacher educators trying to get their prospective teachers to engage genuinely and constructively with race and ethnicity tend to agree with Marilyn Cochran-Smith (2004, p. 101) that, for both instructors and students,

> [t]o teach lessons about race and racism in teacher education is to struggle to unlearn racism itself – to interrogate the assumptions that are deeply embedded in the curriculum, to own our own complicity in maintaining existing systems of privilege and oppression, and to grapple with our own failure.

Conclusion

Despite persistent efforts of many teachers to ignore the existence and deny the salience of race and ethnicity in education, evidence to the contrary is compelling. As this chapter demonstrated, race and ethnicity issues are real and pervasive in US society and schools, and they matter in multiple ways in teaching and learning. Ethnic and racial demographics are becoming increasingly problematic as student populations become more diverse racially, ethnically, linguistically, culturally, and socially. A similar trend is apparent among teachers, but the actual diversity increase is miniscule, and when compared to the diversity of students it is insignificant. Hence, the undeniable reality is that most students of colour in the United States are taught by White teachers. This demographic gap is not, in itself, the biggest problem. Certainly, more teachers of colour are needed, and their presence serves valuable image and identity purposes for both mainstream and minority students. However, the larger issue is the failure of many European and Americans teachers of colour to understand, accept, and respond positively to the significance of race and ethnicity in their teaching. Some of the reasons for these attitudes and behaviours were provided, along with how they can be countered, and the positive effects that are produced by the explicit inclusion of race and ethnicity in teaching and learning.

Evidence from different kinds of programme interventions for different ethnic groups and teachers at different levels of education (elementary, secondary, college) demonstrate consistently that ethnic-responsive and race-responsive curricula and instruction improve the academic achievement, identity development, school adjustment, and personal efficacy of diverse students. Similarly, teacher education curricula that help teachers to better understand the complexities, realities, and salience of race and ethnicity undeniably improve their competence and confidence in dealing with these issues in classroom practices. These interventions and the results they produce are encouraging and illuminating, but much more is needed to extend their effects and sustainability.

In addition to producing tangible results in several achievement measures, race and ethnic-responsive education has the potential to inspire trust, stimulate ownership, and reactivate belief in the transformative and redemptive potential of education among alienated and disenchanted student populations. As Howard (2010, p. 150) suggests:

> Hope is a source of strength, an asset of possibility, and a tangible way of grasping for a reality that is not seen, but is believed to be within reach. Hope offers a response to the anxiety, stress, pain, suffering, misery, anger, and angst that seem to have become staples in urban, rural, and suburban communities across the nation. Each of us has a moral responsibility to ponder what role we are taking to challenge injustice, what questions we are posing to eradicate discrimination, and what actions we are engaged in to end exclusion and oppression no matter what shape or form [they] take...Our work must operate from a paradigm of possibility, a stance of empowerment, a firm belief in the intellectual prowess...and unlimited potential that...students from diverse backgrounds bring from home to their schools everyday.

Race and ethnic-responsive teaching is this beacon of hope for both students and teachers. It represents a realistic promise of a better future for student populations in settings and circumstances now considered by many to be hopeless.

References

Au, K.H. and Kawakami, A.J. (1994) 'Cultural congruence in instruction', in Hollins, E.R., King, J.E. and Hayman, W.C. (eds), *Teaching Diverse Populations: Formulating a Knowledge Base*, Albany, State University of New York Press, 5–23.
Barber, B.R. (1992) *An Aristocracy of Everyone: The Politics of Education and the Future of America*, New York, Oxford University Press.

Bennett, C. (2002) 'Enhancing diversity at a Big Ten university through Project TEAM: a case study in teacher education', *Educational Researcher*, 31 (2), 21–29.

Bennett, C., Cole, D. and Thompson, J-N. (2000) 'Preparing teachers of color at a predominately White university: a case study of Project TEAM', *Teaching and Teacher Education*, 16 (4), 445–464.

Boger, J.C. and Orfield, G. (eds) (2005) *School Resegregation: Must the South Turn Back?* Chapel Hill, University of North Carolina Press.

Boggs, S.T., Watson-Gegeo, K. and McMillen, G. (1985) *Speaking, Relating, and Learning: A Study of Hawaiian Children at Home and at School*, Norwood, NJ, Ablex.

Centre for Public Education (2012) 'The changing demographics of the United States and their schools'. Available from www.centerforpubliceducation.org. [Accessed on 15 January 2013]

Cochran-Smith, M. (1995) 'Uncertain allies: Understanding the boundaries of race and teaching', *Harvard Educational Review*, 65 (4), 541–570.

Cochran-Smith, M. (2000) 'Blind vision: Unlearning racism in teacher education', *Harvard Educational Review*, 70 (2), 157–190.

Cochran-Smith, M. (2004) *Walking the Road: Race, Diversity, and Social Justice in Teacher Education*, New York, Teachers College Press.

Feistritzer, C.M. (2011) 'Profile of teachers in the US'. Available from www. pot2011final-blog-pdf. [Accessed on 10 January 2013]

Gay, G. (2002) 'Preparing for culturally responsive teaching', *Journal of Teacher Education*, 53 (2), 106–116.

Gay, G. and Jackson, C. (2006) 'Resisting resistance in multicultural teacher education', in Pang, V. O. (ed.), *Principles and Practices of Multicultural Education*, Westport, CT, Praeger, 201–221.

Gonzáles, N., Moll, L.C. and Amanti, C. (2005) *Funds of Knowledge: Theorizing Practices in Households, Communities, and Classrooms*, Mahwah, NJ, Erlbaum.

Hawley, W.D. and Nieto, S. (2010) 'Another inconvenient truth: Race and ethnicity matter', *Educational Leadership*, 68 (3), 66–71.

Howard, T.C. (2010) *'Why Race and Culture Matter in Schools: Closing the Achievement Gap in America's Classrooms*, New York, Teachers College Press.

Ladson-Billings, G. (2001) *Crossing Over to Canaan: The Journey of New Teachers in Diverse Classrooms*, San Francisco, Jossey-Bass.

Lee, C.D. (2001) 'Is Charlie Brown Chinese? A cultural modeling activity system for underachieving students', *American Educational Research Journal*, 38 (1), 97–143.

Lee, C.D. (2007) *Culture, Literacy, and Learning: Taking Bloom in the Midst of the Whirlwind*, New York, Teachers College Press.

Lee, C.D. (2009) 'Cultural influences on learning', in Banks, J.A. (ed.), *The Routledge International Companion to Multicultural Education*, New York, Routledge, 239–251.

Lipka, J. (1998) *Transforming the Culture of Schools: Yup'ik Eskimo Examples*, Mahwah, NJ, Erlbaum.

Lipka, J., Andrew-Ihrke, D. and Yanez, E.E. (2011) 'Yup'ik cosmology to school mathematics: The power of symmetry and proportional measuring', *Quarterly Review of Education*, 42 (2), 157–183.

Lynch, M. and Engle, J. (2010a) 'Big gaps small gaps: some colleges and universities do better than others in graduating African American students'. Available from edtrust.org/dc/resources/publications/big-gaps-small-gaps-in-serving-afri-can-american-students. [Accessed on 23 March 2013]

Lynch, M. and Engle, J. (2010b) 'Big gaps small gaps: some colleges and universities do better than others in graduating Hispanic students'. Available from edtrust.org/dc/resources/publications/college-results-online. [Accessed on 23 March 2013]

McCarty, T.L. (2002) *A Place to be Navajo: Rough Rock and the Struggle for Self-determination in Indigenous Schooling*, Mahwah, NJ, Erlbaum.

McLean Donaldson, K.B. (2001) *Shattering the Denial: Protocols for the Classroom and Beyond*, Westport, CT, Bergin and Garvey.

National Centre of Education Statistics (2010) 'Characteristics of the 100 largest public elementary and secondary school districts in the United States: 2008–09 (2010)'. Available from nces.ed.gov/pubs2010/largest0809/.asp. [Accessed on 10 January 2013]

National Centre of Education Statistics (2011) 'Fast Facts: Race and ethnicity of college faculty'. Available from nces.ed.gov/FastFacts/display.asp?id=61. [Accessed on 21 March 2013]

National Centre of Education Statistics (2012a) 'Participation in education: Elementary and secondary enrollment (2012)'. Available from nces.ed.gov/programs/coe/indicator_1er.asp. [Accessed on 8 January 2013]

National Center of Education Statistics (2012b) 'The condition of education'. Available from nces.ed.gov/pubsearch/pubsinfo.asp?pubid=2012045. [Accessed on 10 January 2013]

Orfield, G., Kucsera, J. and Siegel-Hawley, G. (2012) 'E Pluribus...separation: deepening double segregation for more students'. Available from civilrightsproject.ucla.edu/ofield_Epluribus_Reised_complete_2012.pdf. [Accessed on 10 March 2013]

Sleeter, C. (2001) 'Foreword', in McLean Donaldson, K.B. (ed.), *Shattering the Denial: Protocols for the Classroom and Beyond*, Westport, CT, Bergin and Garvey, ix–xiii.

Tatum, B.D. (2007) *Can We Talk About Race? And Other Conversations in an Era of School Resegregation*, Boston, Beacon Press.

Tharp, R.G. and Gallimore, R. (1988) *Rousing Minds to Life: Teaching, Learning, and Schooling in Social Context*, Cambridge, Cambridge University Press.

US Census Bureau (2010) 'Two or more races population'. Available from www.census.gov/prod/cen2010/briefs/c2010br-13.pdf. [Accessed on 8 January 2013]

Villegas, A.M. and Lucas, P. (2002) *Educating Culturally Responsive Teachers: A Coherent Approach*, Albany, State University of New York Press.

Wigginton, E. (1985) *Sometimes a Shining Moment: The Foxfire Experience*, Garden City, NY, Anchor Press/Doubleday.

Wigginton, E. (ed.) (1991) *Foxfire: 25 Years*, New York, Doubleday.

5
Journeys to Success: An Appreciative Inquiry into the Academic Attainment of Black and Minority Ethnic Students at a Post-1992 London University

Julie Hall, Jo Peat and Sandra Craig

Introduction

The Race Relations Amendment Act (2000) calls for public bodies, including schools and universities, to monitor admissions and progress by ethnicity and to develop action plans. In response to the act a number of educational interventions and research projects have been initiated in the school sector. Schools that have been effective in raising Black attainment have successfully used a combination of strategies, which include:

- having high expectations of all pupils;
- monitoring attainment and tackling gaps between groups of pupils;
- celebrating diversity and promoting a sense of belonging for all pupils;
- including Black culture explicitly in the curriculum;
- promoting motivational peer and adult academic mentoring.

(Adapted from *Priority Review: Exclusion of Black Pupils – Getting it. Getting it right* DfES, 2006).

In 2008 a report from the Equality Challenge Unit – Ethnicity, Gender and Degree Attainment, indicated that universities still have some way to go in raising the attainment of BME students at undergraduate level. According to HEFCE (2010), between 2002 and 2006, 37 per cent of

BME students achieved a first or a 2:1, compared with 62 per cent of White students in the study. As reported, 'even after controlling for the majority of factors which we would expect to have an impact on attainment, being from a minority ethnic community (except the 'Other Black', 'Mixed' and 'Other' groups) is still statistically significant in explaining final attainment, although the gap has been significantly reduced' (Broecke and Nicholls, 2007, p. 4). In addition to legal and moral imperatives, as the investment in higher education by individual students and/or their parents, carers or employers becomes more important, it is in the interest of universities to ensure that all students, regardless of ethnic origin, have the best chances of meeting their academic potential.

In April 2009 this case-study university was invited to join the HE Academy/Equality Challenge Unit National Summit Programme to investigate this degree-attainment gap along with 11 other universities. Supported by academics linked to the Summit Programme, each university developed a year-long project, which reflected particular concerns identified, in initial analysis of attainment data, by ethnicity. At this university a small project team representing the Learning and Teaching Enhancement Unit (LTEU), the Students Union and the School of Arts, set out to investigate, through Appreciative Inquiry, those factors which had contributed to the success of BME students in four discipline areas – Psychology, History, Computing and Education. There was high-level support for the project as the attainment of BME students was seen as being critical to the university's commitment to social justice, which meant that any lack of parity in academic attainment between students had to be addressed.

Methodology

The methodology chosen to investigate the factors that contributed to a positive learning experience at the university for BME students was Appreciative Inquiry (Cooperrider and Srivaster, 1987). Cooperrider and Srivaster (1987) suggest that the purpose of Appreciative Inquiry is to focus on positive aspirations and outcomes, centring on asking questions in such a way as to foster positive relationships and build on present potential. This method can be used as a driver for change, allowing for reflection and action on those experiences which have contributed to a positive outcome, in this instance in the learning environment.

The aim of using AI in this project was to facilitate a positive dialogue about learning, teaching and assessment experiences, and about the social interactions between lecturers and students and amongst students themselves. This approach appeared a viable complement to conventional forms of action research, as it engendered a feeling of social inclusion, a consultative process and solution-focused thinking rather than dwelling on difficulties and barriers. The team felt that participants would enjoy exploring the attitudes, patterns and actions of people successfully engaging with their learning. Data on positive experiences would be of value, both to other participants and to those teaching and supporting learning. In addition, the project encompassed empowerment evaluation (Ncube and Wasburn, 2006), allowing participants to be part of the evaluation process and the beneficiaries of change. The design of the questions encouraged students to focus on positive aspects of their experiences in higher education. The questions were supplemented by a pictorial representation of the university by the students, collaborating in smaller groups across the disciplines. The project was managed by a successful undergraduate, a high-achieving Black female who was a mature student. This was a key feature in the design of the project, echoing the work of McCulloch (2008), which points to the importance of the student as co-producer of knowledge, rather than as passive recipient or consumer. This strategy enabled access to other students in a way that would have been impossible for staff, also allowing for the modelling of good practice in involving students in the process rather than limiting their engagement to the product (McCulloch, 2008; Burke and Jackson, 2007).

Sixty students from years two and three on four undergraduate programmes (History, Psychology, Education and Computing) were self-nominated for inclusion in the project. At this institution, BME students are in the majority of undergraduate students in Computing and Psychology, are approximately half of the Education cohort and are a minority in the History cohort. Although self-nomination necessarily meant that more motivated and concerned students were involved, the advantages of self-nomination ensured a sample of students who identified themselves as Black and minority ethnic, rather than the project manager organising the selection.

Drawing on collaborative or participatory methodological frameworks, the research team felt that self-nomination allowed for richer research relations, fostering an environment for open, conversational exchange and debate. Focus groups were used, not only as a means of data collection, but as a medium for conversations with participants – understanding knowledge as co-constructed through an interactive process. This method empowered participants, enabling them to comment in their own words, whilst being stimulated by thoughts and comments from their peers. Contributions could, furthermore, be encouraged from people reluctant to be interviewed alone, who felt they had little to say or who may not usually have participated in surveys (Robson, 2002).

Cognisant of the possibility that focus groups can be dominated by particular individuals, the project manager ensured expert facilitation to minimise this and any conflict between personalities (Robson, 2011). The intention was to develop a rich picture of factors, which students identified as having a positive impact on their learning whilst providing an opportunity for students to learn from each other and contribute to an important strategic initiative in order to improve student attainment.

A thematic analysis of the data was undertaken. Alerted to issues of 'data mining', the project team – and particularly the representative from the Students Union – encouraged more students to contribute to the analysis and consider ways of presenting the findings to a wider audience. An event for students and staff, co-hosted by the LTEU with the Students Union in the case-study university, ensured that early findings were interrogated in public. In parallel the project team ensured a high level of contact with course leaders in the four discipline areas and, throughout the project, provided the opportunity to engage in reflection and professional development. Through this, academic staff were encouraged to consider their approaches to teaching and student engagement on the programmes (Moon, 2000).

Findings

Analysis of the data indicated four overarching themes:

Expectations, care and respect

She never misses a meeting and rearranges for a more convenient time if she is unavailable.

This recurring theme relates to students' perceptions of staff, whom they felt had cared for them or motivated them to do well. Comments centred upon examples of care evidenced through reliability, communicating an expectation of high standards and of 'noticing' the student. Students highlighted a professional approach to providing support: 'It's great when I make an appointment and the tutor is there at the time they said and ready to help.' Students were very conscious that academic staff had other commitments and, therefore, were highly appreciative of those who offered tutorial time regularly. This helped to clarify uncertainties caused by the plethora of advice provided in induction and the early weeks at university. Sharing narrative accounts of the ways in which students navigated the support available meant that awareness was raised amongst all participants about 'what worked'. Successful students had benefited from clear messages about academic staff 'office hours', whereas others misinterpreted such messages on their programmes, understanding that 'office hours' meant that staff were engaged in office work and were therefore unavailable.

Small acts, such as personal communications between staff and students resulted in the student feeling legitimised and motivated: 'I got a note saying: "Well done! This is good!" and I ran round the room and showed everyone.' Students commonly raised the importance of being noticed and lecturers caring that they did well and were achieving. Some mentioned text messages from staff about attendance as evidence that someone cared. Students also appreciated staff who noticed when students were not engaged in the learning environment and acted on this: 'I like it when someone notices and makes a point when people don't work hard enough.' 'It's great when people hold up rules about getting late to class. It sets the standard high.'

For many students, 'caring' clearly involved encouragement to strive for higher grades: students need to know from the outset that the academic staff have high expectations of them. This helps to counteract some of the misinterpretations that students raised in conversations – for example, that the first year 'didn't count' and that 'people are unlikely to get a first in this subject'. One student summed up the comments of many others when she said: 'I love it when I meet a lecturer who has high expectations of us. When they don't, you set your sights lower, then get less than you could have achieved because you kind of think – that's all someone like me can manage.'

Teaching and learning

Some lecturers do more than just talk at us.

The teaching style that students highlighted as being particularly helpful in encouraging them to achieve combined clarity with energy, enthusiasm and active learning. All students recalled particular staff who taught with passion or conviction. They identified classes which provided them with opportunities for discussion, where their comments were encouraged and valued and where they could ask questions and talk things through with their lecturers and peers. 'You make friends and you learn more when you get into groups and talk through things in seminars.' Students appreciated staff who encouraged them to work collaboratively, either online or face to face, because once relationships were established 'we can ask each other for help when we are stuck.' Students highlighted those lecturers who welcomed their contributions and who celebrated the individual and alternative perspectives they brought to their learning These were often contrasted with more passive, PowerPoint-led sessions, where students were 'talked at'.

In the focus groups, much discussion centred upon the extent to which students felt they could seek out lecturers for advice and were proactive in using group and individual tutorials. When asked, the project manager shared her insights about student–staff interactions and, as a result, many students who had never before done so began to consider how they might work more effectively with their lecturers. The Psychology team, for example, reported a significant rise in requests for tutorial appointments from the students involved in the project. Some second-year students began to see their personal tutors for the very first time. One student echoed the words of a number of others when, in one focus group, she declared,: 'Oh, I see now. If I'm not scared to talk to my tutor I can use her to help me understand how to get better marks.'

Assessment and standards

It's great when I am told I can do better and I am shown how.

A common theme in the focus groups was the cathartic feeling of coming to understand how assessment criteria were applied and how one might improve in order to gain better grades. Students identified this knowledge as critical to their chances of doing well. Many shared instances when deep learning had occurred in relation to understanding the academic standards expected. Typical comments included:

- I love it when it's clear what I need to do to improve and there is help there.
- It's great when I am told I can do better and I am shown how.
- In the third year I finally came to understand the conventions of academic writing.

When talking about assessment, many students reported that feedback worked best when it offered a message that 'people have high expectations of me'. A typical comment was, 'I work best when I am able to stagger the effort I put in and get feedback. I hate it when I have to get so many things done to meet a deadline and it all ends up rushed.' As a result, many had appreciated opportunities to consult with academic staff or academic development staff to improve their writing before submitting work. This academic advice alleviated some of the stress around high-stakes summative assessment, particularly on those programmes with common hand-in dates at particular times of the year. One student's remark reflected many others when she said: 'It was great when I got the chance to practise my writing and get some feedback before I handed it in.'

Transitions from one year to the next were seen as exciting and challenging, and students enjoyed sharing their experiences of these transitions. Some students reported having to overcome the shock of changed expectations for second-year work or third-year dissertations. Students who took modules across programmes seemed particularly vulnerable to mixed messages about academic writing conventions or when staff asked for different approaches to referencing or structuring a report. Successful students were able to calculate and monitor the way their grades would contribute to their final degree classification. Others admitted to feelings of confusion about the ways in which their final degree marks would be calculated, and some third-year students were struggling to estimate their final degree score. Discussion in the focus groups centred on how helpful it was to seek advice from lecturers and peers which allowed for clarification of this process and a resulting feeling of students knowing what they needed to do to aim for the classification of degree they wanted. This topic led to some of the richest discussions amongst the students.

Feeling part of the university curriculum and community

Particularly in focus groups with Education and History students, participants appreciated modules which allowed them to relate their personal or professional experiences to their studies. A number of students reported choosing these disciplines because of a desire to explore their own cultural heritages or experiences. Some shared positive examples of being invited to use their family histories as the basis for academic work. This contrasted with other students who were frustrated that their lives seemed undervalued in the context of their studies. Across the discipline areas, students valued opportunities to study issues which had an impact upon their lives in a direct and personal way. One student's comment in a focus group was greeted with much clapping of hands when she declared: 'When you're learning, there should be the same opportunities for all of us to relate to the material and not obstacles which exist for some groups and not White people.'

Students welcomed opportunities to feel a legitimate part of a university community through cross-university activities, and many reported a number of events which had helped them settle in at the beginning. These included social events with staff and mature-student events organised through the Students Union and clubs and societies. Students who felt they were doing particularly well reported wanting to construct an identity as a student at this university rather than purely around their programme. They were able to achieve this identity through active engagement with such initiatives as the Student Ambassador Scheme and the Student Representative Programme. Students appreciated relaxed, informal spaces outside of the canteen, where they could meet and interact with peers. Visual representations of the ideal university included 'chill-out zones', a greater variety of food and increased access to lecturers and those offering pastoral support and advice.

Conclusions

Many of the factors identified by BME students as having a positive impact on academic success have been identified in other research around effective teaching and learning (Gibbs, 2010; Mann, 2001; Race, 1999, 2010; Boud, 2007; Crozier et al., 2008; Hall, 2005; Hockings, 2009; Zepke and Leach, 2007).

A powerful message from this research is that the university must consider how it communicates to students that they are valued and that expectations of them are high. This can be contrasted with an approach, which may be well meaning but which is perceived within a discourse of deficit: 'You might struggle so here is all the support we can offer you.' Few disciplinary differences were uncovered beyond the references to programme choice and an expectation that there would be more opportunities in some programmes to locate learning in individual lived experience. In addition the data do not suggest any particular factors related to gender or entry tariffs.

The process of engaging 60 BME students across the university in the project has, in itself, indicated to students that the university is taking parity of attainment seriously. The focus groups provided a valuable opportunity for students to explore factors which may contribute to academic success, and to create a plan of action in response. The project manager role was critical to the project's success, acting as both a role model and a guide. One student commented: 'She shared some of her experiences, and others and I could relate to her, and her talk was really grabbing and I wanted to hear more.' Another student commented that the message she took from the project was 'getting the most out of your studies and being one of the best, and ... really liked that way of thinking'. The students valued the process as an opportunity to collaborate in order to help the university learn from their experiences while focusing on dialogue around strategies for success. One student explained it thus: 'An open debate and a discussion is better than completing a question-naire. A debate is more interactive and I'd like to hear more.'

Singh (2008) argues:

> Attempts to address the issue of BME (under)achievement in HE have been dominated by reactive measures driven less by a moral impera-tive to do justice and more by regulatory imperatives. This has led to an absolute reliance on positivistic approaches to research the problem and tick-box solutions.

Singh goes on to suggest three institutional and individual stages to developing an antiracist mindset, from critical unconsciousness to critical consciousness. This research project provided the information and the impetus to move from Stage 2 (critical complacency) to Stage 3 (critical consciousness). It is Stage 3 that involves reframing trans-formation and two-way dialogue. In order to do this, dissemination of the findings has happened at all levels within the institution. This has ranged from project reports to strategic university committees, depart-mental action plans, presentations to programme teams and to confer-ences. Student-designed postcards, sent to all staff and those involved in the project to raise awareness of the findings and maintain interest in the issues have been particularly powerful. Professional develop-ment on the issues raised by the project has led to programme teams seeking out opportunities to review curricula and pedagogic practices (Singh, 2008).

The most powerful aspect of our research has been hearing the stories directly from the students and then using these stories as catalysts for transformation with academic colleagues and across the institution. A salutary lesson from this has been that, in some quarters, a first response to this work was that of a deficit model, pathologising and 'othering' the students (Kubota, 2001, 2004). A great deal of work will be needed to eradicate such erroneous misconceptions, but these student voices will, ultimately, push universities to address attainment issues and grapple with and combat racism in higher education. These students, for example, actually pointed to their involvement in the research as contributing to better grades:

'I have got a couple of firsts which has never happen before...I don't know if it's because of the research, but I did feel that I'd put in a lot more effort and changed the way I work, I got a first in my exam and a first in my coursework, which really boosted me.'

'We'd never heard of Appreciative Inquiry before but it sounded positive, you know? Appreciative Inquiry, and it was obviously targeted and aimed at us...there's definitely been an improvement in grades and in our attitudes to the grades...My goal's different and that's really important, 'cause now, really, I don't know but at the time I came away really thinking that now I can so get a first, why can't I there's no reason not to...just felt a little bit more empowered...for me overall the message from it was, it changed my goal from thinking, I can just get through this, to thinking, I can do really well'.

References

Boud, D.J. (2007) *Rethinking Assessment for Higher Education: Learning for the Longer Term*, London, Routledge.

Broecke, S. and Nichols, T. (2007) *Ethnicity and Degree Attainment*. DfES Research Report RW92. Available from www.dfes.gov.uk/research/data/uploadfiles/rw92. pdf. [Accessed on 20 April 2007]

Burke, P.J. and Jackson, S. (2007) *Reconceptualising Lifelong Learning: Feminist Interventions*, London, Routledge.

Cooperrider, D.L. and Srivastva, S. (1987) 'Appreciative inquiry in organizational life', in Pasmore, W. and Woodman, R. (eds), *Research In Organizational Change and Development*, vol. 1, Greenwich, CT, JAI Press, 129–169.

Crozier, G., Reay, D., Clayton, J., Colliander, L. and Grinstead, J. (2008) 'Different strokes for different folks: diverse students in diverse institutions – experiences of higher education', *Research Papers in Education* (Special issue on challenges of diversity for widening participation in UK higher education), 23 (2) 167–177.

DfES (2006) *Priority Review: Exclusion of Black Pupils – Getting It. Getting It Right*. DfES, London.

Equality Challenge Unit (2008) *Ethnicity, Gender and Degree Attainment*, Report.

Gibbs, G. (2010) *Dimensions of Quality*, York; HEA, Available from http://www. heacademy.ac.uk/assets/documents/evidence_informed_practice/Dimensions_ of_Quality.pdf.

Hall, J. (2005) in Richardson, B. (ed.), *Tell It Like It Is – How Our Schools Fail Black Children*, Home Office, London, Trentham.

HEFCE (2010) Student ethnicity – Profile and progression of entrants to full-time, first degree study, Home Office Communication Directorate (2003), Changes to the Law against Racial Discrimination.

Hockings, C. (2009) 'Reaching the students that student-centred learning cannot reach', *British Educational Research Journal*, 35 (1) 83–99.

Kubota, R. (2001) 'Discursive constructions of the images of U.S. classrooms', *TESOL Quarterly*, 35, 9–38.

Kubota, R. (2004) 'Critical multiculturalism and second language education', in Norton, B. and Toohey, K. (eds), *Critical Pedagogies and Language Learning*, Cambridge, Cambridge University Press, 30–54.

Mann, S. (2001) 'Alternative perspectives on the student experience: alienation and engagement', *Studies in Higher Education*, 26 (1) 7–19.

McCulloch, A. (2008) 'The student as co-producer: learning from public administration about the student-university relationship', *Studies in Higher Education*, 34 (2), 171–183.

Moon, J. (2000) *Short Courses and Workshops: Improving the Impact of Learning and Teaching Professional Development*, London, Kogan Page. Available on http://www.multiverse.ac.uk/index.aspx. [Accessed on 10 June 2010]

Ncube, L.B. and Wasburn, M.H (2006) 'Strategic collaboration for ethical leadership: a mentoring framework for business and organizational decision making', *Journal of Leadership and Organizational Studies* (Baker College), 13 (1), 77–92.

Race, P. (1999) *Enhancing Student Learning*, Birmingham: SEDA Special 10, SEDA Publications.

Race, P. (2010) *Making Learning Happen*, 2nd edition, London, Sage Publications.

Robson, C. (2002) *Real World Research*, Oxford, Blackwell.

Robson, C. (2011) *Real World Research*, 3rd edition, Oxford, Wiley.

Singh, G. (2008) 'Race equality and higher education: shifting the paradigm', *Higher Education Academy Conference – 'National Student Survey Conference: Using the Data for Quality Enhancement'*, at the National College for School Leadership, Nottingham, 8 May 2008.

Zepke, N. and Leach, L. (2007) 'Improving student outcomes in higher education: New Zealand teachers' views on teaching students from diverse backgrounds', *Teaching in Higher Education*, 12 (5–6), 655–668.

6
Initial Teacher Education: The Practice of Whiteness

Vini Lander

Introduction

This chapter will discuss how initial teacher education – with respect to preparing and enabling student teachers to teach with confidence, knowledge and understanding in the ethnically diverse classrooms in England – receives little attention in the pre-service teacher education programmes. The chapter will illustrate the current position with respect to teacher training and education in England regarding race equality, and will show that there is very little content related to preparing teachers to understand their own racialised positions as powerful professionals, within either predominantly White or multiethnic classrooms. There is almost no education or training to help student teachers to understand the constructs of race and ethnicity; there is even less attention given to how student teachers can work with pupils to address racist incidents and how they can use the curriculum as a vehicle to develop children's understanding of multicultural Britain, or how to educate children and young people beyond the stereotypes rehearsed and promoted in the media every day.

The chapter draws on the theoretical framework of *Whiteness*. This will be delineated using some current research in England, but drawing predominantly on work in the United States. It will use research regarding the inadequacy of teacher education to increase understandings of how it perpetuates Whiteness through the lack of engagement, and at times sheer reluctance of White educators to understand their own positions as racialised beings within a context whereby the racialised 'Other' is marginalised in order to maintain an unspoken hierarchy of dominance and supremacy (Gillborn, 2005, 2008).

As 2011 receded into history, two events associated with race and crime made the headlines. One the one hand, the news was permeated with discussions about the callous killing of an Indian student, Anuj Bidve, in Salford, Manchester, UK (BBC, 2011a), and it was interesting to note how the first reports avoided the use of the term racist in favour of recasting it as a hate crime. At the same time, in December 2011 the judge in the Stephen Lawrence trial summed up the arguments presented by the defence and the prosecution as a 'hate crime' undertaken twenty years ago for which no one had been convicted at the time (BBC, 2011b). These two events are visible tips of an iceberg which represents the failure of our education system, at all levels, to educate about and against racism – through the failure to develop a 'racial literacy' (Skerrett, 2011) with teachers and children. These crimes are not solely due to the failure of the education system, but due to a collective failure to develop our racial literacy in a way that moves us on to think about and tackle the deep-rooted everyday racism in society.

We need to educate our teachers and children alike to be able to understand our multiethnic society based on facts and informed discussions in classrooms rather than acquiring that understanding from media headlines. Our failure to do so to date within initial teacher education (ITE) means teachers are unable to construct robust counterarguments which can disrupt the barrage of negative headlines about minority ethnic groups, a barrage which influences children's understandings of our society. For example, a teacher recently conveyed how a group of seven–eight-year-old children watched a film in which a woman was robbed. According to the teacher, it was clear that the robber in the film was White. The children were asked to write about the lady, and one child wrote, 'She is skint because the Black man nicked her money.' The teacher asked the child why they had written this and the child said, 'I just thought he was a Black man.' Apart from this initial question from the teacher, there was no followup. We have to ask why? Could it be that this teacher did not know how to follow this up? It may have been because the teacher did not have the training or the racial literacy with which to tackle this child's stereotypical notions of Black men.

It is the responsibility of teacher education, both initial and continuing, to keep race equality on the agenda (regardless of the geographical location of the school) and to have the courage to move beyond the three S's: 'Saris, Steelbands, Samosas' (Troyna and Ball, 1985) and, nowadays, the D for Diwali approach, or 'Africa Week', to address and examine how being White and the discourse of Whiteness are perpetuated through teacher education – education in such a way as to re-centre the majority narrative and to side-step the legislation (except, at times, in the cases of overt racism) to allow silent and injurious covert racism (Gillborn, 2008) to inflict its every-day damage on society as a whole.

If we cannot educate new teachers to understand and act with knowledge to challenge the dominant discourse of Whiteness through the curriculum and the resources and approaches they use, then we will still be paying lip service to race equality in the next century whilst Black and minority ethnic (BME) children continue to be the victims of overt and covert racism, as evidenced by racist attacks, by the high number of BME people in prison, the high numbers of BME pupils excluded from school, the underachievement of certain BME groups (Gillborn, 2008) and, no doubt, the higher number of BME young people making up the unemployment statistics in times of recession (Ball et al., 2012; TUC, 2012).

In the 'Key Facts about Race in the UK', the Runnymede Trust (2012) notes, that since 'the murder of Stephen Lawrence in 1993, 89 more people have lost their lives at the hands of racists in the UK; that if you have an African or Asian surname you need to send twice as many applications as someone with an English name to get an interview[,] and that whilst 300 Black Caribbean students attained the appropriately high grades in their A-Levels to gain entry to Oxford University[,] only one gained a place'. It seems that despite the everyday assumptions of the proverbial 'man or woman in the street' that race or racism are not issues in twenty-first century Britain[,] the facts do not support such an assertion. It is these everyday understandings that student teachers bring to their preparation to become teachers that remain unchallenged and so new teachers remain uneducated about race and racism in Britain.

The context – teacher education in England

This section provides a brief overview of how initial teacher preparation has changed in England, and how these changes have impacted on notions of teacher professionalism, equality and, specifically, the absence of references to racial, ethnic and cultural diversity. There is insufficient space to provide an in-depth discussion about this reduction and erasure, but readers ought to reflect on how this process of erasure in policy documents that govern initial teacher education has gathered momentum and met little resistance from the education community. This is because hand-in-hand with such changes there has been greater control of student teacher numbers through surveillance via institutional inspections.

The landscape of teacher education in England has changed rapidly over approximately the last three decades. These changes continue apace as this chapter is being written. However, the changes in initial teacher education started to gather momentum with the election of Margaret Thatcher in 1979. The introduction of the first set of teacher competences in 1984 (Circular 3/84) and subsequent sets of competences introduced through government circulars, such as in Circulars 9/92 for secondary trainee teachers and 14/93 for primary trainee teachers, were designed to improve trainee teachers' subject knowledge and understanding. The changes in the standards that govern teacher education have shifted the notion of teacher professionalism from the autonomous professional (one who could make decisions based on professional knowledge and understanding) to a more technicist model of the teacher – one who 'can do' (Furlong et al., 2000). In these changes some key elements have been lost: specifically, the need to prepare children and their teachers to be actively engaged in understanding the nature of society around them and to fulfil high standards through a framework of social justice and inclusion. The nomenclature has also changed: for example from *initial teacher education* to *initial teacher training*; from *student teacher* to *trainee teacher* and from *teacher educator* to *teacher trainer*. The move from 'educating' teachers to one of 'training' teachers is widely recognised as a reductive change (Furlong et al., 2000). Just as the nomenclature has changed, so has the role of universities in preparing teachers. A student studying to be a teacher on a postgraduate programme at a university must spend 24 weeks in school (DfE, 2012a, p. 4) and with the introduction in England of School Direct (DfE, 2013), the role of universities has been further reduced. School Direct is likely to produce teacher practitioners for local rather than national or global contexts. Individuals with a first degree who want to become teachers can now do so through training in a school environment without the need to engage in any higher education, thereby becoming the apprentice teacher who will learn the skills of their trade 'on the job'. Therefore, if their school is in a predominantly White area with little ethnic diversity, it is likely that these trainee teachers (I use this term deliberately) will be insufficiently prepared for ethnically diverse classrooms and may perpetuate narrow perspectives in the education they offer children in their classrooms.

As the standards which govern initial teacher preparation have evolved from competences to the Teachers' Standards of 2012, scholars have traced the reduction in references to social justice and ethnic diversity and a transformation of the notion of equality. Scholars working in the intersecting areas of race equality and teacher education have traced the minimal presence, erasure and absence of references to race and ethnicity within the statutory frameworks, that have come and gone, governing teacher education. Gaine (1995) noted how the establishment of CATE (Council of the Accreditation of Teachers Education) started the central control of teacher education, and also how the criteria emphasised teachers' subject knowledge rather than the preparation of teachers to work in an increasingly ethnically diverse Britain.

The recommendation of the Swann Report (DES, 1985) that student teachers gain experience in multiracial schools was largely ignored (Race, 2011). Menter (1989, p. 460) noted how the CATE criteria introduced the *technical* model of the teacher, whilst removing the 'education disciplines' of sociology, philosophy and psychology that were the underpinning conceptual framework of teacher education. These criteria enabled aspiring teachers to understand how children learned within the contexts of their own development, their families, schools and society. Menter (1989) noted how the technicist approach silenced professional dialogue about racism and sexism, thereby limiting student teachers' understanding and their ability to challenge the practices which embed educational inequality.

As the model of the teacher has moved from educator to technicist teacher, the debate about multicultural education has run apace with these changes. Multicultural education was seen as a response to the presence of an increasing Black and minority ethnic population in Britain (Tomlinson, 2008). The notions of multicultural education prevalent at the time within schools is, as described by Troyna and Ball (1983), the three S's – Saris, Steel Bands and Samosas – and in initial teacher education (ITE) it was based on, notes Siraj-Blatchford (1993), the *problems* faced by schools due to the presence of children and students from BME groups rather than the evident racism in the schools. Sadly, in my experience not much has changed; in fact, in ITE there is now even less done on multicultural education or race equality than in the 1980s. The 'problem' of ethnic minorities, or the deficit model of difference, be that ethnic or linguistic, is still prevalent in the discourse today.

The 1990s heralded the death knell of any multicultural education within ITE courses, as the whole sector was publicly attacked and pilloried by the political Right wing, which set the agenda for ITE. Gaine (1995) notes that teaching was cast as a 'technical skill' with no space for theory, and so started the distancing of higher education from the preparation of teachers. This gap has been growing ever since. As the gap has widened, the preparation of teachers to understand race, racism, and issues of equality and inequality have also diminished.

Jones (2000), writing after the murder of Stephen Lawrence, urged that beginning teachers *needed* to understand racism, and he noted how ITE educated (or, rather, trained) teachers to teach in a society within an assumed cultural homogeneity. He argued that it is no wonder that ITE fails to develop student teachers' understanding of key concepts such as, equality, social justice, equality of opportunity and inequality. This lack of knowledge renders them ineffectual in their stated goal of achieving equality of outcomes for their pupils.

Despite initiatives such as Multiverse (Smith, 2012) – a web-based resource related to ethnic, cultural and linguistic diversity to support teachers, student teachers and teacher educators to understand how to work in diverse classrooms – the absence of references related to ethnic diversity are apparent in the current Teachers' Standards 2012 (DfE, 2012b).

In her analysis of the teaching standards in England from 1983–2012, Smith (2012, p. 3) notes that

> conceptualisations of equality however, tend to be concerned primarily with removing perceived obstacles and providing remedial tools to educational success. 'Equality of opportunity' is premised on individualised notions of discrimination which can therefore be overcome by actions of individuals.

Smith's analysis of the teaching standards as policy documents related to the political hue of each successive government provides a timeline of how the deficit notion of difference has become embedded, how each set of standards has served to centre an assimilationist agenda and, thereby, promote White middle class hegemony and maintain the status quo (Smith, 2012, p. 10).

Bryan (2012) examines the Teachers' Standards 2012 (DfE, 2012b) with reference to the inclusion of the term 'fundamental British values', found in Part Two, entitled 'Personal and Professional Conduct.' There it states that teachers should not undermine fundamental British values (BERA Race, Ethnicity and Education Special Interest Group Conference October 2012). In her critique, Bryan (2012) explains how this phrase is drawn from the Prevent Strategy, a counter-terrorism policy targeted at Islamist terrorism. She argues that, not only does the inclusion of this phrase bestow the role of cultural and moral custodian on the teacher, but in addition it conceptualises the teacher's role from a particular perspective, thus signalling an integration of the teacher into the roles of custodian and promoter of national values. These values are listed as:

'democracy, the rule of law, individual liberty and mutual respect, and tolerance of those with different faiths and beliefs' (DfE, 2012b) and as such are not uniquely British. Thus, the project of teacher as technicist is also coupled with the conception of the teacher as custodian of British values and therefore accountable for upholding them. This signals the beginning of a new concept of who teaches and becomes a teacher.

The assimilationist approach exemplified by the Teachers' Standards 2012 needs to be considered alongside three other elements:

1. Pupil demographics;
2. Teacher demographics; and
3. The results of the annual Newly Qualified Teacher (NQT) survey.

In relation to pupil demographics, the data show that schools in England are becoming more ethnically diverse. In 2011 over a quarter of pupils in primary/elementary schools were from minority ethnic backgrounds, and almost 20 per cent spoke English as an additional language. Yet, the data for teachers' ethnicity show that only 6.4 per cent are from BME backgrounds (DfE, 2011). When the outcomes of the NQT survey for 2012 (DfE, 2012c) are considered with respect to the two questions which are related to ethnic and linguistic diversity, respectively:

- How good was your training in preparing you to teach learners from minority ethnic backgrounds?
- How good was your training to work with learners with English as an additional language?

The responses show that, with respect to the first, only 54 per cent of primary NQTs felt well prepared or very well prepared to teach learners from minority ethnic backgrounds; and with respect to the second question only 49 per cent felt equally well prepared (DfE, 2012c). In each case, approximately half of newly qualified teachers felt they were not very well prepared with respect to working with learners from minority ethnic backgrounds and those for whom English is an additional language. One could consider that these statistics attest to the failure of ITE to prepare the predominantly White classes of student teachers for ethnic and linguistically diverse classrooms, yet the Teachers' Standards 2012 centre an assimilationist agenda (Smith, 2012) which seeks to overlook the identity of minority ethnic pupils in terms of their ethnic, cultural and linguistic heritage, depicted as barriers to learning which should be swept away. The process of ITE fails to prepare student teachers to understand how a child's ethnic and linguistic heritage is part and parcel of who he or she is, and how education can help children to be secure in their own identities.

Whiteness

In reflecting on the evolution of the Teachers' Standards and how, at each stage, the notions of difference are conceived as obstacles, and how the role of the teacher as a technicist is to be the agent of assimilation – and when we consider that the majority of the teacher workforce is White, it is not such a great leap to link the Standards to being a means of centring Whiteness to ensure it is securely embedded in the process of preparing future teachers (Gillborn, 2008; DfE, 2012a; Smith, 2012). This section will discuss the notion of Whiteness as a central organising concept which underpins teacher education policy, curriculum and practice. Whiteness is the concept which exposes how structural inequalities are built into processes and practices. It is an invisible component of how policy makers, policy interpreters and recipients work in both complicit and unknowing ways to advantage one group whilst disadvantaging others, namely those from BME groups.

There is a long history of studying BME groups and their successes or failures within the education system (Coard, 1971; Stone, 1981; Gillborn, 2008; Tomlinson, 2008). The notion, 'difference equals deficit, equals a problem to be solved', prevails in the underlying thinking of some individuals. The 'problem' is always perceived to lie with those who represent the 'different other'. This conceptualisation is still evident in the Teachers' Standards with respect to linguistic diversity, and it determines some teachers' responses to the BME pupils in their classrooms. If we stop to examine this idea of the problem being the racialised 'other', then we expose an underlying assumption of the 'other' as aberrant, which assumes there are those who are non-aberrant or 'normal'. Bonnett (2000) explains how White identity has been forged through the conquering, enslavement and domination of people through the process of colonisation. He traces how groups once thought to be White, such as Arabs and Chinese, were marginalised and re-categorised as non-White over the course of time. He describes the development of a 'hegemonic European-identified racialised whiteness' (Bonnett, 2000, p. 17). It is this group that defines or represents the norm. In contemporary society this equates to the White middle class. This underlying unspoken measure of classification needs to be exposed. Whiteness enables us to turn the spotlight of surveillance from the BME 'other' to examining the hidden operation and exercise of power through Whiteness.

Whiteness is a concept which can be used to expose the inherent structures that perpetuate systemic racism. Garner (2010) describes Whiteness as a social and political construct which underpins structural racism. McIntyre (1997) notes that Whiteness is more than the racial identity, White, and Harris (cited in Ladson-Billings, 2004, p. 57) confirms that it is an identity which carries 'social and material value'. Whiteness is a racialised discourse which has been established over time to privilege White people. It maintains their interests and supremacy and is constructed to advantage White people. Frankenberg (2009, p. 526) notes that 'the term "Whiteness" signals the production and reproduction of dominance rather than subordination, normativity rather than marginality, and privilege rather than disadvantage'. Marx (2006, p. 6) grapples with defining Whiteness in her study of six White pre-service teachers. She concludes that 'Whiteness is much more than a racial discourse[, it is] an amalgamation of qualities including cultures, histories, experiences, discourses and privileges shared by Whites.'

The often-cited article by Peggy McIntosh (1990) in which she delineates 46 privileges which Whites enjoy is now, in the Whiteness literature, a seminal piece that others have built upon. In discussing White advantage, Ryde (2009) acknowledges how as a White person she became aware of the advantages associated with her identity:

> Whiteness has become less neutral and more figural for me. It is as if staring at a blank page I have begun to notice contours and shades that were not at first apparent. So what have I seen? I have noticed that I am advantaged by being White in many subtle ways. (Ryde, 2009, p. 36)

Ryde asserts that being White is not seen in as a racialised identity by the vast majority of White people, and she suggests that therein lie the roots of the problem.

The link between Whiteness and structural racism is often unclear to some people. Chubbuck (cited in Yoon, 2012) suggests that Whiteness is not new and is inseparable from racism. Leonardo (2002) suggests that Whiteness and the perpetuation of racism run in tandem. He notes that Whiteness is identified through an inability or unwillingness to name racism which occurs as a result of the action or inaction of White people, and this leads to inequality. Leonardo adds that Whiteness is premised on the notion of 'othering' ethnicity and the 'naturalisation' of White as the norm, and trying to set aside the historical wrongs of the past as a means of moving on is an attempt to hide the construction of dominance. It is the attempt to hide the operations of privilege and domination that Gillborn (2008) notes is the most dangerous aspect of Whiteness, as is the obliviousness to this aspect under which most White people unknowingly operate on a daily basis. Picower (2009) writes about the tools of Whiteness used daily to perpetuate its centrality. She outlines emotional responses, such as anger and defensiveness; colour-blind racism or, as Frankenberg (1993) would term it, a 'color and power evasive' position which maintains the structures of power. The colour-blind approach can be used to 'justify inaction through denial, thereby maintaining the current power structure and preserving the privileges of the dominant group' (Anderson, 2010, p. 250). Picower (2009) suggests that the other tools of Whiteness, such as silence and the promotion of the ethical, non-racist good self in teachers' discourses, are used adeptly to maintain the status quo. Yoon (2012) shows how Whiteness-at-work within schools in the United States serves to maintain a race-neutral approach to children's questions and curiosity about each other's ethnic-ities and that of visitors – doing so in such a powerful way that it does not enable children to talk about ethnicity and difference and, instead, the discourse is about politeness. Picower (2009) would analyse such deflections as a need by teachers to maintain and protect Whiteness.

The deflections, the protective discourses of goodness and innocence, serve some White teachers well since it helps to keep them unsullied by debates about race, ethnicity and racism, thereby maintaining a false innocence which perpetuates the symbolic violence of structural racism and inequality for those racialised as 'other' in their classrooms. Rodriguez (2009) would classify this stance, not as innocence, but as ignorant, because she asserts that in choosing not to know about, or engage in, exposing the power of Whiteness in the maintenance of structural racism, these people choose to be ignorant: racism is thus perpetuated by this ignorance. Rodriguez thereby exposes the harm that ignorant deflections, silences and inactions ultimately inflict on chil-dren. Whiteness enables us to see White people as a racialised group which benefits from the hidden and neutral conceptions of being White and benefit from the invisible operations of Whiteness which serve to reproduce structural racism.

The Practice of Whiteness in ITE

The ways in which Whiteness is embedded in the process of preparing to teach in ethnically diverse classrooms requires careful documentation and tracking in order to reveal its invisible operations. It is worth noting that the responses NQTs make to the question 'How good was your training in preparing you to teach learners from minority ethnic backgrounds?' has always been one of the questions that returned the lowest positive rates, and even NQTs in multiethnic London did not report to be 100 per cent prepared to teach learners from minority ethnic backgrounds. For Primary NQTs the Teaching Agency (2012c, p. 19) notes:

> In the case of the minority ethnic backgrounds question; NQTs trained by London based providers rated this aspect of their training higher than NQTs trained by providers based in the south west government office region (68 per cent of very good and good responses compared with 38 per cent of very good and good responses). There were similar variations in the responses to the English as an additional language question with 61 per cent of NQTs trained by providers based in London compared with 39 per cent of NQTs trained by providers based in the south west region, rating their training as very good or good.

The evidence shows that at least a third of NQTs in London did not feel very well prepared with respect to teaching pupils from minority ethnic groups. So, at least one-third of new teachers feel inadequately prepared to teach the portion of the pupil population which is increasing rapidly. Why should that be?

Student teachers and Whiteness

Research has shown that White postgraduate secondary student teachers represented a spectrum of views with respect to their training to teach BME students and to deal with racist incidences (Bhopal et al., 2009; Lander, 2011b). The students voiced feelings which ranged from naïve conceptions of race and ethnicity to guilt, anger and inadequacy in the face of the incidents they had to deal with in schools. Those who voiced naïve conceptions of ethnicity had little or 'no exposure' (or contact with) people from ethnically diverse backgrounds; their naivety was shown in the vocabulary they used to refer to BME children, terms such as 'pupils from other cultures', or the outdated and unaccepted term 'coloured'. One used the language of colour blindness, stressing that he 'almost has to stop and think to work out who *they* were because it just didn't stand out'. In another extract, Sebastian notes that he would need to be aware of BME pupils in order to look out for bullying to make sure the child 'has not got problems with the other pupils' (Lander, 2011b, p. 357). It is interesting to note that this student teacher associates ethnicity as a problem which attracts bullying or is otherwise problematic. The data did not show whether this conception was one which Sebastian had formed as part of his preparation to teach, it would be unlikely since this interview occurred three months after the start of his teacher education programme. Deficit notions of BME pupils and colour blindness prevailed in the interviews with the naïve students.

There were student teachers who, through their own appraisal, thought they were better disposed towards aspects of ethnic diversity, which ability they attributed to their world experiences, such as living in London or travelling abroad. However, Stuart appeared as a rabbit in the headlights, startled and shocked by the racism he encountered in school from pupils and teaching assistants. He encapsulates the position that Whiteness is naturalised and neutral, explaining his shock by stating 'everyone likes to believe they are neutral and not racist' (Lander, 2011b, p. 359). The idea that he as a White male is neutral indicates that this is a 'norm' by which he thinks others also operate and inadvertently judge others, which Gillborn (2008) asserts is the cause of passive racism.

In interviews with other student teachers in this cohort, some felt guilty upon recognising their positions as novice teachers who are put into situations in school where they are unable to question practices which lead to disadvantageous outcomes for BME children. For example, Steven described how two African [his term] boys who were new arrivals in England and to the school, who spoke little or no English, were placed in his lower-group English class. He recounts how the school policy of placing in lower groups pupils who had English as an additional language made him feel 'uncomfortable' and 'guilty' because they were placed in the 'wrong group for the wrong reasons' (Lander, 2011b, p. 361). Steven felt guilty that these two Black boys were placed in a group with poor indigenous learning, behaviour and language role models and, as such, the school policy would, he felt, lead to inevitable underachievement for these youngsters.

Other students had a strong sense of their own political positioning. and Sean was vociferous in noting that most student teachers would pay 'lip service to racism' and hide behind their 'pc shield' (pc meaning politically correct) with respect to discussions about racism (Lander, 2011b, p. 361). In deploying the term 'pc' Sean indicates that some teachers want to act in a politically correct (pc) manner, but that behind the shield they act and talk in ways which are not pc. The wonderful, visual metaphor of a shield to hide behind, which relates to Picower's (2009) tools of Whiteness in the maintenance of the ethical good self, is apparent in anti-racist utterances on the surface, but Whiteness, as the dominant discourse, remains undisturbed, embedded and hidden behind the 'pc shield'.

Teacher educators and Whiteness

In my unpublished doctoral thesis (Lander, 2011a), which examined the Whiteness of teacher educators, a similar spectrum of perspectives is evident. The narratives of some White teacher educators illustrate their lack of knowledge and experience related to race, ethnicity and racism. The narratives show how this lack of knowledge compounds their embedded Whiteness, which is evident in the language they used to respond to questions about improving student teachers' understanding of race equality. Whiteness was revealed in a range of strategies or moves to maintain it through the tools of Whiteness (Picower, 2009), such as protection, colour blindness, denial, deflection, innocence, niceness and ignorance.

The tutors appeared to want to protect students from understanding topics such as race, ethnicity or racism and tutors made excuses about why these aspects did not feature on the ITE curriculum or in students' practice. Some tutors felt that the White student teachers had a lot to do in learning to become teachers and did not need to be burdened by additional issues, or they were good people and feared getting things wrong when trying to deal with racism. There were others who drew on the neo-liberal discourse of treating them as individuals, where equality is achieved through removing a barrier for individual children (Smith, 2012) to the rather insidious notion that their own ethnicity is divorced from their teacher self, which hints at a neutrality that teachers should possess.

In making excuses for the student teachers one respondent described the students as 'not straying too far from the garden gate', to indicate they attended their local university and could not be expected to have engaged with race, ethnicity and racism because the university is sited in a predominantly White area of England (Lander, 2011a). So, implying firstly, the students could not be expected to know about these things. Secondly, why would they want to know about them? And, thirdly, what use would it be anyway since most of them would teach in schools within the locality? In this phrase there is validation of maintaining the status quo through the dominant discourse of Whiteness. Tutors were divided about the ITE curriculum on offer, with some noting they do too much; one said, 'We do enough without making a song and dance of it', and others said there was not enough courseworkon these aspects.

Other tutors mentioned that teachers in school were not sufficiently knowledgeable or experienced to support student teachers' under-standing about racism or aspects of ethnicity and, since most of the ITE occurs in schools, there seemed to an air of absolution in this statement. In fact, with training through School Direct sited largely in one school, the Whiteness evident within ITE in universities currently will remain undisturbed without a trace of any ripples through this narrow school-based model.

Colour blindness was believed by a number of tutors to be a virtuous position. They talked about a 'common humanity', and said that ethnicity was only associated with external phenotypic features such as hair or skin colour, which were immaterial to learning. Some tutors talked of ethnicity as an impediment and, therefore, the goal of a teacher and schools was to make 'those pupils invisible'. The colour-blind approach is used in the tutors' narratives to 'justify inaction through denial, thereby maintaining the current power structure and preserving the privileges of the dominant group' (Anderson, 2010, p. 250). Frankenberg (1993) and Anderson (2010) argue that colour blindness is just a means of denying ethnic identity and, in doing so, centring what is considered by some people to be the norm or White identity, so at each turn it becomes a privileged status to preserve.

Tutors who classified themselves as having some knowledge and experience about topics such as race, ethnicity and racism talked about other tutors who drew on notions of the teacher as saviour (Marx, 2006) in helping BME children overcome obstacles to their learning associated with either language or ethnicity. One tutor talked about the 'goodness of primary teachers', when an incident involving a Muslim student teacher being failed on placement was discussed, adding, 'I would be horrified to think that [they] would want somehow to estab-lish a typical group of survivors.' Another tutor believed a racist incident on her course had been 'blown up out of all proportion'. Deflection often involved drawing on or acting ethically or casting ethnicity as a label and the danger of using labels. This was a means of nullifying the debate about ethnicity and racism. However, later in the interview the respondent who did not like labels refers to herself being White working class, thereby illustrating how Whiteness creates, maintains and is oblivious to the contradictions that emerge in the struggle to centre it as a dominant discourse.

Other ways in which Whiteness operates is the recruitment and retention of BME teachers to ITE. Writers such as Carrington and Tomlin (2000), Flintoff et al. (2008) and Wilkins and Lall (2010) have shown how BME trainee teachers in a range of geographical settings and across a range of primary and secondary ITE courses have to negotiate the racism of pupils, teachers and schools to survive, or not, on school placements and to pass their courses. It is not surprising, then, that only 6 per cent of teachers are from BME groups, since their struggle to succeed is against overt racism and institutional racism as it manifests itself in the dominant discourse of Whiteness in ITE.

Ways forward

There are ways in which teacher educators can work against the grain of Whiteness within policy and practice. Whilst the Teachers' Standards 2012 are statutory, most ITE providers construct the ITE curriculum (albeit within a finite number of weeks) within the institutions. The curriculum offered to aspiring teachers can be constructed to support teacher candidates' starting points with reference to race and ethnicity through dedicated lectures, seminars and activities which challenge stereotypes, constructions of otherness and internalised racism, and to be critically reflective about the curriculum and resources they offer children in schools. I work with a team of tutors who endeavour to offer these challenges to all student teachers; we work through dedicated sessions on equality and diversity. All students have to attend the eight sessions (15 hours) in three years on an undergraduate ITE course. Whilst I recognise this is insufficient in developing depth of understanding, it is the first step in mobilising our commitment to race equality and integrating aspects of it within the ITE curriculum. This change has only been possible through the dedication and expertise of a small number of ITE tutors and a senior manager with the power to enact changes within the curriculum. These tutors have devised and delivered the units of learning through large-cohort sessions which are not conducive to developing individual understandings nor do they promote discussion. The evaluation of these sessions by students is predictably varied, but one comment which I consider to be a validation of our attempts (although I am not sure it was meant as such) read: 'There's too much equality and diversity.' Let us hope there will be even more and that more teacher educators have the courage of their convictions to overcome the policy imperatives to shake the embedded prevalent Whiteness in ITE rather than hide behind their 'pc shields' (Lander, 2011b).

References

Anderson, K.J. (2010) *Benign Bigotry: The Psychology of Subtle Prejudice*, Cambridge, Cambridge University Press.

Ball, J., Milmo, D. and Ferguson, B. (2012) 'Half of UK's young Black males are unemployed'. Available at http://www.guardian.co.uk/society/2012/mar/09/half-uk-young-black-men-unemployed. [Accessed on 15 April 2012]

BERA (2012) 'What are Fundamental British values? Race, Ethnicity and Education Special Interest Group Conference', October, at the University of Chichester.

BBC (2011a) 'Indian student murdered in Salford street attack'. Available at http://www.bbc.co.uk/news/uk. [Accessed on 23 December 2011]

BBC (2011b) 'Stephen Lawrence trial: Jury retires to consider verdict'. Available at http://www.bbc.co.uk/news/uk-16355693. [Accessed on 23 December 2011]

Bhopal, K., Harris, R. and Rhamie, J. (2009) 'The teaching of 'race', diversity and inclusion on PGCE courses: a case study analysis of University of Southampton'. Available at http://webarchive.nationalarchives.gov.uk. [Accessed on 14 March 2012]

Bonnett, A. (2000) *White Identities*, Harlow, Pearson.

Bryan, H. (2012) 'Reconstructing the teacher as a post-secular pedagogue: a consideration of the new Teachers' Standards', *Journal of Values and Beliefs Studies in Religion and Education*, 33 (2), 217–228.

Carrington, B. and Tomlin, R. (2000) 'Towards a more inclusive profession: teacher recruitment and ethnicity', *European Journal of Teacher Education*, 23 (2), 139–157.

Coard, B. (1971) *How the West Indian Child is Made ESN in the British School System*, London, New Beacon Books.

Department for Education (DfE) (2013) *School Direct*. Available at http://www.education.gov.uk/schools/careers/traininganddevelopment. [Accessed on 20 January 2013]

Department for Education (DfE) (2012a) *Initial Teacher Training (ITT) Criteria*, London, DfE.

Department for Education (DfE) (2012b) *Teachers' Standards*, London, DfE.

Department for Education (DfE) (2012c) 'The Newly Qualified Teacher Survey 2012'. Available at http://media.education.gov.uk. [Accessed on 14 February 2013]

Department for Education (DfE) (2011) 'First release statistics schools, pupils and their characteristics'. DfE, Available at http://www.education.gov.uk/rsgateway/DB/SFR/s001012/sfr12-2011.pdf. [Accessed on March 15 2012]

Department for Education and Science (DES) (1985) *Education for All*. Report of the Committee of Enquiry into the Education of Children from Minority Ethnic Groups (Swann Report). [Online] Available at http://www.dg.dial.pipex.com/documents/docs3/swann.shtml. [Accessed on 12 March 2012]

Flintoff, A., Chappell, A., Gower, C., Keyworth, S., Lawrence, J., Money, J., Squires, S.L. and Webb, L. (2008) *Black and Minority Ethnic Trainees' Experiences of Physical Education Initial Teacher Training: Report for the Training and Development Agency*, Leeds, Carnegie Research Institute.

Frankenberg, R. (1993) *White Women, Race Matters: The Social Construction of Whiteness*, London, Routledge.

Frankenberg, R. (2009) 'White women, race matters', in Taylor, E., Gillborn, D. and Ladson-Billings, G. (eds), *Foundations of Critical Race Theory in Education*, Abingdon, Routledge, 519–533.

Furlong, J., Barton, L., Miles, S., Whiting, C. and Whitty, G. (2000) *Teacher Education in Transition: Re-forming Professionalism?* Buckingham, Open University Press.

Gaine, C. (1995) *Still No Problem Here*, Stoke-on-Trent, Trentham.

Garner, S. (2010) *Racisms An Introduction*, London, Sage.

Gillborn, D. (2005) 'Education policy as an act of White supremacy: Whiteness, Critical Race Theory and education reform', *Journal of Education Policy*, 20 (4) 485–505.

Gillborn, D. (2008) *Racism and Education Coincidence or Conspiracy?* Abingdon, Routledge.

Jones, R. (2000) 'Out of the abyss: the current state of multicultural education in primary education', *Education*, 3–13, 28 (1), 60–64.

Ladson-Billings, G. (2004) 'Just what is Critical Race Theory and what is it doing in a *nice* field like education?' in Ladson-Billings, G. and Gillborn, D. (eds), *The RoutledgeFalmer Reader in Multicultural Education*, Abingdon, RoutledgeFalmer, 49–67.

Lander, V. (2011a) 'Race encounters in ITE: tutors' narratives on race equality in initial teacher education (ITE)'. Unpublished Thesis, Institute of Education, London.

Lander, V. (2011b) 'Race, culture and all that: an exploration of the perspectives of White secondary student teachers about race equality issues in their initial teacher education', *Race, Ethnicity and Education*, 14 (3), 351–364.

Leonardo, Z. (2002) 'The souls of White folk: critical pedagogy, whiteness studies and globalization discourse', *Race Ethnicity and Education*, 5 (1), 29–50.

Marx, S. (2006) *Revealing the Invisible Confronting Passive Racism in Teacher Education*, New York, Routledge.

McIntosh, P. (1990) 'White privilege: unpacking the invisible knapsack', *Independent School*, Winter 90, 49 (2).

McIntyre, A. (1997) *Making Meaning of Whiteness*, Albany, State University of New York Press.

Menter, I. (1989) 'Teaching practice stasis: racism, sexism and school experience in initial teacher education', *British Journal of Sociology of Education*, 10 (4), 459–473.

Picower, B. (2009) 'The unexamined Whiteness of teaching: how White teachers maintain and enact dominant racial ideologies', *Race, Ethnicity and Education*, 12 (2), 197–215.

Race, R. (2011) *Multiculturalism and Education*, London, Continuum.

Rodriguez, D. (2009) 'The usual suspects: negotiating White student resistance and teacher authority in a predominantly White classroom', *Cultural Studies-Critical Methodologies*, 19 (4), 483–508.

Runnymede Trust (2012) 'Key facts about race in the UK'. Available at www.runnymede.org.uk. [Accessed on 2 February 2012]

Ryde, J. (2009) *Being White in the Helping Professions*, London, Jessica Kingsley Publishers.

Siraj-Blatchford, I. (ed.) (1993) *'Race', Gender and the Education of Teachers*, Buckingham, Open University Press.

Skerrett, A. (2011) English teachers' racial literacy knowledge and practice, *Race, Ethnicity and Education*, 14 (3), 313–330.

Smith, H.J. (2012) 'A critique of the teaching standards in England (1984–2012): discourses of equality and maintaining the status quo', *Journal of Education Policy*, iFirst Article 1–22.

Stone, M. (1981) *The Education of the Black Child in Britain*, London, Fontana.

Tomlinson, S. (2008) *Race and Education Policy and Politics in Britain*, Maidenhead, Open University Press.

Troyna, B. and Ball, W. (1985) 'Styles of LEA policy intervention in multicultural/ antiracist education', *Educational Review*, 37 (2) 165–173.

TUC (Trades Union Council UK) (2012) 'Young Black men have experienced sharpest unemployment rise since 2010', Available at http://www.tuc.org.uk/economy/tuc-21533-f0.cfm. [Accessed on 12 March 2013]

Wilkins, C. and Lall, R. (2010) 'Getting by or getting on? Black student teachers' experiences of teacher education', *Race Equality Teaching*, 28 (2), 19–26.

Yoon, I. (2012) 'The paradoxical nature of whiteness-at-work in the daily life of schools and teacher communities', *Race, Ethnicity and Education*, 15 (5), 587–613.

7
Beyond Kung Fu and Takeaways? Negotiation of British Chinese Identities in Schools

Ada Mau

You can be British and Chinese, right? – Jackie, aged 17

British Chinese pupils have been seen as a 'successful' group in the British education system in the last decade. A significant portion of Chinese heritage pupils are UK-born and some have parents and/or grandparents that have been settled in the UK since the post-war era. Increasingly, many families have moved away from the catering trade that has been strongly associated with the UK Chinese population. Many of these young people are well integrated socially and academically at school. The emergence of new forms of identity among the younger generation has created greater diversity within the ever-evolving British Chinese 'community'. This chapter explores the emergent British Chinese identity in which young people recognise their flexible, relational and complex hybridised British Chinese identities, including the possibility of being both British and Chinese.

From behind the counter to 'model' pupils

This chapter draws on the findings of doctoral research that focused on British Chinese pupils who were UK-born/raised and had limited knowledge of Chinese language(s). This study built on an unexplored area which emerged from an earlier Economic Social Research Council-funded study[1] (Francis et al., 2008) that sought to examine the experience and identities of British Chinese pupils who attended weekend, complementary schools to learn their heritage language(s), as well as other earlier studies that examined the experiences of British Chinese young people (e.g., Wong, 1992; Parker, 1995; Song, 1997; Woodrow and Sham, 2001, Francis and Archer, 2004).

Although British Chinese pupils are now widely seen as high-achieving and successful in schools in England, only a few decades ago their academic prospects and well-being were in fact a worrying concern for educationalists and the British government. There were concerns over English-language ability among British Chinese children, particularly those who had spent their early years abroad (Jackson and Garvey 1974; Benton and Gomez 2008). In the early 1980s, only 52 per cent of Chinese pupils in London at secondary school were fluent in English (Chan, 1986; Runnymede Trust, 1986). Some teachers also worried about the impacts of the 'takeaway lifestyle', which often involved young people helping out at their family-run takeaways outside of school hours (Jackson and Garvey, 1974; Baxter, 1988). Parker (1995) and Song's (1997) research on British Chinese young people illustrated that working at their family catering business was significant to the British Chinese experience for many who grew up in the UK. In their research on British Chinese families and pupils in Greater Manchester, Sham and Woodrow (1998, 2001) concluded that British Chinese children appeared to live in a 'cocoon' within British society, under distinctive socialisation practices which prevented them from integrating at school and into wider society. Parker (1997) also argued that British Chinese youths were sometimes portrayed as being associated with triad gangs and positioned as potential outsiders in British society.

However, as the post-war Chinese migrant population has become more settled in the UK, British Chinese pupils' academic performance has been steadily improving, and their test results have become better than all other ethnic groups, including White British. In 1998, a higher portion of pupils of Chinese ethnicity achieved Level 4 in Key Stage 2 English and Maths than for any other ethnic group (DfES, 2006). Among pupils at state-funded schools in England during the academic year 2011–2012, British Chinese pupils remained the highest-attaining ethnic group. The percentage of British Chinese pupils achieving 5 or more GCSEs at grade A* to C or equivalent, including English and mathematics GCSEs or iGCSEs, is 17.6 percentage points above the national average (DfE, 2013). Unlike other ethnic groups, pupils of Chinese descent also generally perform well across all socioeconomic backgrounds. Their 'secret' to academic success attracted attention from educationalists and the public (e.g., Mansell, 2011; Ritchie, 2011). OECD top-ranking results of pupils from Hong Kong and Shanghai (OECD, 2010), as well as 'Tiger Mother/Chinese style parenting' further perpetuated the image of the 'success' of children of Chinese descent.

On the other hand, their high level of academic achievement often means issues faced by British Chinese pupils tend to be overlooked as their performance is not perceived to suffer as a result. The UK Chinese are often perceived by the general public as a silent and self-sufficient community (Chan et al., 2007). Compared with other minority ethnic groups in the UK, the Chinese community is more dispersed geographically to suit the catering business and, therefore, tends to make up only a small number in each area. As a result, the 'community' is in some ways less visible, and this settlement pattern often leads to them being neglected, for example in terms of service provision (NIMHE, 2004). Nevertheless, a number of studies suggest that British Chinese young people have been experiencing significant levels of racism and discrimination (Parker, 1995; Verma et al., 1999; Archer and Francis, 2004; Adamson et al., 2009), but British Chinese pupils are frequently absent from discussions around racism and racialisation within schools. In Francis and Archer's (2004) study of British Chinese pupils in the London area, teachers seemed to assume that British Chinese pupils did not encounter racism, while the parents and young people interviewed told a different story.

The 'hidden' problems experienced within the education system are perhaps a reflection of wider issues experienced by the UK Chinese population for a long time. Earlier research by Parker (1995) and Song (1997) documented the racism regularly experienced by young people helping at their family-run catering businesses. A growing number of individuals within the UK-born/raised generations of British Chinese (e.g., Thorpe and Yeh, 2011; Chen et al., 2011; Chan, 2012), have voiced their concerns over how the British Chinese population has stayed 'invisible' and has put up with racism/stereotypes for too long. This chapter aims to explore the mainstream schooling experience and emerging identities within 'second/third generation' British Chinese pupils in the UK. Although they generally appear to be well integrated into the British schools, they continue to experience regular yet subtle forms of racism and racialisation. This chapter also explores if their seemingly 'integrated' status enables full participation in school life and treatment as full members of British society.

With regard to understanding of identity and ethnicity, postcolonial and sociological work has been drawn on to develop nuanced understandings of identity, culture and ethnicity, being attentive to the ways in which these play out within a multicultural British society and global context. The identities generated within diasporic communities synthesise a host of different cultural elements, challenging and transcending 'old' boundaries (Bhabha, 1990). The concepts of 'hybridity' (Bhabha, 1994) and 'orientalism' (Said, 1978) are used to highlight how the British Chinese pupils are able to flexibly negotiate their identities but are also confined by certain essentialised, dominant discourses. As Hall (1990, p. 235) explains, the diasporic experience is defined 'not by essence or purity, but by the recognition of a necessary heterogeneity and diversity', and the concept of identity 'lives with and through, not despite, difference; by *hybridity*'. This chapter discusses the range of complex, changing, hybridised social and learner identities negotiated and experienced by British Chinese pupils. The study uses a conceptual framework that understands identities and culture as processes of 'becoming' – unstable moments that are subject to the continuous flows of history, culture, context and power (Hall, 1990) and which are intersected by structural axes of 'race', gender, class and other elements. The positioning of British Chinese pupils will also be examined in relation to the integration discourse on new migrants and settled minority ethnic populations.

The data discussed is mainly drawn from individual interviews with 38 secondary schools and sixth form-aged British Chinese young people across Southern England. There were 13 boys and 25 girls, of whom 33 were UK-born, and four out of the five non-UK-born pupils (birth places comprised of Hong Kong, Malaysia, Australia and the United States) moved to the UK before school age. The majority of the pupils (28) had both parents of Chinese heritage, and 10 pupils were of mixed Chinese heritage (with White British or other ethnic backgrounds). Their Chinese parents or grandparents came from a wide range of geographical locations, including Hong Kong, Mainland China, Malaysia, Singapore, Brunei and Mauritius. The majority of the participants were English-dominant or monolingual speakers with limited knowledge of the Chinese language. The terms 'second' or 'third' generations are explicitly not used to describe these young people because such descriptions do not accurately represent the complex migration history, pattern and experiences in some of the families, nor the changing nature of migration in the increasingly mobile and globalised world. The heterogeneous British Chinese 'community' has become even more diverse due to the recent influx of new migrants from Mainland China, but these recent arrivals are not the focus of the discussions in this chapter.

Successfully integrated? Ticking all the right boxes?

Although the British model of 'integration' has never been clearly defined (Saggar and Somerville, 2012), there have been on-going public debates about migration into the UK and integration. Recent concerns on migrants and existing minority ethnic populations often reflect a perception that people from certain linguistic, ethnic or religious backgrounds are not 'integrating' into British society and instead self-segregate. For instance, after the riots that occurred in Northern England in the summer of 2001, the lack of a 'good' level of English and growing up in Punjabi- or Bangla-speaking households were identified by a local MP in Bradford as causes for young Asian men rioting and joining in criminal activities (Blackledge, 2004). South Asian pupils have been criticised for not mixing with their White peers and not fully participating in school (Crozier and Davies, 2008). Trevor Phillips (2005), former chair of the Commission for Racial Equality and Commission for Equality and Human Rights, controversially argued that young people from ethnic minorities were 'alarmingly' not having friendship groups that crossed racial/ethnic boundaries.

Taking part at school

The British Chinese 'community' has been perceived as keeping to themselves. Although their isolation is not generally seen as a 'threat', as in the case of the British Muslim population, the ability of the British Chinese to integrate has also been questioned. In Sham and Woodrow's (1998, 2001) study of British Chinese children in Manchester who predominantly came from families linked to the catering trade, it was reported that the children appeared to live in a 'cocoon' within British society, under distinctive socialisation practices. Sham and Woodrow found that these pupils tended not to participate in extra-curricular activities and often stayed within their friendship group of other Chinese heritage pupils.

However, the British Chinese pupils from this recent study reflected different experiences and behaviours than those in earlier research. These young people came from a wider range of socioeconomic backgrounds and family migration trajectories. English was their dominant, sometimes only, language, and they generally appeared to be highly integrated into their school lives. There was a high tendency toward participation in extra-curricular activities at school, with 79 per cent of pupils (30) interviewed taking part, or having previously taken part, in school activities (e.g., clubs, teams, orchestra, etc.). A number of the participants were in fact extremely active and involved in many activities at school. For instance, Emma (17) was in the school orchestra, badminton team, film society and also helped to raise funds for a national charity. Patrick (aged 17) was a prefect and used to be in the football and basketball teams, while Neve (aged 15), Louise (aged 17) and Jackie (aged 17) all belonged to a number of musical groups at their schools.

One of the factors that contributed to the difference in level of participation compared to Sham and Woodrow's (1998, 2001) findings was the fact that the practice of 'helping out' at the family takeaway was not the norm among participants. In Sham and Woodrow's study, 93 per cent of the total sample came from catering backgrounds, and 63 per cent of their parents were takeaway or restaurant owners. Sham and Woodrow reported that the majority of their participants believed that they ought to go home from school as soon as possible to help their parents in their business or to do homework. However, this more recent study saw only nine pupils (24 per cent) whose families operated and owned catering businesses. Christy (aged 16) explained that she was asked by teachers to assist newcomers from China to adjust; however, she could not be further involved after school because she had to help out at her parents' takeaway. Christy's experience, in fact, represented the minority, rather than the norm, among this sample, and the obligation to work at family catering establishments did not seem to be a major determining factor in preventing participation in school activities.

The interviewees, across a range of socioeconomic statuses, appeared to have more freedom and resources to fully participate in school activities than did previous generations of British Chinese. Nevertheless, it was perhaps unsurprising that the few pupils who were exceptionally active at school were from higher socioeconomic backgrounds, undoubtedly linked to having more economic and social capital from their families and schools. Louise (aged 17), who attended a selective private school and whose parents were professionals, reported being very busy with a range of school activities, as well as with commitments and lessons outside mainstream education. However, Louise was highly aware of the stereotypes of being quiet and non-participatory that have been cast on British Chinese people, and she explained that her involvement with activities was a way to challenge such assumptions:

> I think also Chinese people are often very stereotyped as people who don't take part in community, in the wider community activities, in the British community, which is why I try to do a lot of volunteering at the library, and in Guiding. Because in Guiding, at the district meetings, every single volunteer there is Wh– is Caucasian, there aren't any Indian or Chinese volunteers there at all, and I remember thinking it was really strange when I was younger, and it's not the reason why I volunteer at Guides but I think it's something that I have in mind;

it's kind of like I don't like being stereotyped as someone who would just go home and do maths homework which is what a lot of people perceived of me.

Whilst Louise might have successfully defied the stereotypes, her narrative illustrated that she felt a burden to persistently prove them wrong within a racialised discourse that narrowly defines British Chinese young people. Although British Chinese pupils might generally be successful academically, Archer and Francis (2007) argue that they are still being pathologised as the 'wrong' type of learner: they are repressed/quiet and too focused on academic studies (i.e., 'just go home and do maths homework' and 'people who don't take part in community'). Woodrow and Sham (2001) cautioned that tight family unity, brought about by the catering trade lifestyle and stronger enforcement of 'Chinese culture' within the home sphere, contributed to young people not integrating socially at school, nor adopting different learning styles. Archer and Francis (2007) found that although teachers praised this cultural valuing of education in Chinese families, some expressed concerns that these values and practices could be too pushy and would restrict children's overall development. Intriguingly, the stereotype of strict 'Chinese style' parents seemed to be largely absent from the participants' descriptions within this sample. More than two-thirds of the pupils interviewed felt that their parents saw them as good pupils to various degrees. A few interviewees revealed that there was some pressure or high expectation from their parents to perform well, but most, like Grace (aged 14), did not feel that their parents were too strict:

Most of the time they'd like me to be top of the class, so a bit of pressure, but generally, yeah, they don't really mind about the effort as long as I get good marks, they're fine with it.

The sense of 'oppressive home cultures' or 'tiger mother' style, ultra-strict parenting that is seen in the stereotypes of Chinese parents/ families was not representative of these young people's experiences. Furthermore, the behaviour of 'pushy' and 'strict' Chinese parents, particularly those from the migrant generation working long hours and with limited education and English language skills, can be understood as their way to offer support to their children in academic work (Archer and Francis, 2007). While a few of the pupils described their parents being too busy or unable to help with schoolwork, a number of pupils also reported that their parents provided support when required. For example, Christine (aged 12) said her Hong Kong Chinese parents, who were educated in the UK, sometimes helped her with school reports by reading them and would 'go on the computer' with her.

Mixing with school friends

Additionally, the friendship group patterns of this study differ significantly from Woodrow and Sham's (2001) cohort, who preferred spending time with their Chinese friends and were discouraged by their parents to mix with White British children. Amongst the young people in this study, the majority of pupils described having school friends from non-Chinese backgrounds or a mix of ethnicities. Only two pupils mentioned having friendship groups that consisted of mostly Chinese: for example, Shirley (aged 13), who described 'most of my friends are, like, Chinese, and I have not very much friends in English school'. As a result of the small population and dispersed settlement patterns, British Chinese pupils generally only make up a small number, if any, at a school. Having non-Chinese school friends was conceivably not completely a personal decision for some of the young people living outside of metropolitan areas. However, a high number of pupils described their friendship groups as consisting of people from a mix of ethnicities. Matthew (aged 15) depicted his friendship group as 'really mixed, I've got White friends, Indian, Chinese', while Winnie (aged 13) simply said that her school friends were 'all different races'.

A large majority, 34 (89 per cent) of the interviewed pupils also reported feeling 'happy' to various degrees at their schools, and nine of these pupils expressed being 'really' or 'very' happy at school. Some interviewees enjoyed the relationships they formed at school: for instance, Grace (aged 14) felt that 'everyone's really friendly there, you feel like you're part of the community and, um, yeah you can get involved in a lot of stuff'. Some pupils were pleased with their learning or school facilities. However, three pupils admitted being unhappy at school. While Josephine (aged 14) reported disliking schoolwork, Callum (aged 13) and Ian (aged 17) described suffering from racist bullying at school (further discussion on this issue to come). When the participants were also asked if they fitted in or felt they belonged at their schools, an even higher portion of the pupils (36, 95 per cent) responded positively. The majority of these pupils appeared to be well integrated at their schools and engaged in social mixing, far from living in a 'cocoon' (Woodrow and Sham, 2001). Kinming (aged 15), who reported being 'very happy' at his school with supportive teachers and friends, felt very much part of his school community:

Yeah I mean when you were born here, you know, speak the language, integrating with the others, I mean I get on well with people in this, in the school, get on well with people with the same nationality, yeah, it's not bad.

These accounts also challenge the stereotypes of a homogenous, 'Chinese', approach to education among British Chinese families and of their tendency to keep to themselves. The maturation of the settled UK Chinese population and changing societal conditions (e.g., improved employment opportunities for ethnic minorities) helps to give young people more freedom to participate in school life.

Speaking English (and Chinese)

As mentioned earlier, the ability (or lack of) to speak English is often used in the popular discourse to question the willingness of migrants and ethnic minority communities to integrate and their right to belong in the UK. In Francis and Archer's (2004) research on British Chinese pupils in London, some pupils interviewed expressed dismay when non-Chinese assumed that they were not able to speak fluent English and, on the other hand, other pupils who came from outside the UK and/or with English as an additional language reported being ridiculed and having their right to belong questioned due to their accent or English non-fluency (Archer and Francis, 2007). Due to the dominance of the English language in education and everyday life in England, many British-born/ raised pupils from linguistic minority families only attain a certain level of knowledge of their parents' and/or grandparents' language(s) (as seen in previous research: i.e., Li, 1994; Creese et al., 2007), while English is their more dominant or developed language, even when initially taught the non-English language at home. Like the participants in this study, many British Chinese children use English as their dominant language. Nine of the British Chinese young people were monolingual English speakers who had no, or virtually no, Chinese-language knowledge (in any dialect), and nine others had some level of comprehension in Chinese but did not speak it. Additionally, five of the interviewees reported that their UK-born/raised Chinese parents had little or no Chinese language skills themselves. In Francis's (2005) study on British Chinese pupils in London, those who were recent immigrants experienced ridicule due to their accented English, seen as a sign of their foreignness and a reason to question their belonging in Britain. The pupils in this more recent study were all fluent English speakers – in fact, when being about their sense of 'Britishness', a number of young people cited speaking English and growing up/attending school in England as their reasons for feeling British/English.

However, having English as their dominant or only language did not always prevent language-based marginalisation and racial abuse due to their embodiment of 'Chinese' appearance. The majority of the pupils reported being asked to speak or write Chinese by their schoolmates or teachers, irrespective of their actual knowledge of the language. Ian (aged 17), who did not know any Chinese, reported frequently being asked 'do you speak Chinese?', but also accepted that it was generally an 'innocent' query and 'a fair question to be asked'. Charlotte (aged 14) commented that some schoolmates 'feel that I should know and stuff, ask me about it [Chinese]'; although such incidents did not take place regularly, she revealed 'feeling a bit embarrassed' about such situations. These requests to speak Chinese left Alice (aged 14) 'scared and worried', as she recounted how certain 'horrible' people at her school would 'tell me to say it [Chinese] to them but I'm shy, cause they gonna like, take the mick out of it and stuff'. On one hand, these British Chinese pupils, along with other minority ethnic young people, are expected to speak English and integrate and participate in the English school system and British society. Conversely, they are also expected to maintain and perform their 'exotic' Otherness on demand.

New identities, old stereotypes and racism

Unlike previous generations of British Chinese, who often drew their cultural reference points from Hong Kong and China (Parker, 1995; Woodrow and Sham, 2001), many of these young people in this study felt very much at home in the UK, while still feeling connected with their Chinese heritage at the same time. Parker's (1995) study of British Chinese youth found segmented identities among his respondents. He observed the tendency in the past for British Chinese young people's identities to be compartmentalised into private/Chinese and public/British worlds, as their identification with Hong Kong-based popular culture (e.g., Cantonese music and fashion) could only be experienced and expressed in Chinese networks but carried no cultural currency among their school peers or in the wider society. Most of the British Chinese pupils in this updated study articulated their identifications with Chineseness and Britishness in much more hybridised, fluid, relational, and flexible terms. A number of pupils confidently asserted their right to be and feel both British and Chinese. Neve (aged 15), of mixed White British and Mauritius Chinese heritage, described how she challenged people who did not think she looked 'British':

And then you get people who argue with you and they say you can't be like Chinese and British, and you like, 'Oh yes I can!' (laughs), you clearly can.

These young people communicated a range of complex identities, and the level of feeling British/Chinese or both varied across the sample. Some pupils felt strongly about their identities and experiences but others had not thought about these issues too much and regarded their experience of growing up with Chinese heritage in Britain as just 'normal'. Two of the mixed-heritage pupils also reported not feeling particularly connected to any specific culture or identity – one of them, Federico (aged 15), of Italian and Malaysian Chinese heritage, claimed that he 'just feel a person of the world really'.

Many of these young people reported feeling British to various extents, often in conjunction with feeling Chinese. A large number of the young people attributed their sense of Britishness to speaking English and growing up in the UK. As mentioned earlier, school was often viewed as a site for them to relate to their British identity. Amy (aged 15) articulated this popular view by saying that 'school, education, like I know about the news and, um, I've got, I know about Britain and I live here, so I feel British'; and Charlotte (aged 14) felt that the fact that 'I fit in with my English [school] friends and stuff' made her feel British. However, on the other hand, being at school also highlighted their Chinese identities and being 'different' in relation to their peers and the dominant culture for some others. Often, their own sense of Britishness/Chineseness was constructed relational to feeling and being different from others in a specific context.

> Depending where I am really, I mostly feel more English. But for English people I probably am more Chinese, if you see what I'm saying, but overall I probably am more English than I am Chinese. (Nicky, aged 16)

> Yeah, but it's quite kind of different times really. Like when I'm around Chinese people I feel more Chinese but when I'm with my friends from school I also feel a little bit Chinese as well because I know I'm different from them and I have a different history to them as well. (Grace, aged 14)

Nevertheless, the participants in this study generally seemed to have a positive attitude towards being British Chinese and 'different', though some admitted the experience included some difficulties. Many young people felt that growing up with Chinese heritage made them 'special'. Grace (aged 14) considered her Chinese background made her life more interesting through being 'slightly more different and unique or individual compared to other people around you'. Emma (aged 17) felt that being British Chinese gave her the 'best of both worlds', as she got to 'pick up the really good parts of the Chinese culture and kind of fuse them with parts of English'.

On the other hand, some pupils articulated the tensions and complexities they had to cope with by being in 'both worlds' as racialised, visible minorities. Callum (aged 13) appreciated that he got to 'do lots of different things other people don't get to do' due to being part Chinese, but he also experienced the downside as being picked on at school and being called 'chinky' and 'yellow'. Kit (aged 15) shared similar sentiments; she described that 'there might be some points when it's hard like bullying and racism, but other times it feels good to be different'. A number of young people talked about the racial stereotypes and racism they experienced at school, and the types of incidents included racist slurs and 'jokes', physical violence and more subtle forms of exoticisation and stereotypes. While overt racist acts, such as fighting and having food thrown at the victim, seemed less common, covert and sometimes unintentional types of racism and racialisation took place more regularly and were challenging to tackle. In addition to the 'good at maths' and 'Kung Fu' stereotypes, a significant portion of pupils were regularly reminded of their Otherness at school and asked to perform their Chineseness by teachers and other pupils. Archer and Francis (2007) argue that such performances demand young people to present 'pure' and 'exotic' representations of their Chineseness/racialised Otherness is a form of 'New Orientalism', built on the concept of orientalism (Said, 1978).

The rise of China as an economic superpower has prompted increased interest in China and Chinese culture in the UK. Although such attention could raise the profile of British Chinese, it could also create or enforce essentialised versions of Chineseness. As mentioned earlier, a number of pupils described frequently being asked to 'say something in Chinese' by their peers and teachers; although some pupils appreciated the curiosity and interest, others felt embarrassed, annoyed or scared by these repeated requests to perform their Otherness on demand. Kit (age 15), who could speak some Cantonese, described her discomfort with these encounters:

Yes, when they find out that I can speak Chinese, they be, like, 'Oh say something to me in Chinese!', like, 'How do you say my name in

Chinese?' And 'Say hello in Chinese', and I, I don't know what to do because I feel, like, shy and embarrassed.

For some of the participants, such repeated incidents of being asked to perform their Chineseness created anxieties, and to some young people, such experiences made them feel weary about having to explain themselves repeatedly or/and uneasy at being singled out. However, unlike being subjected to racial slurs, it is difficult for young people to challenge or report these seemingly harmless, and often unintentional, cases of marginalisation. The potential negative effects of the repeated subtle marginalisation could be contextualised through examining Kit's narratives and the observation at our interview. She reported that her teachers commented on her being 'quiet', but in the few hours I spent with her and a few other British Chinese young people in a local youth group, she did not appear to be particularly quiet or shy compared to other interviewees I encountered. She was accommodating and seemed comfortable answering all the questions in the interview, expanding on some answers without probing. In the school context, the quietness or shyness of some British Chinese pupils cannot be understood as simply a result of Chinese 'culture' or upbringing; maintaining a low profile and keeping to oneself is a survival mechanism for some to avoid such continual, awkward confrontations in their everyday racism and marginalisation, as seen in previous research on British Chinese young people (Parker, 1995; Archer and Francis, 2007).

Moreover, school officials and teachers might not understand these issues and unknowingly contribute to racialisation and cultural exoticisation of minority ethnic pupils at school. Jessica (aged 16), who could speak some Cantonese, stated that she regularly got asked to speak Chinese publicly at school:

Because at my school, they, erm, had an international language day, like sometimes in September, and then they used to call me up because I spoke Chinese (laughs), and like, 'Oh speak a bit of Chinese, Jess!', in front of like a whole assembly, that's what I used to do.

Because of the perceived familiarity and prominence of China, Chinese people and 'culture' in the popular imagination, it is inherently difficult for British Chinese young people – irrespective of their background and knowledge of Chinese language or culture – to disassociate from or reject this racialised position as 'Chinese'. 'Cultural' events at schools, such as Chinese New Year celebrations or 'language day' could introduce

Chinese 'culture' to the wider public. However, these events could potentially fall into the superficial and tokenistic 'saris, samosas and steel
bands' 'multiculturalism' approach (Troyna, 1983; Race, 2011) if they
simply reinforce and promote fixed and essentialised exotic imageries.
Such incidents become more awkward for pupils such as Jessica to challenge, especially when school officials or teachers, often unintentionally, impose such oppressions.

Conclusion

Despite their apparent integration and 'success' at school, UK born/raised
Chinese pupils continue to encounter overt racism and covert marginalisation based on their racialised embodiment. Compared to counterparts from previous generations, children from settled British Chinese
families, particularly those who have moved away from the catering
trade, might get more resources and freedom to participate in school
life and community. Younger generations generally express a rootedness
and sense of belonging in British society, and they negotiate through a
range of flexible and hybridised British Chinese identities as discussed in
this chapter. Due to the growth of the UK Chinese population and the
prominence of China on the world stage, the British Chinese 'community' is no longer invisible. However, racial stereotypes and racism, as
well as simplistic, essentialised notions of Britishness and Chineseness
tied to dominant discourses in 'race' and 'culture', continue to position these young people as racialised Others and perpetual outsiders,
no matter how settled, 'integrated' and academically successful they
have become. Schools need to recognise that racism is far from being a
problem of the past for many ethnic and linguistic minority pupils, and
this study highlights the various forms of racism and racialisation experienced by British Chinese pupils. The overwhelming focus in educational
policy since the 1980s on 'standards and achievement' and 'aspirations',
driven by neo-liberal ideas, sidelines other educational needs such as
inclusion and equalities. As suggested by Archer and Francis (2007), the
education system as a whole needs to engage more meaningfully with
the complexity of racialised identities and inequalities.

  This research illustrates that despite their apparent 'success' in 'integrating', the persistence of the processes of racism and Othering creates
barriers for British Chinese pupils to be accepted as authentically 'British'.
The fact that British Chinese young people appear to be 'ticking all the
right boxes' and still experience exclusion illustrates the impossibility
for individuals from minority ethnic/cultural groups of being accepted
as equal members of society within a system that privileges a certain

version of Britishness; integration becomes a futile one-sided exercise. Unlike earlier generations which faced regular crude racism working at their family takeaway counters and felt leaving Britain was a way to escape this predicament (Parker, 1995; Song, 1999), the current generation of young people who are not connected to the catering trade might find dealing with more subtle forms of Othering and racism at school more manageable and tolerable.

One should, however, not be complacent about how racial inequalities affect British Chinese pupils. The same 'Kung Fu' stereotypes being described by Parker's (1997) respondents in the 1990s unfortunately still ring true today. Because of the nature of racism or racialisation being experienced by the group is generally more physiologically based and subtle, the impact could be more difficult to detect. Society's perception of their perceived difference, along with expectations from within the British Chinese 'community', regularly reinforce their sense of being 'different', as described by many of the participants. Being different could be both a source of pride and pain, as articulated by the young people in this research. However, it is also this feeling that prompted some of the young people to contest their positioning and belonging in Britain. Moreover, those with limited power to resist have to find ways to 'deal with' or 'go around' these issues, as did older generations that had to navigate the labour market structure to strategically avoid racism and competition, with heavy social and personal costs. Furthermore, perhaps it is the strategy of 'going around' problems and the system that allows British Chinese to partially fit in and achieve segmented success but still remain unrepresented in public life, even though Chinese people have been settling in Britain for more than a century. Perhaps the more prominent contemporary profile of the British Chinese 'community' will provide new opportunities for young British Chinese to be more assertive when expressing their hybridised identities and be accepted and self-perceived as full members of British society.

Note

1. ESRC project 'British-Chinese Pupils' Identities, Achievement and Complementary Schooling' (RES000231513).

References

Adamson, S., Chan, C.K., Cole, B., Craig, G., Lau, C. and Law, I. (2009) *Hidden from Public View: Racism against the UK's Chinese population*, London, The Monitoring Group.

Archer, L. and Francis, B. (2007) *Understanding Minority Ethnic Achievement: Race, Gender, Class and 'Success'*, London, Routledge.

Baxter, S. (1988) 'A Political Economy of the Ethnic Chinese Catering Industry', PhD thesis, Aston University.

Benton, G. and Gomez, E.T. (2008) *Chinese in Britain, 1800–200: Economy, Transnationalism, Identity*, New York, Palgrave Macmillan.

Bhabha, H.K. (1990) *Nation and Narration*, London, Routledge.

Bhabha, H.K. (1994) *The Location of Culture*, London, Routledge.

Blackledge, A. (2004) 'Identity in multilingual Britain', in Pavlenko, A. and Blackledge, A. (eds), *Negotiation of Identities in Multilingual Contexts*, Clevedon, Multilingual Matters, 68–92.

Chan, A. (1986) *Employment Prospects of Chinese Youth in Britain*, Commission for Racial Equality.

Chan, C.K., Cole, B. and Bowpitt, G. (2007) '"Beyond silent organizations": a reflection of the UK Chinese people and their community organizations', *Critical Social Policy*, 27 (4), 509–533.

Chan, E. (2012) 'Chinese Britons have put up with racism for too long', *The Guardian*, 11 January 2012. Available at http://www.guardian.co.uk/commentisfree/2012/jan/11/british-chinese-racism. [Accessed on 11 January 2012]

Chen, A., Sheen, L. and Needa. V. (2011) *In The Mirror – Three Women, Three Stories, from the Chinese Diaspora*, New Diorama Theatre, London, 9–12 November 2011.

Creese, A., Barac, B., Blackledge, A., Hamid, S., Lytra, V., Martin, P., Wei, L., Wu, C. and Yagcioglu-Ali, D. (2007) *Investigating Multilingualism in Complementary Schools in Four Communities*: *Full Research Report*, ESRC End of Award Report, RES-000-23-1180, Swindon, ESRC.

Crozier, G. and Davies, J. (2008) '"The Trouble is They Don't Mix": Self-segregation or enforced exclusion? Teachers' Constructions of South Asian Students', *Race, Ethnicity and Education*, 11 (3), 285–301.

Department for Education and Skills (DfES) (2006) *Statistics of Education: Trends in Attainment Gaps, 2005*, London, HMSO.

Department of Education (DfE) (2013) *GCSE and Equivalent Attainment by Pupil Characteristics in England*, 2011/12 SFR 04/2013. Available at http://www.education.gov.uk/rsgateway/DB/SFR/s001111/sfr04–2013.pdf. [Accessed on 30 January 2013]

Francis, B. (2005) British-Chinese Pupils Constructions of Education, Gender and Post-16 Pathways: ESRC Full Research Report, R000239585. Swindon: ESRC.

Francis, B. and Archer, L. (2004) *British-Chinese Pupils' Constructions of Education, Gender & Post-16 Pathways*, Economic and Social Research Council (R000239585).

Francis, B., Archer, L. and Mau, A. (2008) *British-Chinese Pupils' Identities, Achievement and Complementary Schooling*, Economic and Social Research Council (RES000231513).

Hall, S. (1990) 'Cultural identity and diaspora', in Rutherford, J. (ed.), *Identity: Community, Culture, Difference*, London, Lawrence and Wishart, 222–237.

Li, W. (1994) *Three Generations Two Languages One Family: Language Choice and Language Shift in a Chinese Community in Britain*, Clevedon, Multilingual Matters.

Jackson, B. and Garvey, A. (1974) 'The Chinese children of Britain', *New Society*, 30 (626), 912.

Mansell, W. (2011) 'Hidden tigers: why do Chinese children do so well at school?', *The Guardian*, 7 February 2011. Available at http://www.guardian.co.uk/education/2011/feb/07/chinese-children-school-do-well. [Accessed on 22 August 2012]

NIMHE (2004) *Celebrating Our Cultures: Guidelines for Mental Health Promotion with Black and Minority Communities*, National Institute for Mental Health in England.

OECD (2010) *PISA 2009 Results: Executive Summary*, Paris, OECD.

Parker, D. (1995) *Through Different Eyes: The Cultural Identities of Young Chinese People in Britain*, Aldershot, Ashgate.

Parker, D. (1997) 'Rethinking British Chinese identities', in Skelton, T. and Valentine, G. (eds), *Cool Places: Geographies of Youth Cultures*, London, Routledge, 66–82.

Phillips, T. (2005) 'After 7/7: Sleepwalking to segregation', speech to the Manchester Council for Community Relations, 22 September 2005.

Race, R. (2011) *Multiculturalism and Education*, London, Continuum.

Ritchie, M. (2011) 'The China syndrome features', *TES Newspaper*, 4 March 2011. Available at http://www.tes.co.uk/article.aspx?storycode=6071857. [Accessed on 22 August 2012]

Runnymede Trust (1986) *The Chinese Community in Britain: The Home Affairs Committee Report in Context*, London, Runnymede Trust.

Saggar, S. and Somerville, W. (2012) *Building a British Model of Integration in an Era of Immigration: Policy Lessons for Government*, Washington, D.C., Migration Policy Institute.

Said, E. (1978) *Orientalism*, London, Routledge.

Sham, S. and Woodrow, D. (1998) 'Chinese children and their families in England', *Research Papers in Education*, 13 (2), 203–226.

Song, M. (1997) 'Children's labour in ethnic family businesses: the case of Chinese takeaway businesses in Britain', *Ethnic and Racial Studies*, 20 (4), 690–716.

Song, M. (1999) *Helping Out: Children's Labour in Ethnic Businesses*, Philadelphia: Temple University Press.

Thorpe, A. and Yeh, D. (2011) 'Contesting "British Chinese" Culture: Forms, Histories, Identities', University of Reading, UK, 24–25 September 2011.

Troyna, B. (1983) 'Multiracial education: just another Brick in the wall?', *New Community*, 10, 424–428.

Verma, G., Chan, Y., Bagley, C., Sham, S., Darby, D., Woodrow, D. and Skinner, G. (1999) *Chinese Adolescents in Britain and Hong Kong: Identity and Aspirations*, Aldershot, Ashgate.

Wong, L.Y.F. (1992) *Education of Chinese Children in Britain and the USA*, Clevedon, Multilingual Matters.

Woodrow, D. and Sham, S. (2001) 'Chinese pupils and their learning preferences', *Race, Ethnicity and Education*, 4 (4), 377–394.

8
Overcoming Disciplinary Boundaries: Connecting Language, Education and (Anti)racism

Stephen May

Introduction: The problem of paradigmatic closure

One of the historical artefacts of the construction of academic disciplines is a tendency towards paradigmatic closure – that is, an often unreflexive and hermetic defence of the particular academic paradigm within which one is situated and a related dismissal of alternative paradigms. Bernstein (1990, 2000) describes these self-regulating academic communities as 'singulars'. Singulars, for Bernstein, are characterised by strong boundary maintenance (classification), which is supported culturally (via professional associations, networks, and writing) and psychologically (in students, teachers, and researchers). As a result, 'singulars develop strong autonomous self-sealing and narcissistic identities' (Bernstein, 2000, p. 54). The only means by which to avoid these hermetic tendencies is to develop interdisciplinary and/or applied fields of enquiry, which Bernstein describes as 'regions'. For Bernstein, regions are 'created by a recontextualising [and, one might add, expansion] of singulars' (Bernstein, 2000, p. 9). From this, potential new lines of enquiry can be drawn from related disciplines. As Becher and Trowler (2001) observe of this:

> It often happens that adjoining disciplinary groups lay claim to the same pieces of intellectual territory. This does not necessarily entail a conflict between them. In some cases, depending on the nature of the claimants and the disposition of the no man's land, it may involve a straightforward division of interest; in others it may mark a growing unification of ideas and approaches. (Becher and Trowler, 2001, p. 60)

How does this apply to the field of race, ethnicity and education? Quite simply this applies because the field's academic history has been bedevilled, more than most, by paradigm wars and a related unwillingness to engage constructively across disciplinary and topic boundaries. This was at its most marked, and most visceral, in the multicultural versus antiracist paradigm wars in Britain in the 1980s. Antiracist educators at the time, drawing on a neo-Marxist academic frame, rejected multicultural education tout court – as an irredeemably 'deracialised' discourse of schooling; an educational approach which reified culture and cultural difference, and which failed to address the central issue of racism within society (Gillborn, 1990; Troyna, 1987, 1993; May, 1994a, 1994b). While the antiracist academic and political critique had considerable merit, particularly in highlighting the limitations of benevolent or liberal multiculturalism, the antagonisms underpinning this critique unnecessarily bifurcated the field at the time. Indeed, the bifurcation contributed eventually to the wider political and academic marginalisation within Britain of both multicultural *and* antiracist education (see Modood, 2007; Modood and May, 2001).

This declamatory pattern within the field of race, ethnicity and education has since been taken up in other national contexts, albeit around somewhat different academic axes. Thus, in the 1990s in the United States, the emergence of critical race theory (CRT) as the 'new' educational paradigm to explain and contest racism within education (albeit borrowed from legal studies in the first instance) was again predicated on a radical dismissal of existing academic work in multiculturalism and multicultural education (see, e.g., Ladson-Billings, 2005; Ladson-Billings and Tate, 1995; Dixson and Rousseau, 2006; Tate, 1997).

These developments highlight another feature apparent in this process of disciplinary demarcations within our field, a tendency to assume that one's national context defines the parameters of analysis. This was a particular feature of critical race theory in its initial years, with its predicational assumptions about colour racism and the black-white dichotomy arising directly from the history of slavery in the United States. CRT has since been re-applied to the British context by the likes of Gillborn (2008) and Preston (2007), and expanded theoretically by Taylor, Gillborn and Ladson-Billings (2009), although it remains to be seen whether CRT is able to establish a meaningful foothold outside of the United States. A key reason impeding this potential development, of course, is that the analytical use of race underpinning CRT (and wider academic and public discourse on race) is itself a predominantly US phenomenon, since European social theorists have long dispensed with this reified and unscientific concept, most often preferring the more multifaceted nature of ethnicity instead (Fenton, 2010).

It is here that Critical Multiculturalism (CM), in particular, provides a useful alternative – one that attempts to bridge the disciplinary (and epistemic) divides that still pervade our field. CM also emerged in the 1990s but, unlike CRT, combines a focus on both the dynamic, complex articulations involved in identity formation (ethnicity, gender, sexuality, etc.), and the multiplicity of racism*s* – moving beyond colour racism and the black-white dichotomy to incorporate cultural and religious racisms, particularly in relation to their (re)invocation post 9/11 (see, e.g., May, 1999a, 1999b; May and Sleeter, 2010a, 2010b; Sleeter and Delgado Bernal, 2004). Critical multiculturalism thus allows for a complex, dynamic analysis of our multiple identities, how these intersect or articulate and, more broadly, how they are constructed and/or situated in relation to wider power relations. In so doing, it draws on related notions of CRT, where appropriate, although it would be fair to say that the reciprocity of theoretical engagement from CRT is largely still forthcoming (May, 2009).

Be that as it may, what both CRT and CM – as well as other paradigms within the field of race, ethnicity and education – still have in common is a repeated failure to incorporate a substantive analysis of the role of *language* as a key form of educational racism and discrimination. This returns us to the disciplinary strictures of the academic fields within which we are situated. Multicultural and antiracist scholars (of whatever ilk) continue to focus primarily on the overt racism and discrimination facing 'students of color' which, in the United States, is most often directed toward African Americans and Latinos and, in Britain, toward Black British and British Asians. And yet, while both Latinos and British Asians also consistently face linguistic discrimination (as do those African Americans who speak Ebonics; see Baugh, 2002), its academic analysis has been left largely to scholars of sociolinguistics, language policy and bilingual education (see, e.g., García, 2009; Kubota and Lin, 2009; although see Nieto and Bode, 2012 for an exception). This is all the more perplexing given that language, along with religion (Modood, 2007), has come to be a key symbol in the retrenchment of multiculturalism as public policy, particularly, post 9/11 (May, 2012, 2014). In the remainder of this chapter, I want to examine one key example where the interconnections between language, racism and education are unequivocally foregrounded – the debate about bilingual education for Latinos in the United States, and the wider English Only movement of which it is a part. In so doing, I will also argue that it is high time that scholars of race, ethnicity and education take this debate far more seriously than they have hitherto.

Language and racism: the contest over bilingual education in the United States

The 'English Only' movement

The contest over bilingual education in the United States is situated within a wider political movement – the 'English Only' movement – which emerged, at least in its contemporary manifestation, in the early 1980s. The raison-d'être of the movement is to ensure the formal ascendancy of English within education and wider civil society in the United States. Initially, the key political goal was to change the US Constitution via an English language amendment (ELA) that would make English, for the first time, an official rather than a de facto national language.[1] Senator Hayakawa was the first to propose an ELA in 1981, arguing that his principal concern in so doing was to help clarify the 'confusing signals' being sent to 'immigrant' groups over the preceding decade. Such signals included the provision of bilingual (voting) ballots, which he considered 'contradictory' and 'logically conflicting' with the requirements of naturalised citizens to 'read, write and speak' English. Existing bilingual education programs, particularly those that maintained student bilingualism throughout schooling, were also regarded as 'being dishonest with linguistic minority groups' – promoting (most often) the maintenance of Spanish alongside that of English and thus, in his view, delimiting opportunities for both the integration of Latinos in the United States and their upward educational and wider social mobility.

The themes expressed by Hayakawa at the beginning of the 1980s were to spawn a movement. While his ELA failed, the publicity that it garnered led Hayakawa to join forces with John Tanton to establish the organisation 'U.S. English' in 1983. US English is not the only organisation of its type but it is certainly the most prominent, having grown rapidly in both numbers and profile from the time of its inception.[2] During the 1980s, a further five ELAs were tabled under the auspices of the English Only movement, a pattern that has continued to the present.

A key reason why none of these proposals has been successful thus far is largely due to the care and caution with which constitutional amendments are treated (see Marshall, 1986). However, the English Only movement has continued to lobby vigorously for restrictionist language policies at the federal level, while also increasingly focusing on changing state-level language policies (Ricento and Wright, 2008; Schildkraut, 2005). As Daniels (1990, p. 8) observes of the latter route, 'the overall strategy [here] seems to be to get some official-English law on the books of a majority of states and to continually fan public resentment over schooling policies that "degrade English" and "cater" to immigrants'. In this regard, they have been far more successful. Using their considerable organisational, lobbying and media skills, the English Only movement has effectively used the vehicle of popular state referenda (originally, implemented as a progressive measure to avoid the special-interest lobbying endemic to US politics) to endorse and implement restrictionist language policies. The first of these, California's Proposition 63, was passed in 1986 by a majority of 73 per cent to 27 per cent – albeit on a very low voter turnout – and included a significant degree of Latino voter support (MacKaye, 1990). Since then, over 30 states have adopted English as their official language; the latest (in 2010) being Oklahoma and Utah.[3] Many of these statutes and amendments are largely symbolic, although some states have implemented specific punitive measures against bilingual education, as we shall see shortly. Nonetheless, all are concerned with declaring English as the official language of the state, and most are aimed at ensuring that English is the only language of government activity (see Crawford, 2000, 2008).

The political rhetoric of the English Only movement builds on a long history of alarmist, and highly racialised, discourse with respect to language and national identity in the United States and the 'threat' of the bi/multilingual immigrant (Shell, 1993). The 'Americanization Movement', which arose in the late nineteeth century and culminated with the First World War, is a clear precursor here (see Schmid, 2001; Schmidt, 2000). What distinguishes the present English Only movement, however, is its national profile and organisation (previous debates about language were usually confined to local or state arenas) and, relatedly, the increasingly wide support that it seems to have garnered with the American public (Donahue, 1995; Schmidt, 2008).

The widespread public support enjoyed by the English Only movement over the last three decades has been built upon a deliberate 'discourse of disinformation' (Cummins, 1995; see also Krashen, 1999) that involves two key dimensions. The first promulgates English as essential for social mobility in US society or, rather, that a lack of English *consigns* one inevitably to the social and economic margins. The second trumpets the greater efficacy of English-only education over bilingual education alternatives, arguing that only via English-only education can the upward educational and wider social trajectories of Latinos in the United States be ensured. In the 1980s, for example, Linda Chávez, a former president of US English, argued: 'Hispanics who learn English will be able to avail themselves of opportunities. Those who do not will be relegated to second-class citizenship' (Crawford, 1992, p. 172). In the 1990s, this sentiment was encapsulated in a US English advertisement in 1998: 'Deprive a child of an education. Handicap a young life outside the classroom. Restrict social mobility. If it came at the hand of a parent it would be called child abuse. At the hand of our schools ... it's called "bilingual educa-tion"' (Dicker, 2000, p. 53). And in the late 1990s and early 2000s, this leitmotif was most prominently associated with Ron Unz, a prominent software entrepreneur and conservative public figure, and his organi-sation 'English for the Children'. Targeting four key US states that allow for citizen-initiated referenda, Unz has over the last 15 years successfully promoted public propositions delimiting or dismantling bilingual education in three of these states. The most prominent of these is California's Proposition 227 (1998), which saw 61 per cent support the measure overall, *including* 37 per cent of Latino voters. However, Unz was also successful in sponsoring similar measures in Arizona in 2000 (63 per cent) and in Massachusetts in 2002 (68 per cent). Only in Colorado in 2002 (44 per cent) was a comparable measure defeated, although, controversially, this was because those opposing the measure played on the fears of Anglo parents that this would result in the reintroduction of too many Latino students into mainstream classrooms (Crawford, 2007).

In combination, these discourses have clearly been highly effective in shifting political and public opinion against bilingual education in the United States. For example, prior to the Arizona referendum (Proposition 203) the *New York Times* ran a front-page story in August 2000 strongly supporting the apparently incontrovertible educational merits of its California precursor, Proposition 227. Subsequently, it was revealed that the claims made in the article simply repeated key talking points in Unz's campaign, although, not surprisingly, it still had a powerful effect on strengthening public support for Proposition 203 (Wiley and Wright, 2004; Wright, 2005). The apparent efficacy of English-only education was also central to George W. Bush's 2001 flagship policy, *No Child Left Behind* (NCLB), which has since been left largely intact by the Obama administration. NCLB saw the revocation of the 1968 Bilingual Education Act on the premise that English-language instruction and assessment are best for all students. Ongoing advocacy of NCLB throughout the last decade has continued to tout its positive effects for bilingual students (Menken, 2008).

The problem is that both these core presumptions are contradicted by a welter of educational, and wider, social research. With respect to language and mobility, for example, racism and discrimination remain far more salient factors for minoritised groups than the acquisition/use of English language, per se, a pattern well-trailed in the fields of sociolinguistics and language policy (see, e.g., Blommaert, 2010; May, 2014; Phillipson, 2010). The relationship between English language use and Latino social mobility bears this out specifically, since 25 per cent of Latinos currently live at or below the poverty line, a rate that is *at least twice as high* as the proportion of Latinos who are not English-speaking (García, 1995; San Miguel and Valencia, 1998). Meanwhile, the supposed merits of English-only education actually fall far short of their bilingual education counterparts. Menken (2008) has documented the clearly negative educational effects that NCLB English-language testing policies have had on bilingual students over the last decade. She found in New York City, for example, that as a result of NCLB's requirement to be assessed in English, with no recourse to one's first language, bilingual students ranged from 20 to 50 percentage points below native English speakers. This finding is widely corroborated in other research on bilingual students (see, e.g., Baker, 2011; García, 2009; May, 2008, 2010 for useful overviews).

Insisting on the merits of English-only education in the face of such evidence, as the English Only movement continues to do, demonstrates a remarkable degree of cynicism. But this cynicism becomes breathtaking when measured against another variable: the funding of these English-only programs. In this respect, the English Only movement is again clearly found wanting. Many who supported the establishment of official state-level English policies, for example, including the Unz-led referenda against bilingual education, logically assumed that a principal concern of the legislation was to expand the opportunities for immigrants to learn English. However, logical or not, this has proved not to be the case. While US English spent lavishly to get ELA measures on the ballot throughout the 1980s and 1990s, it declined to support legislation creating a modestly funded federal program for adult learners of English. As a result of public criticism, US English did make some subsequent effort to fund similar ventures, but these efforts have remained largely desultory and continue to constitute only the barest minimum of their total funding efforts (Dicker, 2003; Schmidt, 2008). As Crawford concludes:

One thing is clear. Rather than promote English proficiency, 99 percent of the organization's efforts go toward restricting the use of other languages.... English Only is a label that has stuck, despite the protests of US English, because it accurately sums up the group's logic: That people will speak English only if they are forced to. That the crutch of bilingual education must be yanked away or newcomers will be permanently handicapped. That immigrants are too lazy or dim-witted to accept 'the primacy of English' on their own. (Crawford, 1992, p. 176)

The return of the nativist

If US English and like-minded proponents such as Ron Unz are not actually concerned with extending opportunities to minority-language speakers to learn English, despite all their rhetoric proclaiming just that, there must be another, more sinister agenda at work. In this respect, it is interesting to note that all previous movements that advocated English-only policies did so as part of a wider nativist and anti-immigrationist agenda. The current English Only movement, despite its disavowals, is no exception to this trend – in effect, it provides us with a modern variant of the Americanization movement of the late 19th–early twentieth century. The links that the organisation, US English, has with anti-immigrationist groups would appear to confirm this, not least because the co-founder of US English, John Tanton, was also previously the founder of a smaller anti-immigration organisation, 'Federation for American Immigration Reform' (FAIR: see Schmidt, 2008). The principal concern of Tanton, and other anti-immigrationists involved in the English Only movement, if it is not already all too clearly apparent, is the rapidly rising Latino population in the United States. In the 2000 census, of the nearly 47 million aged over five who spoke a language other than English at home, 28 million were Spanish speakers (Wiley, 2005). By 2009, the population of Latino Americans had grown to 48.4 million or 16 per cent of the total population, overtaking African Americans to become the largest minority in the United States. It is further suggested that by the year 2050 Latino communities will have increased to 30 per cent of the total population, outnumbering the combined total of African Americans, Asian Americans and Native Americans (US Census Bureau, 2010). This will coincide with a concomitant decline in the number of white Americans. It is this population growth – what Tanton has termed 'the Latin onslaught' on the United States – which is the real concern of many English Only advocates. Zentella (1997) has coined the term 'Hispanophobia' to describe it.

Tanton's own Hispanophobia was exposed when an internal memorandum he wrote in 1986 was made public two years later, causing his resignation from US English. In it, he discusses a range of cultural threats posed by 'Spanish-speaking immigrants', including a lack of involvement in public affairs, Roman Catholicism, 'low educability', high school-dropout rates and 'high fertility'. Among a range of questions raised in relation to these concerns were: 'Perhaps this is the first instance in which those with their pants up are going to get caught with their pants down'. 'Will the present [white] majority peaceably hand over its political power to a group that is simply more fertile'? 'As whites see their power and control over their lives declining, will they simply go quietly into the night? Or will there be an explosion?' (Crawford, 1992, p. 173). A number of notable public supporters of the organization also resigned at the time because of the anti-Latino and anti-Catholic sentiments expressed, including Linda Chávez, the then President of US English.

Despite this setback, US English has continued to garner increasingly wide support, as we have seen. And this is where the present English Only movement differs fundamentally from its predecessors. In short, it cannot *simply* be a nativist movement – or, rather, it cannot just be a simple (transparent) nativist movement – since, one would expect, it would not have generated the broad following that it has. This would appear to be confirmed by the extent of the movement's appeal to many minority language speakers themselves, as demonstrated in the support for California's Proposition 227 among Latino voters. Indeed, its prominent minority supporters have been regularly paraded by the movement as the epitome of the 'good alien' (Tarver, 1994); the success stories of immigration and the embodiment of the American dream.

In addition to its organisational reach and public disinformation strategies, discussed above, a broader sociological reason for the success of the English Only movement lies in is its ability to *invert* the usual immigration and language axis. Where previous movements concentrated primarily on concerns over immigration, from which arose (subsequent) language policies, the English Only movement attempts the reverse, thus making it far more politically palatable. In short, it concentrates almost solely on the status of the English language in the USA as a convenient proxy for a more overtly racialised politics. By extension, it highlights the 'threat' of Spanish to the cultural and linguistic hegemony of the dominant white, English-speaking elite – in the process, using Spanish as a racialised marker of Latino identity (Cobas and Feagin, 2008; Feagin and Cobas, 2008). The approach adopted here is similar to the 'new racism' which substitutes (at least ostensibly) culturalist arguments about race for biological ones. Deutsch (1975, p. 7) has observed that 'language is an automatic signaling system, second only to race, in identifying targets for privilege or discrimination'. Crawford argues along more specific lines:

> ...explicit racial loyalties are no longer acceptable in political discourse. Language loyalties, on the other hand, remain largely devoid of associations with social injustice. While race is immutable, immigrants can and often do exchange their mother tongue for another. And so, for those who resent the presence of Hispanics and Asians, language politics has become a convenient surrogate for racial politics. (Crawford, 1989, p. 14)

Racialising the disciplines: the case of political theory

The English Only movement remains highly active and influential in American public life, using language and education as a racialised battleground in its attempt to delimit the growing demographic, social and political impact of the Latino population in the United States. But what is even more insidious is how their arguments have come to be reconstituted and legitimated academically within 'core' (read: prestigious) academic disciplines, such as political theory. The most notable examples here are in political-theory discussions of multiculturalism within liberal democratic societies, which regularly invoke language as a key variable – either in support of linguistic diversity (see, e.g., Kymlicka, 1995, 2001, 2007), or, more commonly, in opposition to it (see, e.g., Archibugi, 2005; Barry, 2001; Laitin and Reich, 2003; Pogge, 2003). I have discussed these arguments within political theory at length elsewhere (see May, 2003, 2012). However, for my purposes here, I want to focus on a few key exemplars of the general consensus within political theory that 'linguistic diversity is an *obstacle* to [democratic] equality and participation' (Archibugi, 2005, p. 549). Following from this, the role of bilingual education in perpetuating such linguistic diversity is constructed as highly problematic. We can see this clearly in the work of the Italian political theorist, Daniele Archibugi and, in particular, one of the hypothetical examples (so loved by political theorists) that he uses to illustrate his basic point. Taking for his example a state school in an increasingly mixed Anglo/Latino neighbourhood in California,

Archibugi outlines a hypothetical scenario of increasing tension between the two groups with respect to the school's future direction:

> [T]he Hispanic students do not speak English well and their parents speak it even worse. School parents-students meetings end in pandemonium, with the Anglos complaining that their children are starting to make spelling mistakes and the Hispanics protesting because their children are bullied. At the end of a stormy meeting, an Anglo father, citing Samuel Huntingdon, invites the Hispanic community to dream in English. In return, an outraged Mexican slaps him in the face. (2005, p. 547)

Meanwhile, Archibugi (2005, p. 548) also assumes in his scenario that the Anglo parents are middle-class and that most of the Latino parents are 'cleaners', but with aspirations 'to enable their children to live in conditions that will avoid perpetuating the [existing] class division based on different ethnic groups'. In offering potential solutions going forward, he contrasts a multiculturalist response of parallel English and Spanish instruction within the school for the respective groups – bilingual education, in effect – with, in his view, a clearly preferable solution of English language instruction for all. This solution, which he advocates as a 'cosmopolitan alternative' (see May, 2014, for an extended critique), is predicated on the basis that 'American citizens with a good knowledge of English have (1) higher incomes; (2) less risk of being unemployed; (3), less risk of being imprisoned and (4) better hopes for a longer life' (Archibugi, 2005, p. 548). As a salve to the Latino population, however, the cosmopolitan proposal also includes compulsory courses in Spanish language and culture for all, while encouraging Latino parents to learn English in night school and Anglo parents learn 'salsa and other Latin American dances' (ibid.).

The underlying presumptions about language and mobility in Archibugi's scenario are also clearly echoed in comparable accounts. Another prominent political theorist, Thomas Pogge (2003, p. 105), for example, in close accord with Archibugi, observes that many Latinos 'do not speak English well'. Accordingly, in order to best serve the educational interests of Latino children, Pogge specifically endorses an English-only educational approach so as to ensure that Latino students gain the necessary fluency in English to succeed in the wider society. 'The choice of English as the universal language of instruction is justified', Pogge (2003, p. 120) argues, 'by reference to the best interests of children with other native languages, for whom speaking good English (in addition to their native language) will be an enormous advantage in their future social and professional lives'. Pogge (2003, p. 116) also suggests that those (Latino) parents who opt instead for bilingual education may well be 'perpetuating a cultural community irrespective of whether this benefits the children concerned'. For him, this amounts to an illiberal 'chosen inequality' for those children because it 'consigns' them to an educational approach that, in maintaining Spanish (or other languages), wilfully delimits their longer-term mobility in US society. This position is made even starker by Pogge's (2003) intimation that such a choice could possibly warrant the same constraints applied to parents as other child protection laws; equating bilingual education, in effect, with child abuse, a trope that can be directly linked to the wider English Only movement in the United States, discussed earlier.

Two other political theorists, Laitin and Reich (2003, p. 92), argue much the same position, asserting that 'forcing' bilingual education on children will curtail 'their opportunities to learn the language of some broader societal culture'. Relatedly, they fret that these 'individuals have no influence over the language of their parents, yet their parents' language if it is a minority one... constrains social mobility'. As a result, 'those who speak a minority (or dominated) language are more likely to stand *permanently* on the lower-rungs of the socio-economic ladder' (ibid.; my emphasis). Indeed, they proceed to observe that if minority individuals are foolish enough to perpetuate the speaking of a minority language, then they can simply be regarded as 'happy slaves', having no one else to blame but themselves for their subsequent limited social mobility. Suffice it to say that these arguments, dressed up in terms of enhancing social mobility and guarding against ghettoisation, exhibit exactly the same kinds of highly racialised paternalism (and related misinformation about bilingual education) as those of the English Only movement.

Conclusion

What then does the contest over bilingual education in the United States (and related discussions of multiculturalism within political theory) tell us? First, it highlights clearly how language and education can be deployed to overtly (and covertly) racist ends, despite the fact that such practices have seldom gained the attention they deserve in the academic literature on race, ethnicity and education. As I have argued, part of the reason for this is the hermetic nature of disciplinary boundaries and an associated reluctance to emerge from particular academic paradigms.

The Left is particularly prone to the latter – as if any attempt at interdisciplinarity might itself pollute and/or dissipate one's academic and political commitments. But there is also something more insidious at work here. It leaves us prone to the ongoing ascendancy of the Right in such matters. We saw this both academically and politically in Britain in the aftermath of the multicultural/antiracist paradigm wars there (see May, 1994a, b), and we are seeing it again now in our ongoing abnegation of the significance of language to wider debates that link immigration, citizenship, education, race and racism. This abnegation is exemplified in our failure to engage politically with movements such as English Only in the United States, and academically with broadly comparable arguments outlined within arenas such as political theory.

What is required, instead, is what Bernstein (2000) so clearly advocated in his analysis of disciplinary boundaries – a renunciation of singulars (or, at least, a level of critical reflexivity that allows us to move beyond them when needed) and, relatedly, a more regional academic and political approach to these questions. Given the ongoing dismantling of multiculturalist initiatives, exponentially so over the last decade, and the related marginalization of the academic analysis of race, ethnicity and education, reconfiguring our field in this way cannot come a moment too soon.

Notes

1. The U.S. Constitution followed a laissez-faire language policy, deriving from the British model, which specifically eschewed the legislative formality of granting "official status" to English (see Marshall, 1986).
2. In 1983, U.S. English reported having 300 members, in 1984, 35,000 (Marshall, 1986). By 1994, its numbers had grown to some 400,000 members (Edwards, 1994) while, over the course of this time, the organization has also attracted to its ranks many well-known public figures.
3. See www.us-english.org for a current list of U.S. states that have adopted English-only measures.

References

Archibugi, D. (2005) 'The language of democracy: vernacular or Esperanto? a comparison between the multiculturalist and cosmopolitan perspectives', *Political Studies*, 53 (3), 537–555.
Baugh, J. (2002) *Beyond Ebonics: Linguistic Pride and Racial Prejudice*, New York, Oxford University Press.
Baker, C. (2011) *Foundations of Bilingual Education and Bilingualism*, 5th edition, Bristol, Multilingual Matters.

Barry, B. (2001) *Culture and Equality: An Egalitarian Critique of Multiculturalism*, Cambridge, MA, Harvard University Press.

Becher, T. and Trowler, P. (2001) *Academic Tribes and Territories: Intellectual Enquiry and the Culture of Disciplines*, 2nd edition, Philadelphia, Open University Press.

Bernstein, B. (1990) *The Structuring of Pedagogic Discourse, vol. 4: Class, Codes and Control*, London, Routledge.

Bernstein, B. (2000) *Pedagogy, Symbolic Control and Identity: Theory, Research, Critique*, Lanham, MA, Rowman and Littlefield.

Blommaert, J. (2010) *The Sociolinguistics of Globalization*, New York, Cambridge University Press.

Cobas, J. and Feagin, J. (2008) 'Language oppression and resistance: the case of middle class Latinos in the United States', *Ethnic and Racial Studies*, 31,(2), 390–410.

Crawford, J. (1989) *Bilingual Education: History, Politics, Theory and Practice*. Trenton, NJ.: Crane Publishing Co.

Crawford, J. (1992) 'What's behind Official English?' In Crawford, J. (ed.), *Language Loyalties: A Source Book on the Official English Controversy*, Chicago, University of Chicago Press, 171–177.

Crawford, J. (2000) *At War with Diversity: US Language Policy in an Age of Anxiety*, Clevedon, Multilingual Matters.

Crawford, J. (2007) 'Hard Sell: Why Is Bilingual Education so Unpopular with the American Public?' in García, O. and Baker, C. (eds), *Bilingual Education: An Introductory Reader*, Clevedon, Multilingual Matters, 145–161.

Crawford, J. (2008) *Advocating for English Learners: Selected Essays*, Clevedon, Multilingual Matters.

Cummins, J. (1995) 'The discourse of disinformation: The debate on bilingual education and language rights in the United States', in Skutnabb-Kangas, T. and Phillipson, R. (eds), *Linguistic Human Rights: Overcoming Linguistic Discrimination*, Berlin, Mouton de Gruyter, 159–177.

Daniels, H. (1990) 'The roots of language protectionism', in Daniels, H. (ed.), *Not Only English: Affirming America's Multilingual Heritage*, Urbana, IL, National Council of Teachers, 3–12.

Deutsch, K. (1975) 'The political significance of linguistic conflicts', In Savard, J-G. and Vigneault, R. (eds), *Les états multilingues: problèmes et solutions*, Laval, Québec, Les Presses de L'université Laval, 7–28.

Dicker, S. (2000) 'Official English and bilingual education: The controversy over language pluralism in U.S. society', in Kelly Hall, J. and Eggington, W. (eds), *The Sociopolitics of English Language Teaching*, Clevedon, Multilingual Matters, 45–66.

Dicker, S. (2003) *Languages in America*, 2nd edition, Clevedon, Multilingual Matters.

Dixson, A.D. and Rousseau, C.K. (eds) (2006) *Critical Race Theory in Education: All God's Children Got a Song*, New York, Routledge.

Donahue, T. (1995) 'American language policy and compensatory opinion', in Tollefson, J. (ed.), *Power and Inequality in Language Education*, Cambridge, Cambridge University Press, 112–141.

Edwards, J. (1994) *Multilingualism*, London: Routledge.

Feagin, J. and Cobas, J. (2008) 'Latinos/as and white racial frame: The procrustean bed of assimilation', *Sociological Inquiry*, 78(1), 39–53.

Fenton, S. (2010) *Ethnicity*, 2nd edition, Cambridge, Polity Press.

García, O. (1995) 'Spanish language loss as a determinant of income among Latinos in the United States: implications for language policies in schools', in Tollefson, J. (ed.), *Power and Inequality in Language Education*, Cambridge, Cambridge University Press, 142–160.

García, O. (2009) *Bilingual Education in the 21st Century: A Global Perspective*, Malden, MA, Blackwell.

Gillborn, D. (2008) *Racism and Education: Coincidence or Conspiriacy?* London, Routledge.

Gillborn, D. (1990) *'Race', Ethnicity and Education: Teaching and Learning in Multi-ethnic Schools*, London, Unwin-Hyman/Routledge.

Krashen, S. (1999) *Condemned Without Trial: Bogus Arguments Against Bilingual Education*, Portsmouth, NH, Heinemann.

Kubota, R. and Lin, A. (eds) (2009) *Race, Culture, and Identity in Second Language Education: Exploring Critically Engaged Practice*, New York, Routledge.

Kymlicka, W. (1995) *Multicultural Citizenship: A Liberal Theory of Minority Rights*, Oxford, Clarendon Press.

Kymlicka, W. (2001) *Politics in the Vernacular: Nationalism, Multiculturalism, Citizenship*, Oxford, Oxford University Press.

Kymlicka, W. (2007) *Multicultural Odysseys: Navigating the New International Politics of Diversity*, Oxford, Oxford University Press.

Ladson-Billings, G. (2005) 'The Evolving Role of Critical Race Theory in Educational Scholarship', *Race, Ethnicity and Education*, 8 (1), 115–119.

Ladson-Billings, G. and Tate, W. (1995) 'Towards a Critical Race Theory of Education', *Teachers College Record*, 97, 47–68.

Laitin, D. and Reich, R. (2003) 'A liberal democratic approach to language justice', in Kymlicka, W. and Patten, A. (eds), *Language Rights and Political Theory*, Oxford, Oxford University Press, 80–104.

MacKaye, S. (1990) 'California Proposition 63: Language attitudes reflected in the public debate', *Annals of the American Academy of Political and Social Science*, 505 (March), 135–146.

Marshall, D. (1986) 'The question of an official language: Language rights and the English Language Amendment', *International Journal of the Sociology of Language*, 60, 7–75.

May, S. (1994a) *Making Multicultural Education Work*, Clevedon, Multilingual Matters.

May, S. (1994b) 'The case for antiracist education', *British Journal of the Sociology of Education*, 15, 421–428.

May, S. (1999a) 'Critical multiculturalism and cultural difference: avoiding essentialism', in May, S. (ed.), *Critical Multiculturalism: Rethinking Multicultural and Antiracist Education*, London and New York, RoutledgeFalmer, 11–41.

May, S. (ed.) (1999b) *Critical Multiculturalism: Rethinking Multicultural and Antiracist Education*, London, RoutledgeFalmer.

May, S. (2003) 'Misconceiving minority language rights: Implications for liberal political theory', in Kymlicka, W. and Patten, A. (eds), *Language Rights and Political Theory*, Oxford, Oxford University Press, 123–152.

May, S. (2008) 'Bilingual/immersion education: what the research tells us', in Cummins, J. and Hornberger, N. (eds), *Bilingual education: The Encyclopedia of Language and Education*, 2nd edition, vol. 5, New York, Springer, 19–34.

May, S. (2009) 'Critical multiculturalism and education', in Banks, J. (ed.), *Routledge International Companion to Multicultural Education*, New York, Routledge, 33–48.

May, S. (2010) 'Curriculum and the education of cultural and linguistic minorities', in McGraw, B., Baker, E. and Peterson, P. (eds), *International Encyclopedia of Education*, 3rd edition, vol. 1, Oxford, Elsevier, 293–298.

May, S. (2012) *Language and Minority Rights: Ethnicity, Nationalism and the Politics of Language*, 2nd edition, New York, Routledge.

May, S. (2014) 'Justifying educational language right', *Review of Research in Education*, 38 (1), 215–241.

May, S. and Sleeter, C. (2010a) 'Introduction. Critical multiculturalism: theory and praxis', in May, S. and Sleeter, C. (eds), *Critical Multiculturalism: Theory and Praxis*, New York, Routledge, 1–16.

May, S. and Sleeter, C. (eds) (2010b) *Critical Multiculturalism: Theory and Praxis*, New York, Routledge.

Menken, K. (2008) *English Learners Left Behind: Standardized Testing As Language Policy*, Clevedon, Multilingual Matters.

Modood, T. (2007) *Multiculturalism: A Civic Idea*, Cambridge, Polity Press.

Modood, T. and May, S. (2001) 'Multiculturalism and education in Britain: an internally contested debate', *International Journal of Educational Research*, 35 (3), 305–317.

Nieto, S. and Bode, P. (2012) *Affirming Diversity: The Sociopolitical Context of Multicultural Education*, 6th edition, New York, Pearson.

Phillipson, R. (2010) *Linguistic Imperialism Continued*, New York, Routledge.

Pogge, T. (2003) 'Accommodation Rights for Hispanics in the US', in Kymlicka, W. and Patten, A. (eds), *Language Rights and Political Theory*, Oxford, Oxford University Press, 105–122.

Ricento, T. and Wright, W. (2008) 'Language policy and education in the United States', in May, S. and Hornberger, N. (eds), *Encyclopedia of Language and Education*, 2nd edition, vol. 1, *Language Policy and Political Issues in Education*, New York, Springer, 285–300.

San Miguel, G. and Valencia, R. (1998) 'From the Treaty of Guadalupe Hidalgo to Hopwood: the educational plight and struggle of Mexican Americans in the Southwest', *Harvard Educational Review*, 68, 353–412.

Schildkraut, D. (2005) *Press One for English: Language Policy, Public Opinion, and American Identity*, Princeton, NJ., Princeton University Press.

Schmid, C. (2001) *The Politics of Language: Conflict, Identity, and Cultural Pluralism in Comparative Perspective*, New York, Oxford University Press.

Schmidt, R. Sr. (2000) *Language Policy and Identity Politics in the United States*, Philadelphia, Temple University Press.

Schmidt, R. Sr. (2008) 'Defending English in an English-dominant world: the ideology of the 'Official English' movement in the United States', in Duchêne, A. and Heller, M. (eds), *Discourses of Endangerment: Ideology and Interest in the Defense of Languages*, London, Continuum, 197–215.

Shell, M. (1993) 'Babel in America: the politics of language diversity in the United States', *Critical Inquiry*, 20, 103–127.

Sleeter, C.E. and Delgado Bernal, D. (2004) 'Critical pedagogy, critical race theory, and antiracist education: their implications for multicultural education', in J. Banks and C. Banks (eds), *Handbook of Research on Multicultural Education*, 2nd edition, San Francisco, Jossey Bass, 240–260.

Tarver, H. (1994) 'Language and politics in the 1980s: the story of U.S. English', in Pincus, F. and Ehrlich, H. (eds), *Race and Ethnic Conflict: Contending Views on Prejudice, Discrimination and Ethnoviolence*, Boulder, CO, Westview Press, 206–218.

Tate, W. (1997) 'Critical race theory and education: history, theory and implications', in Apple, M. (ed.), *Review of Research in Education*, vol. 22, Itasca IL, F. E. Peacock, 195–247.

Taylor, E., Gillborn, D. and Ladson-Billings, G. (eds) (2009) *Foundations of Critical Race Theory in Education*, New York, Routledge.

Troyna, B. (ed.) (1987) *Racial Inequality in Education*, London, Tavistock.

Troyna, B. (1993) *Racism and Education*, Buckingham, Open University Press.

US Census Bureau (2010) 'Hispanic Americans by the numbers', Retrieved on 28 May 2013 at http://www.infoplease.com/spot/hhmcensus1.html

Wiley, T. (2005) *Literacy and Language Diversity in the United States*, 2nd edition, Washington, D.C., Center for Applied Linguistics and Delta Systems.

Wiley, T. and Wright, W. (2004) 'Against the undertow: the politics of language instruction in the United States', *Educational Policy*, 18 (1), 142–168.

Wright, W. (2005) 'The political spectacle of Arizona's Proposition 203', *Educational Policy*, 19 (5), 662–700.

Zentella, A. (1997) 'The Hispanophobia of the Official English movement in the US', *International Journal of the Sociology of Language*, 127, 71–86.

9
Multiculturalism and Integration

Tariq Modood

There is a lot of confusion about what multiculturalism is and what it is not. This is partly because 'multiculturalism' is too often defined by its critics, whose sole purpose is to create a straw man to knock down. But it is also because both its critics and some of its defenders falsely oppose multiculturalism with integration; and the confusion also partly stems from the fact that there is more than one form of multiculturalism, and they relate to integration in different ways. I would like to use this chapter to clarify the key terms of assimilation, integration, cosmopolitanism and multiculturalism. I hope this helps us better to increase understandings within this debate, to have a clear idea of what is being said or objected to. I would like to think that my analysis will bring people closer to my own advocacy of multiculturalism, but it will have succeeded if it increases understanding of what the issues are. My argument is that discourses of integration and multiculturalism are exercises in conceptualising post-immigration difference and, as such, operate at three distinct levels: as an (implicit) sociology; as a political response; and as a vision of what is the whole in which difference is to be integrated.

Integration

The need for integration arises when an established society is faced by some people who are perceived and treated unfavourably by stand⌐ members (and, typically, who also perceive themselves as 'di⌐ though not necessarily in a negative way). This may relate t⌐ areas or sectors of society and policy, such as employme⌐ housing and so on. For example, someone is integrat⌐ market when s/he is able to enjoy equality of op⌐

145

jobs and careers, including accessing the education and training necessary to compete for such jobs and where the labour market is not segmented into different parts with radically different monetary rewards and working conditions for those with broadly similar qualifications and experience. This is particularly relevant where the segmentation is not, formally or informally, based on criteria such as race, ethnicity, religion and so on, namely the categories of 'difference'. This does not just concern labour markets, but one can apply it more generally.

A core of integration is equality of opportunity in an unsegmented society and where no channelling into or away from a sector of society takes place based on criteria such as race and ethnicity. Integration has a number of components based on opportunities to participate which are context-specific and need to be secured by law and policy initiatives. Integration processes also has a subjective and symbolic dimension, which again will have some context-specific features, but whose features have a more general or macro character: how a minority is perceived by the rest of the country and how members of a minority perceive their relationship to society as a whole. Sectoral integration, however, even when achieved in a number of sectors, is not full integration without some degree of subjective identification with the society or country as a whole – what the Commission on Multi-Ethnic Britain called 'a sense of belonging' (CMEB, 2000) and with the acceptance by the majority that you are a full member of society and have the right to feel that you belong.

Sectoral integration and the general sense of integration can happen at an individual level: an individual may choose to integrate or not, may be given opportunities to participate or not. My interest here is not on individual choices and opportunities themselves when these choices and opportunities are viewed at the level of groups or society as a whole. A sense of belonging is dependent on how others perceive and treat you, not just as an individual but also as a member of a racial group or ethno-religious community. Each policy area will have its own imperatives and difficulties (e.g., whether issues of qualification levels or residential segregation)[1] but there is also a general understanding that we, as members of society, have about what our society is and what it is to be a member – a macro-symbolic conception of society and of integration. This informs popular understanding as well as political ideas and the general terms of policy paradigms. Hence, it has been said by a commission on these topics in Quebec, '[T]he symbolic framework of integration (identity, religion, perception of the Other, collective memory, and on) is no less important than its functional or material framework'

(Bouchard and Taylor, 2008). This is particularly so because the sense of 'crisis' about multiculturalism and integration is operating at this macro-symbolic level. This is evident when one considers how few are the policies that could be said to be about integration or how small are the funds involved compared to the headline importance that the issues regularly achieve. In thinking about policy paradigms, of a general ethos or orientation at a national level, it is therefore important to engage at this macro-symbolic level.

I consider this larger, macro-symbolic sense of integration and implied policy paradigms in terms of four modes of integration [summarised in Table 9.1], namely, assimilation, individualist-integration and two versions of multiculturalism, one of which I will call cosmopolitanism.[2] Each offers its own distinctive take on freedom, equality and civic unity (what might be called 'fraternity' or solidarity), the core values of European democracy. Different interpretations and prioritisations of these concepts suggest embryonic paradigms. The issue or 'problem' these paradigms are addressing is post-immigration 'difference' (Modood, 2007). 'Difference' primarily refers to how people are identified: how they identify themselves (for example as 'white', 'black', 'Chinese', 'Muslim', etc.), how they identify others (again as 'white', 'black', 'Chinese', 'Muslim', etc.) and how they are identified by others ('white', etc.).

These identities fall (not necessarily unambiguously or discretely) within the fields of 'race', ethnicity, religion, culture and nationality as various forms of difference. The problem then, is how to integrate difference, by which I mean the process whereby difference ceases to be problematic. I shall consider four modes of integration (summarised in Table 9.1).

Modes of Integration

Assimilation is where the processes affecting change and the relationship between social groups are seen as one-way; the preferred result is one in which the newcomers do little to disturb the society they are settling in and become as much like their new compatriots as possible.[3] We may think of it as one-way integration. By erasing difference it is also thought that the occasions for discrimination and conflict are not allowed to take root. While 'assimilation' as a term has come to be dropped in favour of 'integration', even today, when some politicians use the term 'integration', they actually, consciously or not, mean what here has been defined as assimilation, so the use of these terms in public discourse must not be taken at their face value but critically inspected.

Table 9.1 Four modes of integration*

	Assimilation	Individualist-Integration	Cosmopolitanism	Multiculturalism
Objects of Policy	Individuals and groups marked by 'difference'.	Individuals marked by 'difference', especially their treatment by discriminatory practices of state and civil society.	Individuals marked by 'difference', especially their treatment by discriminatory practices of state and civil society, and societal ideas, especially of 'us' and 'them'.	Individuals and groups marked by 'difference', especially their treatment by discriminatory practices of state and civil society, and societal ideas, especially of 'us' and 'them'.
Liberty	Minorities must be encouraged to conform to the dominant cultural pattern.	Minorities are free to assimilate or cultivate their identities in private but are discouraged from thinking of themselves as minority, but rather as individuals.	Neither minority nor majority individuals should think of themselves as belonging to a single identity but be free to mix and match.	Members of minorities should be free to assimilate, to mix and match or to cultivate group membership in proportions of their own choice.
Equality	Presence of difference provokes discrimination and so is to be avoided.	Discriminatory treatment must be actively eliminated so everyone is treated as an individual and not on the basis of difference.	Anti-discrimination must be accompanied by the dethroning of the dominant culture.	In addition to anti-discrimination the public sphere must accommodate the presence of new group identities and norms.
Fraternity	A strong, homogeneous national identity.	Absence of discrimination and nurturing of individual autonomy within a national/European, liberal democratic citizenship.	People should be free to unite across communal and national boundaries and should think of themselves as global citizens.	Citizenship and national identity must be remade to include group identities that are important to minorities as well as majorities; the relationship between groups should be dialogical rather than one of domination or uniformity.

Note: * In all cases it is assumed that a backdrop of liberal democratic rights and values are operative to a large degree, and what is highlighted here is in addition or interaction with them.

In the three non-assimilative modes of integration, processes of social interaction are seen as two-way, whereby members of the majority community as well as immigrants and ethnic minorities are required to do something; so the latter cannot alone be blamed for failing to, or not trying to, integrate. The established society is the site of institutions – including employers, civil society and the state – in which integration has to take place, and accordingly they must take the lead. The new (prospective) citizens' rights and opportunities must be made effective through anti-discrimination laws and policies. We need, however, to distinguish between *individualist-integration* and *multiculturalism*. Individualist-integration sees the need for institutional adjustments in relation to migrants or minorities, but sees these as only individual claimants and bearers of rights as equal citizens (Barry, 2001). Minority communities may exist as private associations, but these associations are not recognised or supported in the public sphere.

Multiculturalism is where processes of integration are seen both as two-way and involving groups as well as individuals, and as working differently for different groups (CMEB, 2000; Parekh, 2000; Modood, 2007). In this understanding, each group is distinctive, and thus integration cannot consist of a single template (hence the 'multi'). The 'culturalism' – by no means a happy term either in relation to 'culture' or 'ism' – refers to the fact that the groups in question are likely not just to be marked by newness or phenotype or socio-economic location, but by certain forms of group identities. The integration of groups is in addition to, not as an alternative to, the integration of individuals, anti-discrimination measures and a robust framework of individual rights. Multiculturalism, like most concepts, takes different form in different contexts and at different times. For example, it has been differently understood in the Netherlands than in Britain (Joppke, 2010, Koopmans et al., 2005) and in Quebec compared to in Anglophone Canada (Bouchard and Taylor, 2008). The meaning of any mode of integration is subject to debate and contestation, and its policy originators may start with one meaning as, for example, Roy Jenkins did in the 1960s in relation to race and culture, and others (including late comers to the debate) may push it or extend it in other directions by, say, making religion central, as Muslims in Britain have done (Modood, 2005).

Amongst what is central to multiculturalism is the concept of equality as, indeed, it is to other conceptions of integration. The key difference between individualist-integration and multiculturalism is that the concepts of group and of 'multi' are essential to the latter.

Post-immigration minorities are groups differentiated from the majority society or the norm in society by two kinds of processes. On the one hand, by the fact of negative 'difference' with alienness, inferiorisation, stigmatisation, stereotyping, exclusion, discrimination, racism and so on. On the other hand, by the senses of identity that groups so perceived have of themselves. The two together are the key data for multiculturalism. The differences at issue are those perceived both by outsiders or group members – from the outside in and from the inside out – to constitute not just some form of distinctness but a form of alienness or inferiority that diminishes, or makes difficult, equal membership in the wider society or polity.

Multiculturalism has recently been defined as 'where ethno-cultural-religious minorities are, or are thought of, as rather distinct communities, and where public policy encourages this distinctiveness' (Emmerson, 2011). This, however, is only a third of it. Multiculturalism allows those who wish to encourage such distinctiveness to do so; but it also seeks forms of social unity that are compatible with this – what Hartmann and Gerteis (2005) call 'new conceptions of solidarity', grounded in a concept of equality (Bouchard and Taylor, 2008). Each mode of integration must be understood in terms of its interpretation of free choice, equality and fraternity. Characterisations of multiculturalism that subtract its emphasis on unity are extremely common but incomplete.

Further unpacking multiculturalism and integration

Multicultural accommodation of minorities, then, is different from individualist-integration because it explicitly recognises the social reality of groups, not just of individuals and organisations. There may, however, be considerable complexity about what is meant by social reality of groups or 'groupness' here, and ideas of groups as discrete, homogeneous, unchanging, bounded populations are not realistic when we are thinking of multicultural recognition (Modood, 2007, pp. 93–97). This leads us to *cosmopolitanism*.

Cosmopolitanism emerges by accepting the concept of difference while critiquing or dissolving the concept of groups (Waldron, 1991).[4] Disagreement about the extent to which post-immigration groups exist and/or ought to exist and be given political status means that there are two kinds of multiculturalism (Modood, 1998; Meer and Modood, 2009). While in public discourse, as well as in academia, one or both are referred to as multiculturalism, and often without a full recognition that two different ideas are being expressed; I will reserve the term 'multiculturalism' for the sociological and political position in which groups are a critical feature.[5]

Where 'difference' is positively valorised (or pragmatically accepted) but it is denied that groups exist or, alternatively, exist but should not be politically recognised, this I shall call cosmopolitanism. The contention is that in the early stages of migration and settlement – especially in the context of a legacy of racism, colonialism and European supremacism – forms of social exclusion created or reinforced certain forms of groupness, such as white and black. However, as a result of social mixing, cultural sharing and globalisation in which dominant identities of modernity (such as of race and nation) are dissolving, people have much more fluid and multiple identities, combine them in individual ways and use them in context-sensitive ways (Hall, 1992a). For example, the ways that Caribbean-origin Britons have socially blended into a 'multiculture' and have sought conviviality and sociability rather than separate communities may perhaps not be fully captured as a form of individualistic integration (Gilroy, 2000). While remaining economically marginal and over-represented in relation to the social problems associated with deprived inner city areas, they have become a feature of popular culture in terms of music, dance, youth styles and sport, in all of which they have become significantly over-represented (Hall, 1998). To the extent that football teams, Olympiads and television programmes such as *The X Factor* are central to popular and national identities, Caribbean-origin people are placed at the centre of British national imaginaries. Moreover, Britain and most other countries in Western Europe have recently experienced and are experiencing a new wave of immigration and will continue to do so, including from within the European Union. Given the diversity of the locations from where migrants are coming, the result, it is argued, is not communities, but a churning mass of languages, ethnicities and religions, all cutting across each other and creating a 'super-diversity' (Vertovec, 2007). This may be setting a pattern for the future, and it may be allied to a further argument that globalisation, migration and telecommunications have created populations dispersed across countries that interact more with each other and have a greater sense of loyalty to each other than they might to their fellow citizens.

In what ways does cosmopolitanism go beyond individualist-integration? Its distinctive ethos is that we should value diversity and create the conditions where it is individually chosen. We should oppose all forms of imposition of group identities on individuals and therefore the ideas, images and prejudices by which individuals are inferiorised or portrayed as threatening and so excluded from full membership of society; and we should not require assimilation or conformity to dominant group norms. Yet, a requirement of communal membership can also be oppressive to individuals and their life-chances (Appiah, 1994). Inherited or ascribed identities which slot people into pigeonholes not of their choosing, giving them a script to live by, should be refused (often referred to in the literature as a 'transgression of boundaries'). They not only reduce the options of the kind of person one can be, but they divide society into antagonistic groups.[6] Cosmopolitanism, then, is a conception of multiculturalism as maximum freedom, for minority as well as majority individuals, to mix with, borrow and learn from all (whether they are of your group or not), so individual identities are personal amalgams of bits from various groups and heritages and there is no one dominant social identity to which all must conform. The result will be a society composed of a blend of cultures, a 'multiculture'.

While this is an attractive image of contemporary society and blends easily with the ideas of liberal democracy, it has only a partial fit with even, say, London today, let alone many parts of Britain and continental Europe. In some towns and cities, such as in northern England, there is not a diversity of groups but often just two (for example Asian Muslims and whites) and minority individuals do not float across identities, mixing and matching, but have a strong attachment to one or a few identities. For example, most British Muslims seem to think of themselves in terms of 'Muslim' and/or 'British' (usually both) (Travis, 2002). The fact of super-diversity is emerging alongside rather than displacing the fact of settled, especially postcolonial, communities which have a particular historical relationship with Britain, and the political significance of such communities. Similarly, there are other communities in other European countries with their own historical significance, such as Maghrebians in France and Turks in Germany. Moreover, some groups continue to be much larger than others, and stand out as groups – in their own eyes and those of others – and are at the centre of public policy and debate, especially if they are thought to be failing to integrate. Muslims, for example, seem to be in this category across much of Western Europe, regardless of the degree of conviviality or super-diversity that might be present.

That is not to say that such minority identities are exclusive. Successive surveys have shown that most Muslims in Britain strongly identify with being Muslim, but the majority also identify as British; indeed, they are more likely to identify with 'British' and say they have trust in key British institutions than non-Muslims (Heath and Roberts, 2008); Gallup

(2009) found the same in Germany, albeit less so in France, although Pew Research Center (2006) found much higher levels of national identification in France than other Western European countries. Post-immigration hyphenated identities, such as British-Indian, have become as commonplace in Britain as they have been in the United States for decades. Similarly, diasporic links as described above certainly exist, and are likely to increase, but the net result is not an inevitable erosion of national citizenship – British African-Caribbeans and South Asians have families in their countries of origin and in the United States and Canada, but there is little evidence that most branches of those families do not feel British, American or Canadian.

An important point of difference, then, between the concepts of individualist-integration and multiculturalism proper is that for the latter, the groups in question, the post-immigration minorities, are not of one kind but are a 'multi'. For example, some people will identify with a colour identity like 'black' but there will be others for whom national origin identities (like 'Turkish'), or a regional heritage (like 'Berber'), or a religious identity (like 'Sikh') may be much more meaningful, expressing forms of community and ethnic pride that are struggling for recognition and inclusion. And, of course, these minority identities will interact with wider, societal identities – 'woman', 'working class', 'Londoner', 'British' – in differing ways, expressing the different experiences, locations and aspirations of different groups. So, both the alternative models of multiculturalism as cosmopolitanism and as (what may be called) ethno-religious communitarianism, for which I am reserving the term, multiculturalism, have some grounding and meet the political aspirations of some minority groups. Neither works as a comprehensive sociological or political model, and they should be viewed as complementary (Modood, 1998; CMEB, 2000; Modood and Dobbernack, 2011). Moreover, while recognition of ethnic or religious groups may have a legal dimension, it will for the most part be at the level of civic consultations, political participation, institutional policies (for example, schools and hospitals), discursive representations, especially in relation to the changing discourses of societal unity or national identity, and their remaking.

Regardless of the extent to which recognition of minority identities in this way is formal or informal – led by the state or the semi-autonomous institutions of civil society – it does not challenge, let alone displace, individual rights and the shared dimensions of citizenship. There may, however, be genuine concern that some groups at a particular time and in some areas are becoming too inward-looking. Where the concern is primarily about a lack of positive mixing and interaction between groups at a local level, community cohesion measures – for example, a Christian school offering places to non-Christians or twinning with a non-Christian school – may be an appropriate response (Cantle, 2001). Where the concern is about self-conceptions and discourses more generally, the issue will be about the national or societal identity. Whilst such inwardness has never been part of any theory or policy of multiculturalism, it is clear that it is a fundamental anxiety of the critics of multiculturalism, many of whom go as far as to define multiculturalism in terms of such separatism.[7] It is therefore important to emphasise that multiculturalism is a mode of integration, and that it, no less than hostility to minorities or other modes of integration, should be examined as possible contributory causes of exclusion and segregation (Banting and Kymlicka, 2008).

Ways in which multiculturalism is not dead

This unpacking of what I mean by 'multiculturalism' is also helpful in understanding those who say that multiculturalism has failed (Weldon, 1989; and see Presseurop, 2010 for Angela Merkel's speech on the failure of *multikulti*) or that multiculturalism is dead (Cameron, 2011). They may mean to endorse assimilation, individualistic integration or cosmopolitanism. At the same time they are acknowledging and possibly reinforcing the sociological reality of group difference because their lament is that some groups (especially Muslims) are clearly visible as distinct groups when they should not be; they attribute this fact to a separatist tendency in the groups, encouraged by allegedly multiculturalist policies. The irony is, of course, that the accusatory discourse of 'some groups are not integrating' may actually be reinforcing group identities and therefore contributing to the social conditions that give multiculturalism a sociological pertinence. Moreover, it is not just at the level of sociology that anti-multiculturalists may find themselves using multiculturalist ideas; even while deploying an anti-multiculturalist discourse they may enact multiculturalist policies. For example, they may continue with group consultations, representation and accommodation. The latter have actually increased. The British government has found it necessary to increase the scale and level of consultations with Muslims in Britain since 9/11 and, dissatisfied with existing organisations, has sought to increase the number of organised interlocutors and the channels of communication. Avowedly anti-multiculturalist countries and governments have worked to increase corporatism in practice, for example with the creation by Nicholas Sarkozy of the Conseil Francais du Culte Musulman in 2003 to represent all Muslims to the French government in matters of worship and ritual; and by the creation of the Islam konferenz in Germany in 2005, an exploratory body, yet with an extensive political agenda. These bodies are partly top-down efforts to control Muslims or to channel them into certain formations and away from others; nevertheless, such institutional processes cannot be understood within the conceptual framework of assimilation, individualist integration or cosmopolitanism.

The analytical framework offered helps us also to understand those who say they welcome diversity but seem to be in agreement with critics of multiculturalism. Critics of multiculturalism are usually pointing to the public assertion of strong group identities to mobilise a group to achieve certain policies and/or to demand differential treatment. They are sometimes responded to by those who point to how multiculturalism is working in their neighbourhoods, which they say are multiethnic and where people do not just live peaceably side by side but mix freely and where that mixing is valued above mono-culturalism. Yet such views do not imply support for strong group identities and related policies; on the contrary, their success may be seen to be dependent on the absence of the latter.[8] While this is a reasonable response in its own terms it does not meet the criticism of multiculturalism and in fact may share it. Group-based multiculturalism has become unpopular and is what critics have in mind, although this is obscured by the fact that what I call 'cosmopolitanism' is often referred to by its advocates as 'multiculturalism'.

But what we have to consider is: Can integration of all post-immigration formations be achieved without group-based multiculturalism (Modood, 1998, 2007)? Moreover, a group-based multiculturalism, where group membership is voluntary, may be part of the future in an unintended way, as it is highly compatible with Prime Minister Cameron's vision of a 'Big Society' in which civil society associations based on locality and faith, including inter-faith groups, take over some responsibilities currently undertaken by state agencies. A flagship policy of the Big Society agenda is state funding to create new community-based non-state schools called 'free schools'. Over a quarter of these are led by religious groups; those that started in September 2011 included two Jewish, a Hindu and a Sikh school (Vasagar, 2012). Of the 102 schools approved for funding in July 2012, three were Jewish, one was Hindu, four were Sikh and four were Muslim (BHA, 2012). It is difficult to see how the new Big Society is a break with what is rejected as 'state multiculturalism' (Cameron, 2011). The same trend is found in France, where three Muslim schools have joined the many thousands (mainly Catholic) of state-supported religious schools (Akan, 2009, pp. 246–247), and in Germany, where there are no state funded religious schools but where Islam is increasingly joining the religions that the provincial government funds instruction in within state schools (The Local, 2011; see also DIK, 2009).

The analysis offered here of related macro-symbolic ideas and policy paradigms, each of which consists of a model of society and normative political ideas, includes a sense of unity or fraternity. For modes of integration are not just about sociology (the first level) or politics (second level), but include ideas, however inchoate, of ourselves as a social unity (as displayed at the bottom of Table 9.1). For assimilationists, this consists of a strong, homogeneous national identity. Individualist-integration emphasises the liberal and democratic character of the national polity. Cosmopolitanism is uneasy with the national, an identity that demands allegiance from all citizens whilst creating boundaries between ourselves and the rest of the world. With multiculturalism comes a positive vision of the whole, remade so as to include the previously excluded or marginalised on the basis of equality and sense of belonging. It is at this level that we may fully speak of multicultural integration or multicultural citizenship (Taylor, 1994; Parekh, 2000; Modood, 2007). This third level of multiculturalism, incorporating the sociological fact of diversity, groupness and exclusion, but going beyond individual rights and political accommodation, is perhaps the level that has been least emphasised. Or, at least that is how it seems to many whose understanding of multiculturalism, sometimes polemical but sometimes sincere, is that it is about encouraging minority difference without a counterbalancing emphasis on cross-cutting commonalities and a vision of a greater good. This has led many commentators and politicians to talk of multiculturalism as divisive and productive of segregation.

Theorists of multiculturalism, such as Taylor (1994) and Parekh (2000), related policy documents such as the report of the CMEB (2000) and enactments such as those in Canada and Australia – universally regarded as pioneers and exemplars of state multiculturalism – all appealed to and built on an idea of national citizenship. Hence, from a multiculturalist point of view (though not that of its critics) the recent emphasis on cohesion and citizenship, what has been called 'the civic turn' (Mouritsen, 2008), is a necessary rebalancing of the political multiculturalism of the 1990s, which largely took the form of accommodation of groups while being ambivalent about national identity (Meer and Modood,

2009).[9] This does not invalidate the analysis offered here, that integration without some degree of institutional accommodation is unlikely to be successful. Indeed, for multiculturalists a renewing of national identity has to be distinctly plural and hospitable to the minority identities. It involves 'rethinking the national story' with the minorities as important characters – not obscuring difference but weaving it into a common identity in which all can see themselves, and giving all a sense of belonging to each other (CMEB, 2000, pp. 54–56; Modood, 2007, pp. 145–154).

Conclusion

It may be the case that all the attempted models of integration, especially national models, are in crisis; certainly they are perceived as such. We can, however, have a better sense of what the issues are and therefore what needs to be done if, firstly, we recognise that discourses of integration and multiculturalism are exercises in conceptualising post-immigration difference and, as such, operate at three distinct levels: as an (implicit) sociology; as a political response; and as a vision of what is the whole into which difference is to be integrated. Depending upon the sociology in question, certain political responses are possible or not, or, more reasonable or less. The sociological and political assumptions are thus mutually dependent. Secondly, I have offered a framework in which four distinct political responses – assimilation, individualist-integration, cosmopolitanism and multiculturalism – illuminate each other, and where each successive position attempts to include what is thought to be missing from the predecessor. Each position, however, has its merits and may be appropriate in certain contexts. Each has a particular conception of equal citizenship, but the value of each can only be realised if it is not imposed but is the preferred choice of minority individuals and groups, who of course – being a 'multi' – are bound to choose differently. Thus, no singular model is likely to be suitable for all groups. To have a reasonable chance of integrating the maximum number of members of minorities, none of these political responses should be dismissed. Ethno-religious communitarianism may currently be viewed as undesirable by European publics and policymakers, but given how Muslims have become central to the prospects of integration on a number of fronts, it is unlikely that integration can be achieved without some element of this approach, which is being practised even by those politicians who are making anti-multiculturalist speeches. Perceptions of Muslims as groups, by themselves and by non-Muslim majorities, are hardening, so the key question is whether they are to be stigmatised as outsiders or recognised as integral to the polity. Finally, we must not overlook the third analytical level, which in many ways is not primarily about minorities but about the majority. The enlargement, hyphenation and internal pluralising of national identities is essential to an integration in which all citizens have not just rights but a sense of belonging to the whole as well as to their own 'little platoon' (Burke, 1982, p. 135).[10]

Notes

1. This chapter is a modified version of the chapter with the same title in H. Mahamdalie (ed.), *Defending Multiculturalism*, Bookmarks, London, 2011, and is based on my contribution to the British Academy 'New Paradigms in Public Policy' project, to whom I am grateful for comments on an earlier draft as well as for allowing me to draw on that contribution.Different groups may integrate to different degrees across sectors. For example, Jews in Britain are highly integrated in relation to employment but are the most segregated religious minority.

2. The concern here is not primarily in relation to socio-economic integration, for which see Loury, Modood and Teles (2005) and Heath and Cheung (2007). The bigger challenge, for another occasion, is to connect the socio-economic with the issues discussed in this chapter. The issues of 'difference', however, are as important as the socio-economic in relation to equal citizenship and have to be understood in their own terms.

3. When US sociologists use the term 'assimilation', they usually mean what is meant by integration in the UK, as in the 'segmented assimilation' proposed by Portes and Zhou (1993).

4. Here, I do not mean the idea that there should be a world government or primarily even the ethical view that one should be a citizen of the world; rather I am characterising a mode of integration within a country that emphasises a mixing of people from all over the world, as in the expression 'London is a cosmopolitan city'. British sociologists sometimes use the term 'multiculture', but this clearly has not carried over into public discourse. It has been suggested to me that the term 'interculturalism' best fits here, but in the place where it is most used in relation to national politics, Quebec, it is closer to what here I call 'individualist-integration'. More generally, it is not clear that 'interculturalism' includes anything that is not or cannot be included in multiculturalism (see Meer and Modood, 2012). I did also consider the term 'diversity' but it is either too descriptive and generic, and does not pick out a mode of integration, or has been appropriated as 'diversity management' by human resource professionals.

5. This is how the term has been used by the leading political theorists, such as Taylor (1994), Kymlicka (1995) and Parekh (2000) and by the Canadian government; it is also consistent with CMEB (2000) and other exponents of multiculturalism – see Modood (2007, pp. 14–20) for details.

6. British exponents of this view tend, however, to put some communal identities in a normative, privileged position. This particularly applies to political blackness and to some extent to non-cultural and non-religious political identities generally (Modood, 1994).
7. A review of the American social science literature found that '[t]he most common conception of multiculturalism in both scholarly circles and popular discourse is a negative one, having to do with what multiculturalism is not or what it stands in opposition to. Multiculturalism, in this usage, represents heterogeneity as opposed to homogeneity, diversity as a counterpoint to unity' (Hartmann and Gerteis, 2005, p. 219, 221–222). They found that if they looked at exponents of multiculturalism, as opposed to critics, such simplistic dichotomies were unsustainable, and they concluded: 'multiculturalism is best understood as a critical-theoretical project, an exercise in cultivating new conceptions of solidarity in the context of dealing with the realities of pervasive and increasing diversity in contemporary societies'.
8. Hence the irony that anti-multiculturalists like President Sarkozy are trying to create corporate representations for Muslims in France; while pro-diversity authors call for the cessation of government meetings with Muslim community leaders (Sen, 2006; Malik, 2011).
9. In the 1990s cosmopolitanism and multiculturalism in Britain began to be linked to a national identity and its modernisation, to, for example, 'Cool Britannia' and 'rebranding Britain' (Leonard, 1997), but others welcomed globalisation as an era of the 'post-national' (Hall, 1992b; Soysal, 1994).
10. 'To be attached to the subdivision, to love the *little platoon* we belong [to in...] we proceed towards a love to our country, and to mankind' (Burke, 1986, p. 135).

References

Akan, M. (2009) 'Laïcité and multiculturalism: the Stasi Report in context', *British Journal of Sociology*, 60 (2), 237–256.

Appiah, K. A. (1994) 'Identity, authenticity, survival: multicultural societies and social reproduction', in Gutmann, A. (ed.), *Multiculturalism: Examining the Politics of Recognition,* Princeton NJ, Princeton University Press, 149–164.

Banting, K. and Kymlicka, W. (2008) *Multiculturalism and the Welfare State: Recognition and Redistribution in Contemporary Democracies,* Oxford, Oxford University Press.

Barry, B. (2001) *Culture and Equality: An Egalitarian Critique of Multiculturalism,* Cambridge, Polity.

BHA (2012) 'BHA: Approved 2013 Free Schools include first "faith" special, alternative provision schools'. Available on http://www.politics.co.uk/opinion-formers/bha-british-humanist-association/article/bha-approved-2013-free-schools-include-first-faith-special-a. [Accessed on 12 July 2012]

Bouchard, G. and Taylor, C. (2008) *Building The Future: A Time for Reconciliation,* Consultation Commission on Accommodation Practices Related to Cultural Differences, Quebec.

Burke, E. (1982) *Reflections on the Revolution in France.* Harmondsworth, Penguin.

Cameron, D. (2011) *PM's speech at Munich Security Conference* [online]. http://www.number10.gov.uk/news/speeches-and-transcripts/2011/02/pms-speech-at-munich-security-conference-60293. [Accessed on 29 March 2011]

Cantle, T. (2001) *Community Cohesion: A Report of the Independent Review Team*, London, Home Office.

Commission on Multi-Ethnic Britain (CMEB) (2000) *The Future of Multi-ethnic Britain: Report of the Commission the Future of Multi-Ethnic Britain*, London, Runnymede Trust.

Deustsche Islam Konfrenz (DIK) (2009) 'Islamic religious education trials in schools'. Available on http://www. deutsche-islam-Konferenz.de/nn_1875202/SubSites/DIK/EN/ ReligionsunterrichtImame/ReligionBildung/Schulversuche/schulversuche-node.html?__nnn=true. [Accessed on 16 February 2009]

Emmerson, M. (2011) *Interculturalism: Europe and its Muslims, In Search of Sound Societal Models*, Brussels, Centre for European Policy Studies.

Gilroy, P. (2000) *Between Camps: Race, Identity and Nationalism at the End of the Colour Line*, London, Allen Lane.

Glazer, N. and Moynihan, D. P. (1963) *Beyond the Melting Pot: The Negroes, Puerto Ricans, Jews, Italians and Irish of New York City*, Cambridge MA, The MIT Press and Harvard University Press.

Hall, S. (1992a) 'New ethnicities', in Donald, J. and Rattansi, A. (eds), *'Race', Culture and Difference*, London, Sage, 252–259.

Hall, S. (1992b) 'The Question of Cultural Identity', in Hall, S. and McGrew, T. (eds), *Modernity and its Futures*, Cambridge, Polity Press, 218–240.

Hall, S. (1998) 'Aspiration and attitude – reflections on black Britain in the nineties', *New Formations*, 33, 38–46.

Hartman, D. and Gerteis, J. (2005) 'Dealing with diversity: mapping multiculturalism in sociological terms', *Sociological Theory*, 23 (2), 218–240.

Heath, A. and Roberts J. (2008) *British Identity: Its Sources and Possible Implications for Civic Attitudes and Behaviour* [online]. Available on http://www.justice.gov.uk/docs/british-identity.pdf. [Accessed on 28 March 2011]

Heath, A.F. and Cheung, S.Y. (2007) *Unequal Chances: Ethnic Minorities in Western Labour Markets*, Oxford, published for the British Academy by Oxford University Press.

Joppke, C. (2010) *Citizenship and immigration*, Cambridge, Polity Books.

Koopmans, R., Statham, P., Giugni, M. and Passy, F. (2005) *Contested Citizenship: Immigration and Cultural Diversity in Europe*, Minneapolis, University of Minesota Press.

Kymlicka, W. (1995) *Multicultural Citizenship*, Oxford, Oxford University Press.

Leonard, M. (1997) *Britain TM: Renewing our Identity*, London, Demos.

Loury, G.C., Modood, T. and Teles, S.M. (eds) (2005) *Ethnicity, Social Mobility, and Public Policy: Comparing the USA and UK*, Cambridge, Cambridge University Press.

Meer, N. and Modood, T. (2009) 'The multicultural state we're in: Muslims, 'multiculture' and the 'civic re-balancing' of British multiculturalism', *Political Studies*, 57, 473–497.

Modood, T. (1998) 'Anti-essentialism, multiculturalism and the 'recognition' of religious minorities', *Journal of Political Philosophy*, 6, 378–399.

Modood, T. (2005) *Multicultural Politics: Racism, Ethnicity and Muslims in Britain*, Edinburgh, Edinburgh University Press.

Modood, T. (2007) *Multiculturalism: A Civic Idea,* Cambridge, Polity.

Modood, T. and Dobbernack J. (2011), 'A left communitarianism? What about multiculturalism?' *Soundings,* 48.

Mouritsen, P. (2008) 'Political responses to cultural conflict: reflections on the ambiguities of the civic turn', in Mouritsen, P. and Jørgensen, K.E. (eds), *Constituting Communities: Political Solutions to Cultural Conflict,* London, Palgrave, 1–30.

Parekh, B.C. (2000) *Rethinking Multiculturalism: Cultural Diversity and Political Theory,* Cambridge MA, Harvard University Press.

Pew Research Center (2006) *The great divide: How Westerners and Muslims view each other* [online]. Available on http://pewglobal.org/2006/06/22/the-great-divide-how-westerners-and-muslims-views-each-other. [Accessed on 28 March 2011]

Portes, A. and Zhou, M. (1993) 'The new second generation: segmented assimilation and its variants', *The Annals of the American Academy of Political and Social Science,* 530, 74–96.

Presseurop (2010) *Mutti Merkel handbags Multikulti* [online]. Available on http://www.presseurop.eu/en/content/article/364091-mutti-merkel-handbags-multi-kulti. [Accessed on 28 March 2011].

Soysal, Y. (1994) *Limits of Citizenship: Migrants and Post National Membership in Europe,* Chicago, Chicago University Press.

Taylor, C. (1994) 'The politics of recognition', in Gutmann, A. (ed.), *Multiculturalism and 'the Politics of Recognition': An Essay,* Princeton NJ, Princeton University Press, 25–73.

The Local. (2011) 'Islamic studies gain foothold in state schools'. Available on http://www.thelocal.de/education/20111222-39667.html. [Accessed 22 December 2011]

Travis, A. (2002) 'The need to belong – but with a strong faith [online]'. Available on http://www.guardian.co.uk/uk/2002/jun/17/september11.religion1. [Accessed on 2 June 2011]

Vasagar, J. (2012) 'Third of new free schools are religious', *The Guardian.* Available on http://www.newstatesman.com/uk-politics/2008/08/religious-state-secular. [Accessed on 13 July 2012]

Vertovec, S. (2007) 'Super-diversity and its implications', *Ethnic and Racial Studies,* 30, 1024–1054.

Waldron, J. (1991) 'Minority cultures and the cosmopolitan alternative', *University of Michigan Journal of Law Reform,* 25, 751.

Weldon, F. (1989) *Sacred Cows,* London, Chatto & Windus.

10

The 'Schooled Identities' of Australian Multiculturalism: Professional Vision, Reflexive Civility and Education for a Culturally Complex World

Greg Noble and Megan Watkins

Since their inception in Australia in the 1970s, multicultural policies have been met with general but qualified public support (Ang, Brand, Noble and Sternberg, 2006; Dunn et al., 2004). The national and international contexts since 2001, however, have heightened anxieties around immigration and social cohesion, evoking the claims of a 'crisis' around multiculturalism (Lentin and Tilley, 2011). This has exacerbated a longstanding lack of clarity about what multiculturalism actually means, both here and overseas (Parekh, 2006; Modood, 2007). In 2011, however, against the international trend, the Australian Government (2011) reasserted its policy commitment to multiculturalism. Yet, multiculturalism is still in a moment of uncertainty and re-evaluation, not just because of criticism from conservative commentators (Donnelly, 2005), but because there is some concern that policies developed in the 1970s and 1980s may no longer be as relevant in Australia's increasingly transnational, culturally complex and technologically mediated societies (Modood, 2007).

Within this wider context, multicultural education has faced challenges to its relevance, framework and modes of delivery. This chapter emerges from a series of projects reassessing multicultural education – its concepts, practices and goals – to ensure schooling practices can function more effectively in promoting cultural inclusion and social justice. It argues that multiculturalism has always entailed competing 'logics', in which demands for cultural recognition existed alongside imperatives towards social justice. However, this is a difficult balance to maintain, and in the last 20 years we have seen an increasing emphasis on cultural difference in defining multicultural education. The schemas of cultural difference that structure teachers' professional practice may, therefore, shape classroom teaching in sometimes problematic ways, *producing* particular kinds of reduced student identities. The chapter concludes then on the need for professional development programs to engage teachers – not just students – in developing the critical capacities for understanding a culturally complex world.

The logics of multicultural education

The notion of 'multicultural education', of course, covers a range of programmes in Australia – English as a Second Language (ESL), community languages, multicultural perspectives across the curriculum, anti-racism programs, intercultural understanding, community liaison and so on. It is not the aim of this chapter to try to write a history of the evolution of multicultural education in Australia – this has been done by others (Martin, 1978; Inglis, 2009; Allan and Hill, 2004). The starting point for us here is that these programmes draw on diverse rationales – notions of social justice, cultural maintenance, community harmony, cultural awareness. Yet the *logics* of many of these rationales are in tension, and these programmes exist in competition for limited educational resources and time. There are, therefore, issues here which teachers have to reconcile in order to fashion adequate responses to cultural diversity within schools and classrooms.

These competing logics can be seen in the foundations of Australian multiculturalism in the 1970s. While it marked a shift from the assimilationism of the White Australia Policy, multiculturalism quickly became a system of funding and administration which locked community organisations into systems of political representation predicated on simplified notions of ethnic community (Jakubowicz, Morrissey and Palser, 1984; Collins et al., 2000). Rather than focus on social reform, wherein ethnic minorities gained access to key institutions through programs promoting participation and equity, a benign multiculturalism of identity politics emerged (Hage, 2002). Cultural groups were deemed equal and their diversity superficially celebrated (Noble and Poynting, 2000, p. 63), resulting in a fetishisation of difference (Modood, 2007) and reducing cultural complexity to essentialised ethnic identities which emphasised boundaries between groups, leaving multiculturalism open to conservative anxieties about the threat to national cohesion.

This foregrounding of a reduced identity politics is largely the result of the marriage of the 'cultural expediency' of the state (Yúdice, 2003) and its need to manage populations, the strategic essentialism of community organisations (Spivak, 1990) which desire to gain recognition and financial support as an identifiable 'community', and social understandings of diversity which rely on stereotypical perceptions of physical and cultural difference. To produce a more effective multicultural education, we believe it is necessary to consider, firstly, the relations between 'official' multicultural discourse and popular and professional understandings of culture, ethnicity and multiculturalism.

These issues are not purely theoretical. In New South Wales (NSW), which has the second largest state education system in the world and one of the most culturally diverse, 30 per cent of students have a language background other than English (LBOTE), with increasing numbers from Asia, Africa and the Middle East; 6 per cent of students are Aboriginal or Torres Strait Islander; while about 12,000 students are from refugee backgrounds. Each year, students from 100 nations representing 130 language groups enter the system. About 11 per cent of the total student population are learning ESL (though it is assessed that many more need ESL), including 7,000 students who are newly arrived from overseas countries (NSW Department of Education and Communities (DEC, 2012).

How we understand these differences has significant consequences for how we approach issues around diversity in schools. We typically identify students in terms of their, or their parents', country of origin, but if we reconfigure those statistics in terms of language background, religion or 'ethnicity' (which is often very provincial), then we get a contrasting angle on diversity; and if we try to factor in several of these elements, then the picture becomes quite complex. Yet, it is not just that Australia is marked by 'the increasingly complex nature of contemporary diversity' (Koleth, 2010); the very nature of that diversity has changed dramatically. Students who are the children or grandchildren of immigrants might happily claim several ancestries and appropriate resources from several cultural origins. Intergenerational change, intermarriage and cultural hybridisation as well as the widening cultural, linguistic and religious diversity of immigrants and their children challenge the assumption of cohesive ethnic communities on which multiculturalism was founded (Ang et al., 2002). Given the increasingly complex forms of diversity in schools, the rationale and programs of delivery within multicultural education need re-examination.

Multicultural schemas of perception

Central to this re-examination must be the ways teachers 'see' and respond to such diversity, because this is crucial to the ways multicultural education is delivered. As well as considering the relation between 'official' multiculturalism and popular perceptions, we need to consider how the 'professional vision' of teachers (Goodwin, 1994) – as well as popular perceptions – encodes issues around diversity, working through particular categories of identity which frame not just how students and their families and communities are seen, but also how educational and behavioural 'problems' are constructed. Bourdieu (1996a, p. 156) argues that schemas of perception frame the actions of participants in a field of practices. Such schemas are unconscious and are converted into 'eternal norms', naturalising the contingencies of the social world, shaping pedagogic actions that reproduce the social categories that are hidden by them (Bourdieu, 1996b, p. 73). Bourdieu focuses on the ways these schemas operate in educational institutions in class terms, whereby the academic criteria for evaluating students hides the social categories underlying the formation of those schemas (Bourdieu, 1996b, pp. 10–11, 167); but we suggest these schemas also operate in *ethnicised* ways. Teachers' 'professional vision', we suggest, entails schemas of difference which facilitate the management of the culturally diverse school – but they may do so in ways that may be progressive in intention but problematic in implementation.

These arguments derive from two research projects, conducted in NSW schools, into understandings of ethnicity, culture, and multiculturalism amongst teachers, parents and students, to explore the possibilities of a more effective curriculum and pedagogy for a culturally complex society. The importance of considering these schemas of difference emerged in an electronic survey of NSW DEC teachers when we asked them to describe their cultural backgrounds. Of the 5,128 responses (almost 10 per cent of the NSW teaching service), the survey recorded 1,155 different responses, with teachers coming from 109 countries of birth, and speaking 131 languages. The variety of forms of self-identification by teachers displays something of the complexity of culturally diverse Australia: they saw themselves in terms of hyphenated identities which combined homeland and Australia (e.g., Greek-Australian), and in terms of nation (e.g., Fijian), faith (e.g., Hindu), language (e.g., Arabic), 'province' (e.g., Yorkshire), 'race' (e.g., South African Coloured), geopolitical region (e.g., Asian). Most importantly they often combined these elements in diverse ways (e.g., Australian with multicultural background:

Aboriginal-Irish-Australian-Chinese-Italian). Yet the complexity the teachers saw in themselves was not matched by how they saw their students, who in interviews were more typically described as belonging to about a dozen categories, such as Chinese, Lebanese, Tongan, Asian, Arabic or Islander (i.e., in terms of a more limited and less complicated array of singular ancestries, regions or languages). Such categories aggregate students, whereas the terms teachers use about themselves highlight their specificity.

The tendency to reduce the ethnicities of students is not simply a pragmatic response to complexity, but it echoes a series of conceptual difficulties around notions of multiculturalism, culture and ethnicity. Ethnicity, for example, was variously defined by teachers in an earlier survey as:

- shared common background
- family background
- the ethnic group you identify with
- a group with their own customs and traditions
- cultural background
- peoples' race or background – genetically?
- to do with the language and colour
- where you come from
- a person's cultural background which is smaller than the dominant culture

Many of these overlap, but others are in contradiction, and some are meaningless. Some see ethnicity as the same as culture; some see it in relation to phenotypical or linguistic features; others see it primarily as a question of self-identification, or as a 'minority', and so on. Our aim is not to ridicule teachers for their inconsistency but to point out that, as intellectual workers, teachers are not well equipped to think through the difficult concepts of cultural difference central to their professional practice. Moreover, they participated in the wider *ethnicisation* of culture, by which we mean the tendency to conflate complex cultural pasts and presents with singular notions of ethnicity. The reduction of the cultures of students represents a way into dealing with issues of diversity that, in practice, 'resolves' the competing conceptual and pedagogic demands of the diverse logics of multiculturalism, but it does not necessarily address students *as they are*.

This 'resolution' of complexity is seen, for example, in the tendency in practice to subsume the various aims of multicultural education under the task of 'cultural awareness'. When we asked teachers to rank the various goals of multicultural education, there was a spread across the various categories, but with the emphasis clearly on the question of equity. However, when teachers were asked what schools could do to foster cultural inclusion, the 'multicultural day' was by far and away the most common response. In other words, a form of 'cultural recognition' was the primary way in which they conceived the school's response to the needs of cultural diversity. Such days, of course, trade on what we might call a cultural imaginary central to the professional vision of teachers: the visible codification of identifiable ethnic communities, the lure of exotic differences and the moral demand for 'tolerance' of those differences.

This cultural imaginary also operates through the teachers' articulation of attributes of student populations. This response is echoed, for example, in the tendency to essentialise ethnicity in explaining the educational performance of students. Chinese students, for example, were seen as successful, but were also seen as passive, reliant on teacher direction, learning by rote, not taught to think, not communicative, but pushed, competitive, and poor socially (Watkins and Noble, 2013). Sometimes this was spelt out as a cultural pathology. One teacher, of Chinese background herself, said that the emphasis on education goes 'deep down to the root, to the Chinese culture...right from 2000 BC...deep down from Confucius upward'. In other words, the attributes of students were accorded a primordial status; yet they are also constructed as a problem. As another said:

> the Chinese community are very successful in terms of their work ethic, in terms of providing opportunities for their children to immerse themselves in anything that is academic. However, I think the sad part about the Chinese community is that they have a programmed life without giving the children the opportunity of growing up as rational, happy, contributing human beings.

This is one way the professional vision of teachers operates to establish ways of justifying the need for multicultural education for educationally 'successful' groups. Yet it is, of course, more clearly seen in the representation of less successful groups, such as 'Pasifika' communities,[1] which are seen as not valuing education or hard work and preferring the sociality of the school. Pasifika students, one teacher claimed,

> respond better to more of a laidback approach with choices but no direction. They don't respond to structures. They respond better to

feeling good about themselves and having a teacher that will relate to them as individuals.

It is not just that these perceptions are problematic, but that they have implications for practice. The 'solution' implied in this response is not pedagogical but couched in terms of the pastoral role of teachers. Moreover, some teachers described attributes as culturally inherent:

[T]heir strength that they bring with them to the classroom is naturally they can sing and dance.

As another argued,

if you leave them to their own devices they will be off because they are not, by nature, they are not students. Some people are students and some people are not, and Islander kids tend not to be students.

Our point is not simply about teachers' use of racist stereotypes in the name of multiculturalism (Wynter, 1990), but that their professional schemas of difference define students' attributes and thus shape practice. This paradigm embodies a bureaucratic essentialism 'useful' for the administration of culturally diverse schools because it gathers diverse populations into an ordered array of categories in a marriage of expedience with the strategic essentialism of ethnic politics through which community organisations gain institutional recognition and resources.

Schooled identities

The bureaucratic essentialism which frames multicultural programs in schools – and its impact upon teachers' practices and understandings of the ethnicity of their students – contributes to the promotion of what can be termed 'schooled identities' that operationalise this cultural imaginary. This is a process by which, despite various forms of sociocultural experience that constitute a student's identity, a narrow conception of their ethnicity is foregrounded, often providing a rationale for their academic performance and behaviour, techniques for addressing perceived learning needs and programs for encouraging cultural maintenance, community harmony and cultural awareness. This notion of 'schooled identities' is more obviously directed towards students whom we term non-Anglo: those with a language background other than English, in particular those students whose difference is more marked compared to the normative Anglo, English-speaking child. 'Anglo' seemed to operate as an ethnically neutral term in these schools. In contrast to their dealings with groups of non-Anglo students, teachers focused on the individual family experiences of students of Anglo background or categories such as class or gender over any notion of 'Anglo' ethnicity in explaining their academic performance. In other words, schools participate in the production of the ethnicised categories they service.

To exemplify how schooled identities operate, we want to focus on the students of 'Pasifika' backgrounds. Pasifika students are an increasingly large group in Sydney schools; many of them perform poorly on national literacy and numeracy tests and so receive attention through a range of state and school-based programs to improve their academic performance. Despite their varied cultural and linguistic backgrounds, not to mention that many of them were born in Australia, they are treated as a cohesive group. Certain programmes may target a particular Islander community but very often the more manageable 'Pasifika' label is applied with differences elided to ensure the requisite numbers for funding and the easier carriage of these programmess in schools. Categorised as a group, 'Pasifika learners' are represented as coming from societies that share much the same cultural system, and consequently their needs seem to be read from off a cultural template, as if their imagined ethnicity not only determined performance at school but the approach to teaching they should receive (Horsley and Walker, 2005).

While there is a need for mechanisms of cultural recognition, the consequences of some manifestations of this recognition can be problematic. Grouping students together as one entity to 'service' their needs may conflate internal cultural, linguistic and educational differences. In one school (Watkins and Noble, 2013), students of diverse backgrounds (Tongan, Samoan, Cook Islands, etc.) were 'lumped together' to make up the numbers for a funded community languages class for 'Pasifika' students, and assuming a shared heritage – but of course they do not share a language. As a consequence, the educational rationale of mother tongue maintenance – that it helps the student acquire the language of the host nation – is replaced by the view that students of the 'same background' will be valorised by such a class and somehow therefore do better at school. This may seem to be progressive from the school's perspective, but it conforms to the logic of ethnic aggregation found in the bureaucratic essentialism of multicultural policy. From there, it is a short step to forms of cultural pathology which obscure our understandings of learning practices, not aid them. Further, such classes mean that students of these 'same backgrounds' are removed from their usual class and thus from conventional lessons in English, maths, or whatever.

This 'lumping together' was commented upon by Sela, one of the Tongan community representatives:

> I hear we have a specific learning style that is the premise that a lot of teachers will work on. Because of the culture we come from, they think that there is – that we have – a different learning style, like the sing and the dance – and the teacher uses that.

In other words, there was a view that students of Pasifika backgrounds would engage more in schoolwork if aspects of 'traditional' culture such as singing and dancing were integrated into the curriculum. But this notion of 'learning style' moved far beyond the incorporation of such activities, and ultimately to affect a teacher's overall pedagogy. One set of professional development materials we found in schools declared that 'Pacific people are tactile and communal by nature and students engage in lessons that are rich in activity and involve group work' (Delmas, 2003, p. 12). Teachers receiving this literature were encouraged to use these perhaps less rigorous pedagogic modes with their Pasifika students, many of whom arguably needed a more structured approach to address their learning needs. Sela pointed out, in fact, that most of the classrooms in her homeland were very formal in orientation.

Putting the issue of the appropriateness of the pedagogy aside, such examples have much to say about the everyday practice of multiculturalism in schools. The simplistic connection that is made here between village life – something many of the students may never have experienced – and a predisposition for group-based learning, reflects the essentialising of ethnicity and the narrow conception of culture that often frames the ways in which cultural diversity is institutionally understood and managed. While a range of valuable and effective programs operate in schools under the umbrella of multicultural education, such as ESL, approaches which take such a narrow perspective on ethnicity have the potential to produce a kind of 'pedagogic apartheid': employing different teaching methodologies for students of perceived different ethnic backgrounds rather than focusing on learning needs, per se. While there is, of course, a cultural dimension to students' performance at school, it is far more complex than a matter of ethnicity. It relates also to class, gender, migration history and family practices. Despite an acknowledgement in education policy documents of the need to cater to the complex nature of cultural diversity and the challenges posed by varied immigration, increased settlement of refugees and transnationalism, 'ethnicity' is still largely understood in common sense terms as an unproblematic category based on clear and timeless boundaries around 'culture' or 'race'. Such an understanding, which fails to capture the hybrid reality of students' ethnicity, is a legacy of multiculturalism itself. As a policy founded on giving recognition to distinct ethnic communities, a notion prevails of ethnicity as being bounded. With these understandings firmly entrenched, there is some difficulty in conceptualising ethnicity in more fluid and heterogeneous terms.

Such a view of ethnicity also frames the ways in which many programs designed to foster cultural maintenance and awareness operate in schools. In our discussion with a group of high school students about the programmes in their school we were intrigued by the comments of a boy named Gary who, while of Tongan background, strongly identified as Australian. Gary had been encouraged to attend the Haka dance group at this school – Haka being a traditional ceremonial dance found in Polynesian societies. Gary explained that one of the good things about the group was that he got to experience his 'own culture'. When the comment was made that it was interesting that he had to come to school to experience his culture, Gary responded, 'Yeah, because, yeah my family are like, not really traditionally Tongan. We tend to blend with the Australian...yeah it is kind of weird.' What was foregrounded by the school, therefore, was Gary's Tongan heritage, and a particular 'traditional' view of that heritage, something the teachers felt obliged to maintain in promoting an ethos of multiculturalism. Yet for Gary, this aspect of his culture was remote, a part of his parents' past that had little connection with his everyday reality in Western Sydney. This is not to say there is no value in honouring these traditions, but there are three key issues here. First, there is no singular version of the Haka, because it varies across regions, so someone is making a choice about which version to teach, and 'recognising' (or *mis*recognising) students through that selection. Second, we have to ask whether it is the role of the school to ensure the maintenance of traditional cultural forms – to teach students their 'own' culture – particularly with students whose forms of identification are at odds with the way they are perceived by the school. Third, we have to consider that far from 'including' this difference, it is being reproduced as an exoticised, but possibly marginalised, difference.

The schemas of difference that operate here may not only serve to pigeonhole students as cultural product of imagined traditions but focusing on multiculturalism as a celebration of difference has little relevance for those who do not see themselves as different, or do not wish to be perceived this way. Also, focusing on multiculturalism is a celebration of a particular kind of difference; a difference linked to a notion of ethnicity as bounded and essentialised rather than the cultural hybridity more reflective of the student population and Australia in general. It is also a difference that sets Anglo students apart – multiculturalism is for others. Such a view was evident in the comments of a young Anglo girl in one of the primary schools we worked in. With their own take on inclusive curriculum as an aspect of multicultural education, this school in the outer western suburbs of Sydney with an ethnically diverse population of students, had set their Year 3 and 5 students, aged 8–10 years, the task of compiling digital photo stories about their cultural backgrounds, highlighting country of birth, customs, food, and so forth. This Year 3 student of Anglo background, however, was unsure she could complete the task. This was not so much because she felt she would have difficulty mastering the technology but, as she said to her teacher, 'I don't have a culture, Miss. I'm not different.' This attempt at inclusive curriculum was not inclusive of *this* child, or at least she saw it that way, which attests to the view that multicultural discourse has tended to exclude Anglo-Australians, particularly those who have not embraced the cosmo-multiculturalism that Hage (1998) critiques – a world quite alien to this working-class Anglo child in outer suburban Sydney. To her, the multicultural project she had been set was something for her classmates who were different – the Pasifika, Croatian, African, Indian and Aboriginal students.

As Ang (2001, p. 98) explains, multiculturalism has failed to provide '"old" Australians with ways of re-imagining themselves as an integral part of the "new" Australia'. Yet, even a child born into this new Australia is having difficulty recognising herself within the multicultural project of contemporary Australia. If Anglo-Australians do not see themselves as being within the cultural imaginary of multiculturalism, the flip side is that the 'differences' of her classmates set them apart and outside the mainstream culture of the nation. Multiculturalism's emphasis on distinct ethnic communities means that, despite the rhetoric of inclusivity, it promotes a kind of 'living-apart-together' (Ang, 2001) which, in schools, translates to educating-apart-together. While we would not necessarily agree with Wynter (1990) that multiculturalism represents little more than another form of racism, the celebration of difference that multicultural education promotes poses an obstacle if the goal is social inclusion, participation and civic belonging in culturally diverse society (Kalantzis, 2001; Gropas and Triandafyllidou, 2012, p. 149).

From multicultural education to reflexive civility

Does this multicultural approach signal the end of a policy in which migration-based nation-states have invested so strongly? We think not for, while there are problems, the term has traction among the populace. As indicated at the beginning, numerous studies in Australia report a general acceptance for cultural diversity, but what was evident in our work with teachers was the lack of conceptual resources for dealing with the lived reality of cultural complexity and the constraints this put on their professional vision. We want to suggest that multicultural education needs to embrace what we might call a 'reflexive civility', similar to Miera's (2007) account of a program of reflexive intercultural education and Harreveld's (2012) conception of 'cosmopolitan capabilities'. Civility, here, refers to a way of imagining and engaging in a shared, civic life which moves beyond the moral imperative that we acknowledge and 'respect' cultural groups and their values and customs to develop the critical capacities for understanding civic life and for living in a multicultural society; it is 'reflexive' then because it entails the capacities to reflect upon and analyse the historical specificity and dynamism of human cultures – as an ensemble of practices, identities and relations – including one's own. A reinvigorated educational programme for a multicultural Australia, then, must approach these elements as a fundamentally *intellectual* task, not simply an ethical one of respect for cultural difference. Such a programme would not just aim to celebrate forms of ancestral identification, nor simply to take into account the diverse backgrounds of students, but it would foster the kinds of critical skills and knowledge that are necessary for students and their teachers to unpack the complexity of culture in the complex societies of the twenty-first century.

This task begins not in the classroom, but in the professional development of teachers. Schools typically prioritise a focus on students as the target of educational change but, as this chapter has implied, this can only happen if teachers develop the critical resources for grappling with cultural complexity. We cannot teach young people the skills to understand and live in a culturally complex world unless the training of teachers equips them with the capacities to foster these skills (Harreveld,

2012; Henry, 2012). This is significant given that, as Timperley and Robinson (2000) argue, the implementation of effective multicultural educational programs is thwarted by a 'professional ethos' of autonomy in schools which actually discourages a collegial but critically reflective evaluation of practice.

Based on the research we have conducted in NSW schools, we would suggest that teachers participate in a programme of professional learning that involves a number of elements:

- the starting point that teachers are intellectual workers, not only practitioners or professionals, whose training in critical and analytical techniques needs to be constantly renewed and applied to their own practice;
- a reflection upon the forms of self-identification that teachers participate in, drawing upon a range of cultural resources: language, homeland and ancestries, faith, and so forth;
- a comparison of this complexity with the ways they talk about their students, the forms of 'complexity reduction' (Watkins, 2011) they engage in to make sense of classroom diversity, and the limitations of this;
- a critical engagement with the cultural dynamics of the contemporary world, shaped not simply by migration, per se, but by transnationalism, intermarriage, generational change, cultural appropriation and hybridisation;
- development of action research models whereby teachers bring these critical capacities to bear upon the circumstances of their own schools and classrooms, but which avoid assumptions of easy solutions based on reified notions of students' 'cultures'.

Such a program would promote an understanding of civic relations as predicated not on the focus on difference, per se, nor on a simplistic understanding of core national values, but on networked and articulated belonging that enables social life. This means understanding what Brubaker (2004) describes as 'ethnicity without groups', seeing ethnicity not in terms of reduced collective identities but as part of a heterogeneous mix of factors that constitute who we are and who we continue to become, and around which people only sometimes mobilise collectively. Moreover, this complexity means not just that each of us belongs to multiple groups, but that different kinds of groups are constituted in diverse ways (Eriksen, 2007, p. 1059). The issue is how people 'inhabit' such complexity as a lived reality.

Rather than a singular conceptualisation of ethnically defined identity, it is the complexity of cultural practices and relations that we should be investigating in classrooms. Culture is recognised as a process defined both by a degree of fluidity and stability. There may be some 'cultural coherence' and stability in relation to customs and language but, as Modood (2007, p. 89) outlines, this does not mean 'people of certain family, ethnic or geographical origins are always to be identified by their origins and indeed supposed to be behaviourally determined by them'. This has been a flaw of much multiculturalism and, so too, multicultural education. Construing culture in terms of practices rather than fixed identities brings to the foreground the idea of culture as a process, making and remaking, adapting and augmenting, appropriating and redefining. Students and teachers, both, need to develop these capacities if multicultural education is to have a meaningful impact.

Acknowledgements

The research upon which this article is based was funded by an Australian Research Council Linkage Project with the NSW DEC and the NSW Institute of Teachers. We wish to acknowledge the generous support of each body.

Note

1. 'Pasifika' is a term often used in Australia to describe students whose background is from one of many nations in the Pacific Ocean, such as Tonga, Samoa, Cook Islands, Fiji, and so on. In Australia, Maori students are often also included, though they are not included in this term in New Zealand. Members of these communities are also often known as Polynesian or 'Islanders'.

References

Allan, R. and Hill, B. (2004) 'Multicultural education in Australia: historical development and current status', in Banks, J. and McGee Banks, C. (eds), *Handbook on Research on Multicultural Education*, San Francisco, Jossey-Bass, 979–996.

Ang, I. (2001) *On Not Speaking Chinese*, London, Routledge.

Ang, I., Brand, J., Noble, G. and Wilding, D. (2002) *Living Diversity*, Artarmon, Special Broadcasting Service.

Ang, I., Brand, J., Noble, G. and Sternberg, J. (2006) *Connecting Diversity*, Artarmon, Special Broadcasting Service.

Australian Government (2011) *The People of Australia: Australia's Multicultural Policy*, Canberra, Department of Immigration and Citizenship. Available at http://www.immi.gov.au/media/publications/multicultural/pdf_doc/people-of-australia-multicultural-policy-booklet.pdf. [Accessed on 7 September 2012]

Bourdieu, P. (1996a) *The Rules of Art*, S. Emanuel (trans.), Cambridge, Polity Press.

Bourdieu, P. (1996b) *The State Nobility*, L. Clough (trans.), Cambridge, Polity Press.

Brubaker, R. (2004) *Ethnicity without Groups*, Cambridge, Cambridge MA, Harvard University Press.

Collins, J., Noble, G., Poynting, S. and Tabar, P. (2000) *Kebabs, Kids, Cops and Crime: Youth, Ethnicity and Crime*, Sydney, Pluto Press.

Delmas, J. (2003) *South Pacific Islander Students and Science Education: Addressing the Disparity*, NSW Premier's Macquarie Bank Science Scholarship Report, Darlinghurst, NSW Department of Education and Communities.

Donnelly, K. (2005) 'Perils of multicultural education', *The Australian*, December 19, 13.

Dunn, K.M., Forrest, J., Burnley, I. and McDonald, A. (2004) 'Constructing racism in Australia', *Australian Journal of Social Issues*, 39 (4), 409–430.

Eriksen, T.H. (2007) 'Complexity in social and cultural integration', *Ethnic and Racial Studies*, 30 (6), 1055–1069.

Goodwin, C. (1994) 'Professional vision', *American Anthropologist*, 96 (3) 606–633.

Gropas, R. and Triandafyllidou, A. (2012) 'Religious diversity and education', in Triandafyllidou, A., Modood, T. and Meer N. (eds), *European Multiculturalism*, Edinburgh, Edinburgh University Press, 145–166.

Hage, G. (2002) *Against Paranoid Nationalism*, Sydney, Pluto Press.

Hage, G. (1998) *White Nation*, Sydney, Pluto Press.

Harreveld, R. (2012) 'Repositioning multiculturalism in teacher education policy and practice: a case for cosmopolitan capabilities', in Wright, H., Singh, M. and Race, R. (eds), *Precarious International Multicultural Education*, Rotterdam, Sense Publishers, 259–276.

Henry, A. (2012) 'The problematics of multiculturalism in a post-racial America', in Wright, H., Singh, M. and Race, R. (eds), *Precarious International Multicultural Education*, Rotterdam, Sense Publishers, 41–60.

Horsley, M. and Walker, R. (2005) 'Pasifika Australia: culturally responsive curriculum and teaching', in McInerney, D. (ed.), *Effective Schools. Vol. 5, Research on Sociocultural Influences on Motivation and Learning*, Greenwich, Information Age Publishing, 327–351.

Inglis, C. (2009) 'Multicultural education in Australia: two generations of evolution', in Banks, J. (ed.), *The Routledge International Companion to Multicultural Education*, New York, Routledge, 109–120.

Jakubowicz, A., Morrissey, M. and Palser, J. (1984) *Ethnicity, Class and Social Policy in Australia*, Social Welfare Research Centre Report No. 46., Kensington, University of New South Wales.

Kalantzis, M. (2001) 'Civic pluralism and total globalisation', in Buckley, B. and Conomos, J. (eds), *Republics of Ideas: Republicanism, Culture, Visual Arts*, Annandale, Pluto and Artspace Visual Arts Centre, 110–123.

Koleth, E. (2010) 'Multiculturalism: a review of Australian policy statements and recent debates in Australia and overseas', Research Paper No. 6, Library, Canberra, Parliament of Australia.

Lentin, A. and Titley, G. (2011) *The Crises of Multiculturalism: Racism in a Neoliberal Age*, London, Zed Books.

Martin, J. (1978) *The Migrant Presence*, Sydney, George Allen and Unwin.

Miera, F. (2007) 'German Education Policy and the Challenge of Migration'. Paper prepared for the EMILIE research project funded by the European Commission

Research DG, Sixth Framework Programme, Frankfurt. Available at http://www. eliamep.gr/eliamep/files/German_Education_policy_and_the_Challenge_of_ Migration.pdf. [Accessed on 7 September 2012]

Modood, T. (2007) *Multiculturalism*, Cambridge, Polity Press.

Noble, G. and Poynting, S. (2000) 'Multicultural education and intercultural understanding: ethnicity, culture and schooling', in Dinham, S. and Scott, C. (eds), *Teaching in Context*, Camberwell, Australian Council for Educational Research Press, 56–81.

NSW Department of Education and Communities (2012) *Key Statistics and Information*. Available at http://www.dec.nsw.gov.au/about-us/statistics-and-research/key-statistics-and-reports. [Accessed on 7 September 2012]

Parekh, B. (2006) *Rethinking Multiculturalism*, 2nd Edition, Houndsmills, Palgrave.

Spivak, G. (1990) *Post-Colonial Critic*, London, Routledge.

Timperley, H.S. and Robinson, V. (2000) 'Workload and the professional culture of teachers', *Educational Management and Administration*, 28 (1), 47–62.

Watkins, M. (2011) 'Complexity reduction, regularities and rules: grappling with cultural diversity in schooling', *Continuum*, 25 (6), 841–856.

Watkins, M. and Noble, G. (2013) *Disposed to Learn: Diversity, Discipline and Dispositions in Schooling*, London,. Bloomsbury.

Wynter, S. (1990) *Do Not Call Us Negroes: How Multicultural Textbooks Perpetuate Racism*, San Francisco, Aspire.

Yúdice, G. (2003) *The Expediency of Culture: Uses of Culture in the Global Era*. Durham NC, Duke University Press.

11
Using Specialist Software to Assist Knowledge Generation: An Example from a Study of Practitioners' Perceptions of Music as a Tool for Ethnic Inclusion in Cross-Community Activities in Northern Ireland

Oscar Odena

Introduction

This chapter discusses how using specialist software for qualitative data analysis may best be reported to substantiate researchers' claims. The first part outlines a generative model of social knowledge development as a means to understand the role researchers play in producing new knowledge, and it suggests where software, if used, may be placed within this model. In the second part of the chapter some possibilities of software for Computer Assisted Qualitative Data Analysis (CAQDAS) to assist researchers in substantiating their assertions are discussed. This is exemplified with an examination of the interview analyses processes employed in a study on using musical activities as a tool for inclusion in intergroup settings in Northern Ireland. Implications for those interested in advancing race and ethnicity within education are considered in the concluding section.

Generating social knowledge

In the second half of the twentieth century social research developed remarkably, a fact evidenced by the coming of age of an increasing number of knowledge areas, with new research centres round the globe and new specialist research handbooks produced by major publishers.

Epistemological developments resulted in qualitative research approaches being incorporated into the academy and perceived as valid means for obtaining useful knowledge. Many journals were, and continue to be, founded which explicitly encourage authors to submit papers embracing a wide variety of research approaches, including qualitative and mixed methods (the growing list of journals listed in the *Journal Citation Reports* is witness to this development).

Depending on the questions asked, on the topic(s) addressed and the context of the enquiry, each knowledge area has traditionally tended to favour particular research practices. This has resulted in some approaches being developed in particular areas and later being used by others working in related fields – for example, ethnography being developed within anthropology studies and later used by educational researchers. Regardless of varying research practices in different traditions, the type of claims made by social researchers would seem to range from (a) isolated observations that capture their initial interest, to (b) the elaboration of (inconclusive) observations when a number of details are put together, and to (c) the development of claims substantiated by corroborated evidence supported by multiple layers of data analyses. Whereas isolated and inconclusive observations may entice readers to think about a particular topic, or even inspire them to re-focus all their working efforts, arguably claims substantiated by corroborated evidence are interpreted and used in a very different way. For example, policy-makers and professional associations may develop new programmes and projects based on such substantiated claims. Looking for alternative explanations and supporting one's claims with systematic analyses processes may be seen as part of the conscientious researcher's work ethic, regardless of knowledge area. Even if the 'eureka' moment,[1] when generating a new theory came from an isolated observation, any new theory would need to be tested systematically against the available data to make sure that it is sound rather than fanciful, and that it will stand the scrutiny of peers. Sometimes this may comprise gathering additional data to examine how the new theory makes sense (or not) in light of the new data. Figure 11.1 below outlines a generative model of social-knowledge development first proposed elsewhere (Odena, 2012a). The arrow on the left represents the degree of in-depth data analyses required to produce new knowledge. In this model, the three types of knowledge claims outlined above are closely linked with the quality of evidence used to support them.

Analysing data from social settings would include a broad variety of activities: from recording the frequency of observed behaviours in a

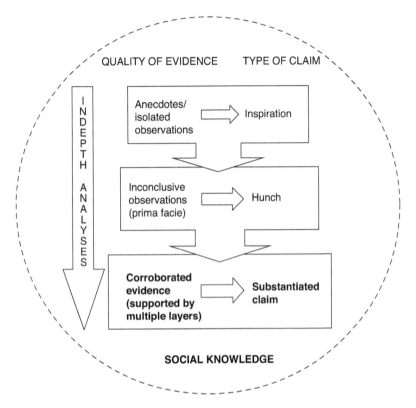

Figure 11.1   A generative model of social knowledge development
Source: Adapted from Odena (2012a).

video extract, to identifying themes in conversations through repeated readings of transcripts, to regularly brainstorming with team members and critical friends to move the interim analysis forward. Regardless of the steps of the analysis process, its ultimate aim would be to make sense of the results, developing from the data some meaning which is relevant to the aim(s) of the enquiry – and if this was not possible, to suggest why not. I would argue that investing time and a degree of planning and reflexion are often preconditions to successful meaning-making in data analysis. Paraphrasing Schön (1983) and Day (1999), two types of reflexion would be needed: reflexion-*in*-analysis and reflexion -*on*-analysis. These would be the reflections done on the spot (*in*), likely to draw on existing frameworks, and the reflection done before and after the analysis (*on*), following a 'process of deliberation enabling analysis, reconstruction and reframing in order to plan for further action' and opening up possibilities for talking with others about analysis processes (Day, 1999, p. 23).

The debate around using software for qualitative data analysis

The above suggested preconditions to successful meaning-making in data analysis – time investment and planning/reflecting – have been affected by the use of Information Communication Technologies (ICTs), changing the work patterns of many social researchers and creating a degree of controversy. Researchers currently use ICTs not just for gathering/managing data and writing up documents, but for assisting in the analysis process. Specialist software employed in CAQDAS can aid the researchers' tasks of testing alternative hypotheses and of creating a multilayered analysis.[2] Some of the advantages described in the CAQDAS literature include increased power for searching and making links across datasets and for keeping track of emerging ideas (Evers, 2011; Fielding and Lee, 1998; Hutchison, Johnston and Breckon, 2010; Konopásek, 2008; Lewins and Silver, 2007; Odena, 2012a). However, for a number of reasons some researchers are wary of using specialist software for qualitative data analysis. For instance, if used rigidly, the software chosen may come to define the analysis it should merely be employed to support, de-contextualising the dataset (e.g., when not enough time is spent by the researcher to reflect upon whether any predefined categories may need modifying/deleting if they do not accurately represent topics emerging from the dataset). Another criticism is that researchers may become carried away with frequency counts in transcripts rather than working toward interpretation of their meaning (Richards, 2002).[3] Ultimately, the relevance of frequency counts would normally depend on the focus of the study and on how the research questions are framed.

Some packages have autocoding facilities (e.g., *Qualrus*), which can be useful for assisting in the analysis of large datasets resulting from structured interviews. However, it has been suggested that overreliance on autocoding is dangerous because it assumes that specific ideas are addressed by interviewees using similar words (Alkin, 2010). When using a software package researchers would need to be aware not only of the new analysis possibilities afforded but of any subtle changes in their own ways of organising, reading and interpreting the datasets; in other words, researchers would need to reflect on how these changes may affect the meaning-making process.

The purpose of this chapter is not to offer a description of the facilities of specialist software packages', but to discuss how these facilities can be used and reported on by researchers to better support their work. Analysis processes are not always discussed in research publications. Sometimes the word limit does not allow for a detailed explanation of methods and methodology, and the authors mention only in passing the analysis approach employed (e.g., thematic analysis, grounded theory) without disclosing in detail the particular processes followed. At other times, due to the publisher's remit, reports focus on results and implications for practice, assuming that a detailed discussion of the research methodology may not be equally interesting. Nevertheless, I would argue that such discussion would be necessary whenever implications for practice are developed from empirical data, in order to show how they are substantiated in the researchers' data analyses. The next section offers an account of a worked example of using specialist software to develop category construction and to substantiate the researchers' conclusions.

An account of a worked example: using software to assist the analysis of interviews on the potential of music as a tool for inclusion in cross-community activities

The example of software use outlined in this section comes from an exploratory study of practitioners' views on the potential of music education activities as a tool for ethnic inclusion in cross-community settings in post-conflict Northern Ireland (Odena, 2009a, 2010, in press). The main aim of the study was to explore how to develop music skills while bringing together children from both main communities – Protestant and Catholic. Seventeen interviewees were purposefully selected following a 'maximum variation sampling' approach, taking into account their potential as 'key informants' as determined by having extended experience with this type of cross-community activity (Cohen, Manion and Morrison, 2011). Interviewees were working in, or had worked in, a wide variety of contexts, including: teacher-education colleges; the inspectorate; Nursery, Primary and Secondary schools; specialist music schools, and out-of-school music projects. The interviews were semi-structured and attempted to explore the participants' backgrounds, their views on music education in Northern Ireland (NI) and advice on how to increase the effectiveness of cross-community projects.

Participants were interviewed in their work settings and, in most cases, they showed the building facilities and invited the researcher to observe some activities and talk with the children and/or any other adults present. Interviews with key informants were digitally recorded and fully transcribed; 230 double-spaced pages of transcriptions were analysed using thematic analysis with the assistance of specialist software (*NVivo*). The analysis process involved reading the transcripts and looking for emerging patterns and ideas to form initial categories, followed by repeated readings until all categories were checked against all responses. With each reading, the names of categories, their number and internal organisation, would develop, as categories were modified, sometimes merged or deleted. Table 11.1 below shows 31 categories and subcategories (indented) that emerged from the initial analysis.

Table 11.1   Initial categorisation of interview transcripts

1. teacher training provided
2. teacher training provided/students going abroad
3. teacher training provided/practicum organisation
4. teacher training provided/student teachers background
5. music education in NI
6. music education in NI/NI size
7. music education in NI/recent improvement
8. music education in NI/past project not cross-community
9. advice
10. advice/difficulties of cross-community education
11. advice/different activities in diff schools
12. cross-community project
13. cross-community project/Marvellous Medicine
14. cross-community project/music at School A
15. cross-community project/music at School A/students backgrounds
16. cross-community project/music at School of M.
17. cross-community project/music at School of M./students' background
18. cross-community project/music at School of M./Music Makers
19. cross-community project/Nursery projects
20. music potential for working together
21. music potential for working together/children's potential
22. music potential for working together/music potential – memories
23. stereotypes & alienation
24. stereotypes & alienation/music as sign of identity
25. egalitarian concerns
26. Education for Mutual Understanding
27. intergenerational differences
28. more key practitioners
29. socio-economic factors
30. teachers' background
31. teachers' self-perception

Subsequently, selected quotations from the above categories were discussed with colleagues and two groups of postgraduate students at Queen's University Belfast. The categorisation was then further refined, resulting in the final list of 11 categories shown in Table 11.2 below. The software assisted in the researcher's grouping of relevant quotations under the emerging categories and subcategories. It also facilitated printed reports with all quotations in any given category from which to select representative quotations for discussion with colleagues. This ensured that the emerging analysis was: (a) regularly double-checked for internal consistency by the researcher, and (b) discussed with local students and colleagues for increased validity and reliability. For example: *Is this addressing the research aim? Are we interpreting the data in a similar way?* When needed, the software capabilities assisted in re-categorising particular quotations and facilitated the constant comparison between the contents of new emerging categories and older categories.

Table 11.2   List of categories, in bold, and subcategories, in *Italics*

---

1. Teacher education
  School placements provided
  Student teachers' background
2. Music education in NI
  Different activities in different schools
3. Project processes and effectiveness
  Barriers for cross-community education
4. Cross-community projects
  'Marvellous Medicine'
  The School of Music's 'Music Makers'
  Nursery projects
  Music at Integrated School A
  Music at Integrated School B
  Grammar School A cross-community project
  Grammar School B music education
5. Music education potential
  Children's potential
  Music potential in participants' paths
6. Music as a sign of identity
  Stereotypes & alienation
7. Education for Mutual Understanding cross-curricular theme
8. Intergenerational differences
9. Information on potential key practitioners
10. Socio-economic factors
11. Participants' backgrounds

Source: Adapted from Odena (2010).

After a number of readings, re-readings and discussions with colleagues, some initial categories were merged with subcategories when these did not actually reveal any distinctive ideas to merit a separate label. For example, the initial subcategory, 'egalitarian concerns', which contained a small number of quotations on young children's educational opportunities, was finally merged with the category 'Socio-economic factors.' The software's flexibility not only assisted in developing categories across settings (e.g., 'Barriers for cross-community education') but also within settings. For instance, a number of subcategories were developed focussing on each type of setting, under category 4 'Cross-community projects':

The final categories focussed on a number of issues, including 'Project processes and effectiveness' and the potential of music activities as a tool for inclusion (e.g., 'Music potential in participants' paths'). Over 90 per cent of the text within the transcripts was finally categorised, and a table with the number of quotations for each category was included in subsequent outputs to show that final categories were not anecdotal. The analysis evidenced how the activities and aims explained by interviewees varied depending on a number of factors, one of the most important being the level of acknowledgment of integration of the educational setting, which appeared to be influenced by the socio-economic environment. For example, in the more prosperous areas of Belfast there were grammar schools with a rich variety of in-school and out-of-school music activities. These would include Irish folk groups (of Catholic/ Nationalist tradition), brass and flute bands (of Protestant/Loyalist tradition) and church choirs, all in the same building and welcoming children from both communities. Parents interested in supporting the development of the musical abilities of their children would take them to these schools regardless of their own religious orientation. Arguably, these were not the children living in economically deprived areas where conflict between and within violent groups and lack of jobs seemed to feed a cycle of low aspirations for young people (Northern Ireland Statistics and Research Agency, 2005; Lloyd, 2009). At the time of data collection (2007–2009) segregation was acute in areas that were labelled as 'hot spots' during 'the troubles'. In these areas prejudice remained, and it was coupled with internal violence exacerbated by socio-economic problems such as high unemployment (McKittrick et al., 2007; Odena, 2010). The quotation below describing a violent attack (with a reference to a Loyalist song) is an example of the low-key violence that was reported regularly in local Northern Ireland newspapers, but was rarely reported in UK-wide media:

Much was made during the week about claims by travel writer Simon Calder that the 'Troubles Murals' are world class tourist attractions...Better not tell about the 18-year-old Protestant motorcyclist who was knocked down by a hit and run driver on the Shankill [a notoriously Loyalist area] during the week. He managed to struggle to his feet in spite of a fractured leg and other injuries. He was approached by three people who wanted to know if he was Catholic or Protestant. They asked him to sing the Sash. He did not know the words. Notwithstanding his fractured leg and no doubt traumatised state, they attacked him. He managed to get away and, while running for his life on his fractured leg, he heard them shouting that they were going to wreck his bike. And if he had made it to an ambulance, it would probably have been attacked by nationalist youths because it had just left the Shankill. (Anderson, 2007, p. 16)

It would need to be pointed out that over 80 conflict-related deaths have occurred since 2000, with evidence that in former 'hot spots' children are still regularly exposed to violence and unresolved feuds.[4] For some young people growing up in these areas, cross-community projects can be the only opportunity to meet with people from the other community in a constructive setting. It is apparent that cross-community music projects have been and continue to be an effective means of addressing prejudice amongst children, although addressing prejudice may have not always been the aim of all projects reported by interviewees, but a welcomed side effect.

The data analysis also highlighted some barriers for this type of project, such as unenthusiastic parents, unsupportive school principals and funding shortages, as well as some remaining negative stereotypes linked with the music traditions of each community. One of the practical suggestions outlined by all interviewees was to avoid any melodies that had a political overlay or could be perceived as having one, unless the activities were carried out in integrated schools (which have an integrated ethos welcoming children from across the divide[5]). Regardless of any barriers, music was perceived as an ideal tool to use in cross-community activities because of the ease children had in working collaboratively in musical tasks, and the potential of music to allow for creative development. Projects and activities described included a one-day visit between two Nurseries, with music and movement activities, a creative music project called 'Music Makers', with over 50 Primary schools – all culminating in a one-day workshop in central Belfast and musical activities in integrated schools. The non-competitive and creative aspect of all of these examples was stressed by two participants involved in coordinating 'Music Makers':

> We really stress the importance that it's not competitive ... [I]t's very much to give the children an opportunity to show off what they have done and ... to encourage the children to be creative and the teachers not to be frightened of creativity. (Teacher educator)

All classes participating in the above project prepared an original composition on a given theme, using voices and school instruments, and they rehearsed a number of common songs. Teachers were offered music training workshops at the start and were regularly asked for feedback, which avoids feedback channelled into the organisation of the project, in a way akin to collaborative action research (e.g., Leitch et al., 2007; Reason and Bradbury, 2008). In addition, the coordinators went into Primary schools to advise and mentor the teachers' development of music skills, running sessions alongside teachers before the final cross-community days in which children sang the common repertoire and played their compositions in front of three to five Primary classes from different schools. Overall, the potential to develop music skills while bringing children from both communities together was acknowledged by the interviewees' many positive experiences in their own education and current work with children:

> [Children] can inspire people like no other group of people can ... [Music] is a superb tool ... I've got to the stage now where I can see children not being aware of their cultural background and if you give them a task to do that involves percussion instruments and music and movement, they will throw themselves into it wholeheartedly and are quite prepared to work with other people in doing that. (Composer and music workshop leader)

Interviewees were enthusiastic with the activities reported, and they observed increased cohesion and positive awareness towards the other main group as a welcome side effect. Nevertheless, in repeated readings of the categorised transcripts, it became clear that most of the one-day activities reported on would only fall within what has been called in the social psychology literature as the beginning stage of intergroup prejudice reduction (e.g., Pettigrew, 1998; Odena, 2010). In this first stage, contact is established, but no lasting change occurs on the perception towards the other group. The projects described may in fact not be as effective in reducing prejudice as one could imagine from a first visit to the cross-community settings or from a quick reading of the transcripts. The specialist software allowed for repeated analyses after break periods in which new literature was read, taking up things where they were left, and assisting in meaning-making by, for example, facilitating repeated readings of all quotations within each category, making sure that no stone was left unturned.

Conclusions: implications for advancing race and ethnicity studies within education.

From the above exploratory study it can be suggested that one-off activities would need continuity with the same actors if the aim is to achieve a more lasting effect in terms of prejudice reduction. It is apparent that the level of integration of the setting affects the choice of activities that can be implemented. Activities that would work in one place may not work or be accepted by participants elsewhere. For instance, melodies with political connotations from the opposite side of the Northern Ireland divide would not be accepted in schools in former hot spots, but the same melodies would be played at public performances of cross-community ensembles in the 'leafy' neighbourhoods of Belfast. A similar principle applies when developing activities across post-conflict societies.

Discussing how to use music as a tool for inclusion with Greek Cypriot teachers in Larnaca, it became clear that their post-conflict society had unique characteristics and complexities, resulting in different school settings (Odena, 2009b). Teachers in Cyprus were eager to learn musical activities used in Northern Ireland to apply them in their schools but they had to first explore and assess the level of integration of their work setting, and in most cases they needed to develop their own activities.[6]

I would argue that an appropriate approach to carry out such exploration would be a collaborative professional enquiry approach, in which professionals willingly explore their own practice with the aim of improving it, periodically reviewing what they do through individual and group work and reflection (Reason and Bradbury, 2008). In addition, practitioners need time and space to develop an understanding of their own values to avoid reinforcing 'the psychological barriers which sustain division' (Donnelly, 2004, p. 263), particularly as the implementation of activities is ultimately up to them.

For the sake of clarity, and to facilitate the assessment of the increasing number of published reports and articles, researchers would need to disclose the amount of data collected and the steps followed in analysing each dataset. This would include explaining how specialist software was used (if any) and a consideration of how its use may have affected the meaning-making process, allowing readers to assess whether the conclusions were built on the data collected, on the authors' personal viewpoints, or a degree of both. These suggestions would apply to any researchers carrying out qualitative analysis of data from social settings.

Acknowledgments

The Bernard van Leer Foundation supported the above study. Thanks to all interviewees for generously giving their time and to colleagues at Queen's University Belfast and the University of Brighton for their support at different stages of the project. Institutions and individuals that provided contacts, literature and feedback were acknowledged in the final report and other relevant outputs (Odena, 2009a, 2010, in press).

Notes

1. Since the beginning of the twentieth century, the creative process has been researched from a variety of disciplines, including psychology, philosophy, aesthetics, musicology and music education. For a review of literature on creativity relevant to formal education, see Odena (2012b). A number of research-based reviews are available with a particular focus on creativity in arts education (e.g., Burnard, 2007), music education (e.g., Odena, 2012c; Welch, 2012) and music psychology (e.g., Webster, 2009). For interested readers, Kaufman and Sternberg's volumes (2006, 2010) offer comprehensive reviews on creativity research and its worldwide development.
2. The CAQDAS Networking Project hosts a non-commercial website based at the University of Surrey, UK, that includes information about all the leading software packages as well as topical sections for beginners and more advanced users (www.surrey.ac.uk/sociology/research/researchcentres/caqdas). A discussion of two particular packages (Odena, 2007) and a problematisation of its uses (Odena, 2012a) are available elsewhere.
3. A comprehensive discussion of the arguments for and against the use of CAQDAS can be found in Lu and Shulman (2008) and Richards (2002).
4. From 1966 to the late 1990s, over 3,700 people were killed and tens of thousands injured due to direct fighting between and within Republican and Loyalist groupings, the British army and the local police (McEvoy et al., 2006; Muldoon, 2004). All these deaths are documented in *Lost lives* (McKittrick et al., 2007), a comprehensive volume that in its latest edition included 75 deaths occurred after [2,000], twenty-five of which resulted from internal Loyalist feuding, taking the death toll up to 3,720. Since then, a number of Catholic police officers have been killed by Nationalist splinter groups, and such dissident violent groupings still exist in both communities.

5. Less than 1 in 10 Primary, Secondary and Grammar schools are currently classified as 'Integrated', balancing their intake between the two main communities, a movement that was started as early as 1981 as a response to the conflict.
   For more information on the segregation of the Northern Ireland education
   system please see Connolly (2009), Gallagher (2004), Integrated Education
   Fund (2012) and Kilpatrick and Leitch (2004).
6. Cyprus was partitioned after an armed conflict that claimed over 5,000 lives
   (1974–1978), leaving the North and South under Turkish and Greek Cypriot
   control, respectively (Bercovitch and Jackson, 1997). Since the opening of
   crossing-points in 2003, people from the North have been allowed to work in
   the South, where salaries are higher and some schools are now accepting children from both communities (Zembylas, Kendeou and Michaelidou, 2011;
   Zembylas and Bekerman, 2012).

References

Alkin, M.C. (2010) *Evaluation Essentials*, New York, Guilford.

Anderson, G. (2007) Welcome to the zoo...', in *The Belfast Telegraph*, Weekender,
Saturday, 11 August, 16.

Bercovitch, J. and Jackson, R. (1997) *International Conflict: A Chronological
Encyclopedia of Conflicts and their Management 1945–1995*, Washington, D.C.,
Congressional Quarterly Press.

Burnard, P. (ed.) (2007) 'Creativity. Section 11', in Bresler, L. (ed.), *International
Handbook of Research in Arts Education*, Dordrecht, Springer, 1173–1290.

Cohen, L., Manion, L. and Morrison, K. (2011) *Research Methods in Education*, 7th
edition, London, Routledge.

Connolly, P. (2009) 'Developing programmes to promote ethnic diversity in early
childhood: lessons from Northern Ireland', Working Paper No. 52, The Hague,
The Netherlands, Bernard van Leer Foundation.

Day, C. (1999) *Developing Teachers: The Challenges of Lifelong Learning*, London,
Falmer Press.

Donnelly, C. (2004) 'Constructing the ethos of tolerance and respect in an integrated school: the role of teachers', *British Educational Research Journal*, 30 (2),
263–278.

Evers, J. (2011) 'From the past into the future: how technological developments change our ways of data collection, transcription and analysis'. *Forum:
Qualitative Social Research*, 12 (1). Available at www.qualitative-research.net/
index.php/fqs/article/view/1636/3161. [Accessed on 28 August 2012]

Fielding, N.G. and Lee, R.M. (1998) *Computer Analysis and Qualitative Research*,
London, Sage.

Gallagher, A.M. (2004) *Education in Divided Societies*, London, Palgrave Macmillan.

Hutchison, A.J., Johnston, L.H. and Breckon, J.D. (2010) 'Using QSR-NVivo
to facilitate the development of a grounded theory project: an account of a
worked example', *International Journal of Social Research Methodology*, 13 (4),
283–302.

Integrated Education Fund (2012) *Who We are Background: History of Integrated
Education*. Available at www.ief.org.uk/aboutus/whoweare. [Accessed on 28
August 2012]

Kaufman, J.C. and Sternberg, R.J. (eds) (2006) *The International Handbook of Creativity*, Cambridge, Cambridge University Press.

Kaufman, J.C. and Sternberg, R.J. (eds) (2010) *The Cambridge Handbook of Creativity*, Cambridge, Cambridge University Press.

Kilpatrick, R. and Leitch, R. (2004) 'Teachers' and pupils' educational experiences and school-based responses to the conflict in Northern Ireland', *Journal of Social Issues*, 60 (3), 563–586.

Konopásek, Z. (2008) 'Making thinking visible with Atlas.ti: computer assisted qualitative analysis as textual practices', *Forum: Qualitative Social Research*, 9 (2). Available at www.qualitative-research.net/index.php/fqs/article/view/420. [Accessed on 28 August 2012]

Leitch, R., Gardner, J., Mitchell, S., Lundy, L., Odena, O., Galanouli, D. and Clough, P. (2007) 'Consulting pupils in Assessment for Learning classrooms: the twists and turns of working with students as co-researchers', *Educational Action Research*, 15 (3), 459–478.

Lewins, A. and Silver, Ch. (2007) *Using Software in Qualitative Research: A Step-by-Step Guide*, London, Sage.

Lloyd, T. (2009) *Stuck in the Middle: Some Young Men's Attitudes and Experience of Violence, Conflict and Safety*, Londonderry, Centre for Young Men's Studies, University of Ulster.

Lu, Ch.-J. and Shulman, S.W. (2008) 'Rigor and flexibility in computer-based qualitative research: introducing the coding analysis toolkit', *International Journal of Multiple Research Approaches*, 2 (1), 105–117.

McEvoy, L., McEvoy, K. and McConnachie, K. (2006) 'Reconciliation as dirty word: conflict, community relations and education in Northern Ireland', *Journal of International Affairs*, 60 (1), 81–106.

McKittrick, D., Kelters, S., Feeney, B. and Thornton, C. (1999) *Lost Lives: The Stories of the Men, Women and Children Who Died As a Result of the Northern Ireland Troubles*, 1st edition, Edinburgh, Mainstream Publishing.

McKittrick, D., Kelters, S., Feeney, B., Thornton, C. and McVea, D. (2007) *Lost Lives: The Stories of the Men, Women and Children Who Died As a Result of the Northern Ireland Troubles*, updated edition, Edinburgh, Mainstream Publishing.

Muldoon, O.T. (2004) 'Children of the troubles: the impact of political violence in Northern Ireland', *Journal of Social Issues*, 60 (3), 453–468.

Northern Ireland Statistics and Research Agency (2005) *Northern Ireland Multiple Deprivation Measure 2005*, Belfast, NI Statistics and Research Agency.

Odena, O. (2007) 'Using specialist software for qualitative data analysis', *Educationline*. Available at www.leeds.ac.uk/educol/documents/165945.pdf. [Accessed on 28 August 2012]

Odena, O. (2009a) *Early Music Education As a Tool for Inclusion and Respect for Diversity: Study Paper for the Bernard van Leer Foundation*. Available at the University of Hertfordshire Research Archive (UHRA) at https://uhra.herts.ac.uk/dspace/handle/2299/6227. [Accessed 28 August 2012]

Odena, O. (2009b) 'Invited keynote speaker on using music education as a tool for inclusion at the International Peace Education and Interculturalism Conference, Cyprus Pedagogical Institute, 18–19 November 2009'. Available in UHRA at https://uhra.herts.ac.uk/dspace/handle/2299/6179. [Accessed on 28 August 2012]

Odena, O. (2010) 'Practitioners' views on cross-community music education projects in Northern Ireland: alienation, socio-economic factors and educational potential', *British Educational Research Journal*, 36 (1), 83–105.

Odena, O. (2012a) 'Using software to tell a trustworthy, convincing and useful story', *International Journal of Social Research Methodology*. Available in iFirst at: www.tandfonline.com/doi/abs/10.1080/13645579.2012.706019. [Accessed on 28 August 2012]

Odena, O. (2012b) 'Creativity in the secondary music classroom', in McPherson, G.E. and Welch, G.F. (eds), *The Oxford Handbook of Music Education*, vol. 1, Oxford, Oxford University Press, 512–528.

Odena, O. (ed.) (2012c) *Musical Creativity: Insights from Music Education Research*, Farnham and Burlington VT, Ashgate.

Odena, O. (in press) 'Musical creativity as a tool for inclusion', in Shiu, E. (ed.), *Creativity Research: An Interdisciplinary and Multidisciplinary Research Handbook*, London, Routledge.

Pettigrew, T.F. (1998) 'Intergroup contact theory', *Annual Review of Psychology*, 49 (1), 65–85.

Reason, P. and Bradbury, H. (eds) (2008) *'The SAGE Handbook of Action Research: Participative Inquiry and Practice*, 2nd edition, London, Sage.

Richards, L. (2002) 'Qualitative computing – a methods revolution?' *International Journal of Social Research Methodology*, 5 (3), 263–276.

Schön, D.A. (1983) *The Reflective Practitioner: How Professionals Think in Action*, London, Basic Books.

Webster, P. (ed.) (2009) 'Part 8: composition and improvisation', in Hallam, S., Cross, I. and Thaut, M. (eds), *The Oxford Handbook of Music Psychology*, Oxford, Oxford University Press, 401–428.

Welch, G. (2012) 'Musical creativity, biography, genre and learning', In Hargreaves, D., Miell, D. and MacDonald, R. (eds), *Musical Imaginations: Multidisciplinary Perspectives on Creativity, Performance and Perception*, Oxford and New York, Oxford University Press, 385–398.

Zembylas, M. and Bekerman, Z. (2012) *Teaching Contested Narratives: Identity, Memory and Reconciliation in Peace Education and Beyond*, Cambridge, Cambridge University Press.

Zembylas, M., Kendeou, P. and Michaelidou, A. (2011) 'The emotional readiness of Greek Cypriot teachers for peaceful co-existence', *European Journal of Education*, 46 (4), 524–539.

12
The Sheer Weight of Whiteness in the Academy: A UK Case Study

Andrew Pilkington

The questions that this chapter addresses have their origins in the murder of a young man. Stephen Lawrence was killed on 22 April 1993 as he waited at a bus stop in South London with his friend, Duwayne Brooks. What prompted a group of White youths to attack him was the colour of Stephen's skin. Stephen was stabbed to death because he was Black (Macpherson, 1999). Although the racist murder of Stephen Lawrence is by no means unique, there is no doubt that it is this case which has received the greatest media attention and resonated most with people across ethnic boundaries (Cottle, 2004). This is due in no small measure to Stephen's parents, Doreen and Neville Lawrence, who exhibited extraordinary resilience in seeking justice for their son and mounted a campaign to that end. While they faced innumerable obstacles, including a flawed police investigation that prevented Stephen's murderers from being successfully prosecuted, their patience and persistence did eventually pay off. They persuaded the incoming Labour government in July 1997 to set up a judicial inquiry into the police investigation of their son's murder, and subsequently two people have been convicted of Stephen's murder and been sent to prison .

The charge of institutional racism

The inquiry was conducted by a former judge of the High Court, Sir William Macpherson of Cluny. The public hearings began on 24 March 1998 and the final report was published on 24 February 1999. The main findings are summarised very crisply:

> The conclusions to be drawn from all the evidence in connection with the investigation of Stephen Lawrence's racist murder are clear.

There is no doubt but that there were fundamental errors. The investigation was marred by a combination of professional incompetence, institutional racism and a failure of leadership by senior officers. A flawed Metropolitan Police Service review failed to expose these inadequacies. The second investigation could not salvage the faults of the first investigation. (Macpherson, 1999, para 46.1)

Although the primary focus of the inquiry was on the police, the report suggested that all major organisations in British society are characterised by institutional racism.

Racism, institutional or otherwise, is not the prerogative of the Police service. It is clear that other agencies including for example those dealing with … education also suffer from the disease. (Macpherson, 1999, para 6.54)

This was an extraordinary admission, since 'for 30 years British officialdom had consistently denied that it had any meaning when applied to Britain' (Parekh, 2000, p. 72). What is also remarkable about the willingness of the government, and indeed myriad other institutions (see Singh, 2000, pp. 34–35), to admit to the charge of institutional racism is not only the fact that the state had steadfastly refused until February 1999 to have any truck with the concept, but also the fact that the concept had originally been coined by two Black-power activists, Carmichael and Hamilton (1967) in the United States.

The report was received with approval by Parliament. In presenting the report to Parliament, Home Secretary Jack Straw expressly accepted the charge of institutional racism laid at the door of 'both the Metropolitan Police Service and in other Police Services and other institutions countrywide' and committed the government to implement all the report's recommendations:

The inquiry's assessment is clear and sensible. In my view, any long-established, white-dominated organisation is liable to have procedures, practices and a culture that tend to exclude or to disadvantage non-white people. The report makes 70 wide-ranging recommendations, and I welcome them all. (Hansard, 1999, col. 391)

Response by higher education to the charge

My concern in this chapter is with higher education (HE) and how universities in England responded to the charge of institutional racism. The leaders of both the major academic unions – Paul Makney of the National Association of Teachers in Further and Higher Education (NATFHE) and David Triesman of the Association of University Teachers (AUT) – publicly accepted in 1999 the charge that higher education institutions (HEIs) were characterised by institutional racism. This is not altogether surprising: research commissioned by the sector on ethnicity and employment in higher education, culminating in a report published a few months after the Macpherson report in June 1999, pointed to disadvantages experienced by academic staff from minority ethnic groups (Carter et al., 1999). The disadvantages related to recruitment, employment status and career progression, with some Black and minority ethnic (BME) staff reporting experiences of racial discrimination and harassment. A few years later, another major study pointed to disadvantages experienced by BME students. The latter were less likely to be found in old universities, more likely to drop out, less likely to be awarded good honours degrees and more likely to do less well in the labour market (Connor et al., 2004).

Three specific questions are addressed in this chapter:

- What factors prompted the higher education sector and, in particular, Midshire University to address race equality?
- How positively has the sector as a whole and the case-study university specifically responded to these pressures?
- How do we explain the response (or lack of response) of the sector and the university?

There is little doubt that the main factors prompting universities to address race equality have been external to the sector. Of critical importance here has been the role of the state. For a brief period in the first few years of the new millennium, the state exerted considerable pressure on universities to address race equality. The state cajoled universities to address race equality through two strategies for higher education, notably those concerned with widening participation and human resources. The first sought to promote equality and diversity in the student body, while the second was concerned with promoting equal opportunities (EO) in staffing. In addition to these colour-blind strategies, the state required universities, along with other public organisations, to develop race-equality policies and action plans following new race-relations legislation in 2000. The pressure eventually subsided and, as I have argued elsewhere, other government agendas prompted by concerns over increasing net migration, disorder and terrorism subsequently marginalised the one concerned with race equality (Pilkington, 2008).

Colour-blind strategies: widening participation and equal opportunities

The government's concern that universities widen participation for students and promote equal opportunities for staff was first made amply clear by the Secretary of State for Education and Employment in his November 1999 funding letter to the Higher Education Funding Council for England (HEFCE), a central body which distributes government funds to higher education institutions in England (HEFCE, 2008). On widening participation, the 1999 funding letter stated: 'Widening access to higher education is a key priority and critical to tackling social exclusion' (HEFCE, 2008, para 19). On equal opportunities, the same letter expressed itself in no uncertain terms:

> I am deeply concerned about the present position on equal opportunities for HE staff. Evidence suggests that only a minority of academic staff in higher education institutions are from an ethnic minority background, are women, or have a disability, and that relatively few from these groups reach senior positions. (HEFCE, 2008, para 27)

The government's concern to widen participation and promote equal opportunities is only partially about race and ethnicity. This is evident from a comparison of successive funding letters (HEFCE, 2008). Blunkett's 1999 funding letter made no reference to race and ethnicity in the section on 'widening access' (HEFCE, 2008, para 19–24) and subsequent funding letters, which continued consistently to prioritise widening participation, followed suit. When it comes to staff as opposed to students, Blunkett's 1999 funding letter was unprecedented in emphasising race equality in the section on 'equal opportunities for HE staff'. Subsequent funding letters, in contrast, when they emphasised the importance of equal opportunities, did not expressly mention race and ethnicity. The emphasis placed on race equality in 1999 reflected the high profile given to the Macpherson report earlier in that year. The absence of any reference to race and ethnicity thereafter indicates that the strategies to widen participation and promote equal opportunities were colour-blind strategies focused on social disadvantage.

How successful were these colour-blind strategies in promoting race equality? However effective these strategies may have been in relation to other equality strands, they do not seem to have made significant inroads in combating race inequality. I have examined the evidence in some depth elsewhere (Pilkington, 2011) and so shall present the main findings here very concisely.

Let us begin with strategies concerned with widening participation. There is little doubt that widening participation is primarily concerned with class. Despite the occasional references made by government Ministers to 'BME learners' (NATFHE, 2000), the needs of these learners are of only marginal concern to key policy makers. The central focus of attention is social class. This is evident in a number of ways:

- The funding letters, as we have already pointed out, never mention race or ethnicity but invariably refer to social class or a proxy measure of it (HEFCE, 2008).
- The performance indicators used in HEFCE documents are wholly class based.
- Many policy documents 'selectively use particular pieces of research to make the case that the under-representation of...ethnic minorities has been largely solved' (Webb, 1997, p. 85). The result is that 'the needs of BME learners are mostly rolled up into generic widening participation policies' which effectively means that 'BME participation...drop...off the agenda' (AimHigher, 2006, p. 2).

Despite the fact that the binary divide between universities and polytechnics was abolished in 1992, the higher-education sector remains highly stratified (Davies et al., 1997). This means that as we 'move to a mass system of higher education...it is increasingly important that we consider the different sorts of higher education that are now on offer' (Reay et al., 2005, p. vii). When we do this, we discover that students from minority ethnic backgrounds are 'far more likely to be negatively positioned within the higher education system and to study less prestigious subjects in less prestigious institutions' (Jary and Jones, 2006, p. 7). A recent study which examined students' choices of higher education revealed that

> while more working class and ethnic minority students are entering university, they are generally entering different universities to their white middle class counterparts. Class tendencies are compounded by race. (Reay et al., 2005, p. 162)

The focus on admissions to the sector as a whole glosses over the differentiated nature of the higher-education sector and overlooks the different rates of return from going to different institutions.

A recent analysis of what institutions do under the heading of widening participation is revealing. HEIs receive funding for widening access and improving retention but, despite the fact that they receive more for improving retention, most activities focus on *access* rather than *success*. Using the student life cycle to identify different stages, Thomas and May (2005) discovered that 64 percent of activities were related to pre-entry, for example aspiration raising, and that only 13 percent of activities were concerned with supporting student success and employability. As the authors put it, 'This study suggests that the sector is prioritising pre-entry and access initiatives at the expense of interventions once students have entered HE' (Thomas et al., 2005, p. 193). This finding is significant and has adverse consequences for minority ethnic groups that are more likely to gain access to the sector but disproportionately face problems in succeeding.

Turning to strategies promoting equal opportunities, we discover that the key ones were evaluated positively in 2005. The evaluations nonetheless reveal significant lacunae. One reveals that many key staff do not believe in the importance of EO (HEFCE, 2005a), while other research indicates that many staff are, in fact, highly sceptical of the efficacy of equal opportunities policies (Deem et al., 2005). Furthermore, analysis of university equal opportunities strategies identifies significant deficiencies in monitoring (HEFCE, 2007, p. 14, para. 143 in HEFCE, 2007) and in target setting (HEFCE, 2007, p. 37, para. 27 in HEFCE, 2007). Since it has been widely recognised for a long time that an organisation intent on preventing or detecting racial discrimination needs to undertake both 'ethnic monitoring and the setting of targets' (Sanders, 1998, p. 38), the evidence pointing to failures in data gathering and target setting suggest that many HEIs have not taken equal opportunities policies seriously, at least when it comes to race.

This suggestion is confirmed by another of the evaluations conducted in 2005: 'activities undertaken...appear to have had the greatest impact on the role and reward of women in the majority of institutions' and, as a result, 'the role of minority ethnic groups...has received much less emphasis...compared to the emphasis on gender equality' (HEFCE, 2005b, p. 10). Further evidence that race issues had been side-lined relative to gender issues was submitted by 'some union stakeholders' who 'believed that the race aspects of job evaluation have not been considered' (HEFCE, 2005b, p. 56). Previous research has indicated that equal opportunities policies in higher education tend to focus on gender rather than race (Neal, 1998; Law et al., 2004). The evidence above that the implementation of equal opportunities strategies entailed a greater concern with gender than race issues suggests that this prioritisation persists.

Race-relations legislation

Let us turn, finally, to an approach that is explicitly concerned with race. The government's major response to the Macpherson report was a legislative initiative, the Race Relations (Amendment) Act (RRAA), 2000. The act extended the scope of the 1976 Race Relations Act by covering public bodies which had been previously exempt and making it unlawful for public authorities to discriminate in carrying out any of their functions. While this act, like previous race relations legislation, prohibited unlawful discrimination, a new approach was also evident. For the first time, a general statutory duty was placed on all public authorities, and specific duties on some authorities, to eliminate racial discrimination (including indirect discrimination), promote good race relations and facilitate equality of opportunity. The act gave the Commission for Racial Equality (CRE) the power to develop a statutory code of practice and provide guidance to public authorities on how to meet the general duty and any specific duties introduced by the home secretary. By enjoining public bodies in this way to develop policies and plans which promote racial equality, the RRAA adopted a very different approach to that embodied in previous race relations-legislation: public authorities were now being required to take a proactive stance to racial equality and thus take the lead in eliminating racial discrimination, promoting good race relations and facilitating equal opportunities.

The deadline in England and Wales for the production of race equality policies with plans of implementation was set for May 2002. The specific duties for HEIs were:

- Prepare and maintain a written race-equality policy and implementation plan;
- Within the policy and plan assess the impact of institutional policies on staff and students from different racial groups;
- Within the policy and plan monitor the applications, admissions and progression of students;
- Within the policy and plan monitor the recruitment and development of staff;
- Within the policy and plan set out arrangements for publishing the race equality policy and the results of monitoring impact assessments and reviews.

What is interesting about these specific duties is what they prioritise. They do not, unlike the 'Anti-Racist Toolkit' produced by Leeds University

(Turney et al., 2002), focus on teaching and research, but on widening participation and equal opportunities (Sharma, 2004). The colour-blind widening participation and equal-opportunity policies may, as we have seen, have bypassed minorities, but it was hoped targeted policies would make a difference.

In order to fulfil its statutory obligations under the RRAA, HEFCE required HEIs to submit their race-equality policies and plans for review in November 2002. The Equality Challenge Unit, a sector-wide advisory body created in 2001, was asked to review them on behalf of HEFCE, with the review itself being undertaken by the Gus John Partnership in terms of a template devised by the Equality Challenge Unit. The outcome of the review entailed placing each policy and plan into one of five categories:

• An exemplar of good practice at this stage in the implementation process (E);
• Good/Good with certain areas needing attention (G);
• Developing appropriately but with significant areas needing attention (D1);
• Developing appropriately but with major work to be done (D2);
• Not yet aligned with the requirements of the RRAA; needing urgent revision (N).

While 34 HEIs were categorised as having developed 'exemplary' policies, 45 HEIs (deemed to be N and D2) were categorised as having submitted policies and plans which did not meet the requirements of the RRAA and required further work (John, 2003). HEIs judged to be D2 or N were required to resubmit their policies and plans within three months. The Office of Public Management (OPM) was commissioned to do a subsequent review in 2003. The policies and plans of 45 HEIs which had initially been judged to be D2 or N were reassessed using the same template and grading system as the initial review. The report in July 2003 concluded that, although the majority of HEIs had made significant progress, 17 were judged to have policies and plans that were categorised as N or D1 and thus were still not compliant with the legislation. These 17 HEIs were again reassessed in 2004 by OPM, at which time only 4 were judged noncompliant (OPM, 2004a). Finally, OPM was commissioned to review, two years after the original deadline for submission of race equality policies and plans, how HEIs were implementing their policies and plans. The review was upbeat: 'This review of progress, two years after initial race equality policies and action plans were developed, shows the considerable progress travelled by the majority of HEIs[;] ... 80 per cent are making fair progress, and of these some are showing real innovation and good practice in different areas' (OPM, 2004b, p. 23). Given that a report published a mere five years earlier (Carter et al., 1999) indicated that only a few HEIs had a race equality policy at all, such an upbeat position is understandable. However, it should be noted that this review, like the compliance reviews, was desk-based and that the reality on the ground may be different. As the final compliance review acknowledges:

> It is important to reiterate that the existence of a strong policy docu-
> ment does not necessarily mean that progress is being made on the
> ground. Indeed, in some instances... policy documents have been
> produced by external consultants, and it is not clear to what extent
> commitments are owned by the university. (OPM, 2004a, p. 12)

So what can we provisionally conclude? Colour-blind government strat-egies to widen participation and promote equal opportunities seem to have had minimal impact in combating race inequality in the period that we have examined. By contrast, the more targeted Race Relations (Amendment) Act seems to have had more impact, at least in the sense of generating race-equality policies and plans.

We need to be circumspect, however. Even when legislation had insisted on the production of race-equality policies and action plans, and guidance had been provided to aid the production process, the requisite policies and action plans were often initially lacking, and significant pressure had to be exerted to ensure minimal compliance. What is more, when (some of) those institutions that had produced exemplary policies were followed up 'eighteen months to two years later, those Institutions had done very little to translate their first class policy into meaningful action that could make a difference to the learning community, and especially to its black students and staff' (John, 2005, pp. 593–594).

This raises an important methodological point. It should be noted that the secondary research I have drawn upon above to evaluate the impact of government strategies and legislation is limited. It is often based on ques-tionnaires to senior staff or based on analysis of written documents. Both methods have their biases. The first method invariably tends to present institutions in a favourable light since senior staff are loath to be publicly self critical and are concerned, in a Goffmanesque way, to manage the impression of their organisations. The second method also tends to present institutions in as favourable a light as possible. There is an acute awareness that public documents present images of the organisational ethos. Those responsible for their production, therefore, are often concerned to massage these images so that they are positive. There is also another danger with documents. This is that we confuse what is written in strategic and policy documents with what actually happens in institutions. Since strategic and policy documents often serve as the public face of the university, an inordinate amount of time can go into getting them just right. This can entail that writing documents and having good policies become substitutes for action: as one of Ahmed's interviewees put it, 'you end up doing the document rather than doing the doing' (Ahmed, 2007, p. 599).

Drilling down: the response of Midshire University

We clearly need to move beyond such methodologies to assess what actually happens on the ground. We need to drill down to find out what is really going on. Here, I shall draw upon an ethnographic investigation of one university in the decade following the publication of the Macpherson report (Pilkington, 2011). The university is a new one in Central England and will be identified as Midshire University.

What is immediately apparent at Midshire University is that at different times more or less attention has been placed on race equality. At certain points, the university has made a serious effort to address the issue of race equality. At other times, the issue has not been on the institution's radar. The development of equal opportunity policies from 1989 onwards eventually led to the development of action plans for different strands of equality. A race-equality plan was devised between 1992 and 1994. This plan was updated and launched in 1996 and, in terms of Carter and colleagues' (1999) typology, merited top marks; it was an 'advanced policy.' Within an extraordinarily short time, however, the policy had been forgotten. Indeed the subsequent requirement under the Race Relations (Amendment) Act to develop, by May 2002, a race-equality policy and action plan was not appropriately met. The policy and plan were awarded bottom marks by the Equality Challenge Unit, and the university was subsequently required to resubmit its policy and action plan to HEFCE within a limited time period. This provided an opportunity for race-equality champions within the university to develop a robust policy and action plan and persuade senior management to put in place appropriate resources to support the policy and plan. It is noteworthy that what prompted the recovery was not the race-relations legislation, per se, but the independent review which indicated the university was non-compliant.

Race equality subsequently had a higher priority within the university. New governance arrangements and the arrival of two equality and diversity officers in 2004 subsequently gave equality and diversity, generally, and race, in particular, higher profiles. And, there is no doubt that for some years significant progress was made. To give an indication of this, I compare below two distinct academic years, 1999–2000 and 2006–2007, in terms of factors pertinent to a university meeting the specific duties of the recent race-relations legislation. While there is a danger of presenting a Panglossian picture, there is no doubt that significant progress was made.

The period 2006–2007, however, was the university's high point in terms of addressing race equality. Since then external pressure from the government has ineluctably declined. Although lip service continues to be paid in government pronouncements and in some strategies toward race equality and ethnic diversity, a discourse centred on community cohesion has become hegemonic and has marginalised discourse concerned with race equality and ethnic diversity (Pilkington, 2008). At Midshire University, this entailed increasing resistance to an equality and diversity agenda and, eventually, the disappearance of any dedicated committees or equality and diversity officers. This development was justified in terms of mainstreaming but has, in fact, entailed a reversal of the progress made in the preceding years to meet the general and specific duties of the race relations legislation (Pilkington, 2011).

Institutional racism and Midshire University

The concept of institutional racism has not fared well in the years that have elapsed since the Macpherson report. The concept is now little used and has been expressly rejected by many academics as lacking analytical subtlety and by many policymakers as outmoded (Pilkington, 2011). Nonetheless, it is revealing for those of us working in universities to reflect upon the ten components of institutional racism identified by the Parekh report (2000, pp. 74–75):

- Is there evidence of 'indirect discrimination' in the services provided for members of minority ethnic groups?
- Are 'employment practices' racially inequitable?
- Is the 'occupational culture' ethnically inclusive?
- Is the 'staffing structure' one in which senior staff are disproportionately white?

- Is there a 'lack of positive action' in involving members of minority ethnic groups in decision-making?
- Do 'management and leadership' consider the task of addressing institutional racism a high priority?
- How widespread is 'professional expertise' in intercultural communication?
- Is there evidence of relevant high quality 'training'?
- How much 'consultation' is there with representatives from minority communities?
- Is there a 'lack of information' on the organisation's impact on minority communities? (Parekh, 2000, pp. 74–75)

It is instructive to compare Midshire University at different points in time in terms of these ten dimensions of institutional racism identified in the Parekh report. Here, I draw upon my ethnographic investigation of Midshire to identify continuities and changes between 1999–2000 and 2006–2007 (Pilkington, 2011).

If we examine both Tables 12.1 and 12.2, we find that there clearly were some changes between 1999 and 2008. The university improved: its monitoring, by ethnicity, of the student experience; it tightened its formal recruitment procedures; it developed a more inclusive culture that exhibits public recognition of diverse identities; it had an equality scheme and action plan that does address race; training in equality and diversity improved, with more staff now cognisant of their obligations under the race relations legislation; and information on the impact of institutional policies and procedures on Black and Asian communities improved.

What is perhaps more significant than these changes, however, are the continuities (note the final column of Table 12.2). These include the following: persistent ethnic differentials in the student experience that adversely impact on BME students and point to possible indirect discrimination: ethnic differentials in staff recruitment that adversely impact on Black and Asian applicants and point to possible indirect discrimination;(some) minority ethnic staff subject to racism and (some) White staff cynical about political correctness; an overwhelmingly White senior staff team, with no evident efforts to transform this situation; low priority given to the implementation of a race-equality action plan; few staff skilled in intercultural issues; many staff not trained in equality and diversity; and few efforts made to consult Black and Asian communities.

The discovery of some significant continuities over time in the approach of the university to race equality is revealing. The comparison, it should be noted, is of a low mark (1999–2000) and high mark

Table 12.1 Promoting race equality by specific duty and academic year

General duty	1999–2000	2006–2007	Verdict
Race equality plan	No specific live race-equality policy or plan	A live specific race-equality policy and plan incorporated since 2006 in a wider Equality Schema and Action Plan	Significant progress
Equality impact assessments of policies	None	Ongoing screening of existing policies and screening of new policies	Significant progress (on student-related policies)
Monitoring student admissions and progress	Poor baseline data and no routine reports; BME mentoring scheme; Christian chaplaincy with no provision for Muslim prayer spaces	Excellent baseline data and routine reports to dedicated Equality and Diversity subcommittees of Senate; BME mentoring scheme; Inter-faith chaplaincy with provision for Muslim prayer spaces	Significant progress
Monitoring staff recruitment and progression	Monitoring data collected but not analysed	Monitoring data collected but not used and no reports to dedicated Equality and Diversity subcommittees of Senate since 2004	No evident progress
Publishing impact assessments, monitoring and reviews	No annual review and no published assessments, monitoring and reviews	Annual progress review and assessments, monitoring and reviews on the Web	Significant progress

(2006–2007) for the university. We would expect to be impressed, above all, by the changes. And, yet, the continuities are striking and illustrate very clearly both the continuing disadvantages faced by minority ethnic groups and also the lack of urgency to transform this situation. It is conceivable, of course, that Midshire University is exceptional (compared to other higher-education institutions) in this respect. And we cannot of course generalise from this case study to the sector as a whole. Nonetheless, what we have found at Midshire University

Table 12.2 The interacting dynamics of institutional racism in Midshire University

Dimension	University	University changes
Indirect discrimination	HIGH/MEDIUM	Some progress While there was an increase in the proportion of students from minority ethnic groups, there continued to be persistent and adverse ethnic differentials.
Unfair employment practices	HIGH	No change
Racism in the occupational culture	MEDIUM/LOW	Some progress While there continued to be little evidence of overt racism and some attempt to be more inclusive, there was evidence that (some, especially support) staff from minority ethnic groups felt marginalised.
White senior management	HIGH	No change
Lack of positive action	HIGH	No change
Low priority given to race equality	HIGH	No change
Low expertise in intercultural issues	HIGH	No change
Inadequate training in race and community relations	MEDIUM	Some progress While the university did not meet its target of 100% staff being trained, progress was made, with 20% trained.
Poor consultation with minority ethnic communities	HIGH	No change
Lack of information on the impact of policies, practices and procedures.	MEDIUM/LOW	Some progress This improved considerably for students but not for staff.

resonates with findings elsewhere (Turney et al., 2002; Bhattacharya, 2002; Major, 2002). Whatever qualms we may have with the analytical utility of institutional racism, what the concept has sensitised us to is 'the sheer weight of Whiteness' in the university (Back, 2004, p. 1). In this sense, the concept has been extremely revealing. It is impossible to comprehend the persistence of racial disadvantage and the failure to combat this without recognising 'how deeply rooted Whiteness is throughout the...system' (Gillborn, 2008, p. 9). While minority ethnic staff are typically conscious of this, it is often the case that, for White staff (including White researchers), 'the Whiteness of the institution goes unnoticed and is rationalised into a day-to-day perception of normality' (Law et al., 2004, p. 97). It is crucial, therefore, that we are reflexive and do not let 'the "whiteness" of the academy.... go unnoticed and uncommented' (Clegg et al., 2003, p. 164; Frankenberg, 2004).

Conclusion

Research continues to demonstrate that individuals from minority ethnic communities disproportionately experience adverse outcomes (Ahmed, 2012). To give two examples, BME academic staff continue to experience significant disadvantage in higher education ten years after the publication of the Macpherson report (Leathwood et al., 2009; ECU, 2011), and BME students continue to be less likely to be awarded good honours degrees (Broecke and Nicholls, 2007; HEA, 2008). And, yet, universities are extraordinarily complacent. They see themselves as liberal and believe existing policies ensure fairness; in the process, they ignore adverse outcomes and do not see combating racial/ethnic inequalities as a priority. This points, in my view, to the sheer weight of Whiteness (if not institutional racism).

Reference List

Ahmed, S. (2007) '"You end up doing the document rather than doing the doing": Diversity, Race Equality and the Politics of Documentation', *Ethnic and Racial Studies*, 30 (2), 235–256.

Ahmed, S. (2012) *On Being Included: Racism and Diversity in Institutional Life*, London, University Press.

Aimhigher (2006) *A Review of Black and Minority Ethnic Participation in Higher Education*. Available at www.aimhigher.ac.uk/sites/practitioner/resources/Conf%20Summary%20report% [Accessed on 20 November 2011)

Bhattacharya, G. (2002) 'The Unwritten Rules of the Game: Imagine Working in a Place Where the Rules Aren't the Same for Everyone', *The Guardian*, 15 January. Available at www.guardian.co.uk/education/2002/jan/15/raceineducation.race1. [Accessed on 24 March 2013)

Broecke, S. and Nicholls, T. (2007) *Ethnicity and Degree Attainment*, Research Report RW92, London, Department for Education and Skills.

Carmichael, S. and Hamilton, C. (1967) *Black Power: The Politics of Liberation in America*, New York, Vintage Books.

Carter, J., Fenton, J. and Modood, T. (1999) *Ethnicity and Employment in Higher Education*, London, Policy Studies Institute.

Clegg, S., Parr, S. and Wan, S. (2003) 'Racialising Discourses in Higher Education', *Teaching in Higher Education*, 8 (2), 155–168.

Connor, H., Tyers, C. and Modood, T. (2004) *Why the Difference? A Close Look at Higher Education Minority Ethnic Students and Graduates*, Research Report RR448, London, Department for Education and Skills.

Cottle, S. (2004) *The Racist Murder of Stephen Lawrence: Media Performance and Public Transformation*, Westport, CT, Greenwood Press.

Davies, P., Williams, J. and Webb, S. (1997) 'Access to higher education in the late twentieth century: policy, power and discourse', in Williams, J. (ed.), *Negotiating Access to Higher Education*, Buckingham, SRHE/Open University Press.

Deem, R., Morley, L. and Tlili, A. (2005) *Negotiating Equity in Higher Education Institutions*. Available at www.hefce.ac.uk/pubs/redreports/2005/rd10_05/rd10_05doc. [Accessed on 30 May 2010)

Equality Challenge Unit (ECU) (2011) *Experience of Black and Minority Ethnic Staff in Higher Education in England*, London, ECU.

Frankenberg, R. (2004) 'On unsteady ground: crafting and engaging in the critical study of Whiteness', in Bulmer, M. and Solomos, J. (eds), *Researching Race and Racism*, London, Routledge, 104–118.

Gillborn, D. (2008) *Racism and Education*, London, Routledge.

Hansard, (1999) 'Stephen Lawrence Inquiry', 24 February. Available at www.publications.parliament.uk/pa/cm199899/cmhansard/vo990224/debtext/90224–21.htm. [Accessed on 23 April 2012)

Higher Education Academy (HEA) (2008) *Ethnicity, Gender and Degree Attainment Project: Final Report*, London, ECU.

HEFCE (2005a) *Equal Opportunities and Diversity for Staff in Higher Education*. Available at http://www.hefce.ac.uk/pubs/hefce/2005/05_19/05.19.pdf. [Accessed on 29 May 2012]

HEFCE (2005b) *HEFCE Race Equality Scheme*. Available at http://www.hefce.ac.uk/pubs/hefce/2005/05_04/ [Accessed on 2 August 2012)

HEFCE (2007) *Rewarding and Developing Staff in Higher Education*. Available at www.hefce.ac.uk/lgm/hr/reward/ [Accessed on 21 August 2012]

HEFCE (2008) *Grant Letter from the Secretary of State to HEFCE*. Available at www.hefce.ac.uk/finance/fundinghe/grant/ [Accessed on 20 August 2012]

Jary, D. and Jones, R. (2006) 'Overview of widening participation policy and practice', in Jary, D. and Jones, R. (eds), *Perspectives and Practice in Widening Participation in the Social Sciences*, Birmingham, C-SAP, 3–30.

John, G. (2003) *Review of Race Equality Policies and Action Plans in HEFCE-funded Higher Education Institutions*. Available at www.hefce.ac.uk/lgm/divers/ecu. [Accessed on 30 October 2012)

John, G. (2005) *Taking a Stand*, Manchester, Gus John Partnership.

Law, I.., Phillips, D. and Turney, L. (eds) (2004) *Institutional Racism in Higher Education*, Stoke on Trent, Trentham Books.

Leathwood, C., Maylor, U. and Moreau, M.P. (2009) *The Experience of Staff Working in Higher Education*, London, Equality Challenge Unit.

Macpherson, W. (1999) *The Stephen Lawrence Inquiry: Report of an Inquiry by Sir William Macpherson of Cluny*, London, HMSO.

Major, L. (2002) 'Incredible Islands', *The Guardian,* January 15. Available at www.guardian.co.uk/education/2002/jan/15/raceineducation.race1. [Accessed on 24 March 2013]

NATFHE (2000) *Learning Through Diversity,* London, NATFHE.

Neal, S. (1998) *The Making of Equal Opportunity Policies in Universities,* Buckingham, SRHE/Open University Press.

Office of Public Management (OPM) (2004a) *Assessment of Race Equality Policies and Plans in HEFCE-funded HEIs.* Available at www.hefce.ac.uk/Pubs/rdreports/2004/rd09_04/ [Accessed on 1 December 2011]

Office of Public Management (OPM) (2004b) *Review of Progress in Race Equality.* Available at www.hefce.ac.uk/Pubs/rdreports/2004/rd09_04/ [Accessed on 1 December 2011]

Parekh, B. (2000) *The Future of Multi-Ethnic Britain,* London, Profile Books.

Pilkington, A. (2008) 'From institutional racism to community cohesion: the changing nature of racial discourse', *Sociological Research Online,* 13 (3). Available at http://www.socresonline.org.uk/13/3/6.html. [Accessed on 24 March 2013]

Pilkington, A. (2011) *Institutional Racism in the Academy: A UK Case Study,* Stoke on Trent, Trentham Books.

Reay, D., David, M. and Ball, S. (2005) *Degrees of Choice,* Stoke on Trent, Trentham Books.

Sanders, P. (1998) 'Tackling racial discrimination', in Blackstone, T., Parekh, B. and Sanders, P. (eds), *Race Relations in Britain,* London, Routledge, 36–52.

Sharma, S. (2004) 'Transforming the curriculum', in Law, I., Phillips, D. and Turney, L. (eds), *Institutional Racism in Higher Education,* Stoke on Trent, Trentham Books, 105–118.

Singh, G. (2000) 'The concept and context of institutional racism', in Marlow, A. and Loveday, B. (eds), *After MacPherson: Policing After the Stephen Lawrence Inquiry,* Lyme Regis, Russell House Publishing, 29–40.

Thomas, L., May, H., Harrop, H., Houston, M., Knox, H., Lee, M., Osborne, M., Pudner, H. and Trotman, C. (2005) *From the Margins to the Mainstream,* London, Universities UK.

Turney, L., Law, I. and Phillips, D. (2002) *Institutional Racism in Higher Education Toolkit Project: Building the Anti-Racist HEI.* Available at www.leeds.ac.uk/cers/toolkit/toolkit.htm. [Accessed on 16 August 2005]

Webb, S. (1997) 'Alternative students? conceptualisations of difference', in Williams, J. (ed.), *Negotiating Access to Higher Education,* Buckingham, SRHE/Open University Press, 65–86.

13

The Multicultural Dilemma, the Integrationist Consensus and the Consequences for Advancing Race and Ethnicity within Education

Richard Race

Introduction

The relationship between multiculturalism and integration has been examined by a number of authors. Similarities and differences between the ideas have been explored and analysed, and the debates are ongoing (Race, 2008; 2011; Cantle, 2012; Modood, 2013). Williams (2013, p. 1) has developed the idea of the *multicultural dilemma*. She describes this idea as the political consequences that relate to the hostility between the host population concerning rising rates of immigration. Katwala (2013, p. 15) defines integration as: 'respect for the law, the ability to speak English, and the desire to contribute positively to society [and a]...commitment to fair treatment'. Katwala (2013) argues that a combination of these factors leads towards an integrationist consensus, but it is people-focused rather than politically focused. The distinction between people and politics is important because both elements shape responses within both the multicultural dilemma and integrationist consensus. Political speeches by Angela Merkel and David Cameron between November 2010 and March 2011, criticised the multicultural project and declared the term was no longer useful and, in fact, integration was the way forward when dealing with society, cultural diversity and immigration in both Germany and the United Kingdom. Within an English context, the integrationist focus can be seen within recent Coalition policy documents in England (DCLG, 2012; Pickles, 2013). An interesting response to Merkel's and Cameron's speeches defended multicultural ideas and the notion of celebrating cultural diversity rather than being hostile towards the continued economic and cultural benefits of immigration (Mahamdallie, 2011).

The objective of this chapter is to underline that multiculturalism and integration must, and needs to focus on more than a debate on immigration (Collier, 2013). The multicultural dilemma and integrationist consensus can be, and are here, applied to other areas, that is, policy and professional practice issues in relation to race and ethnicity in education. The first section of the chapter explores multiculturalism in education (Race, 2011) with the idea of the multicultural dilemma (Williams, 2013) being explored alongside the multicultural backlash (May and Wessendorf, 2010). The practical consequences of this for teachers and how they can teach, let alone advance, race and ethnicity issues will be examined. The next section focuses on the concept of integration and how the idea of the integrationist consensus provides opportunities for diverse educational practice. The notion of integrationist consensus is then applied to Katwala's (2013) examination on how Eltham in South London has changed in relation to race and ethnicity since the death of Stephen Lawrence in 1993. Citizenship education is then examined, highlighting a balanced opinion of its potential (Race, 2011; OFSTED, 2013), but also its integrationist foundations (DfES, 2007; DfE, 2011). The penultimate section applies the notions of multicultural dilemma and integrationist consensus to race and ethnicity issues in education (Forrester and Taylor, 2011) whilst the conclusions analyse the issues of how and what needs to be taught – that is, for students and teachers to provide more diverse curricula in relation to advancing race and ethnicity within education (Race, 2013).

Multiculturalism, race and ethnicity in education

Mahamdallie's (2011) important collection of work defends the ideas of multiculturalism and comes not only at a time when Prime Minister David Cameron delivered his 'End of Multiculturalism' speech in Munich (February 2011), but it also gives both practical and theoretical contexts to the debates that surround 'the multiculturalism backlash' discourse. Vertovec and Wessendorf (2010, p. 26) argue that:

> Across a range of countries, there seems to have arisen a kind of convergence of backlash discourse, idioms and stratagems attacking a presumed multiculturalism. Although each set of public debates has developed within discrete national political contexts, there has subsequently emerged, too, a convergence of policy responses.

Angela Merkel's speech, which preceded Cameron's, has often been misquoted in the English-speaking world, as it focused on German multiculturalism, both its benefits and failings (Race, 2012b, p. 244). The academic highlighting of how the concept of multiculturalism can be used contradicts recent political 'backlash' discourse (Vertovec and Wessendort, 2010; Race, 2011). The importance of multiculturalism, as Triandafyllidou et al. (2012, p. 5) argue in Europe, focuses on, 'the political accommodation by the state and/or a dominant group of all minority cultures defined first and foremost by reference to race, ethnicity or religion'. And in this section of the chapter, we are interested in how this accommodation has occurred concerning race and ethnicity.

Malik (2010) skilfully shows the story of race relations legislation in the UK, influenced by the civil rights movement in the United States during the 1960s and 1970s. Malik (2010, p. 59) highlights 'the official accommodation of diversity'. This can be seen in a wider social policy movement from integration to multiculturalism in the UK, highlighted by the Swann Report (DES: 1985). It can also be argued that anti-racist research was also influencing parts of the education policy debates in the UK during the 1980s (see Stephen May's chapter in this collection). However, despite this anti-racist movement in education, the enquiry into the death of Stephen Lawrence (see Andrew Pilkington's chapter in this collection) and the repeated call for greater representation of cultural diversity in the national curriculum, consequent Equality Act legislation of 2006 and 2010 – preceded by Cantle's (2008) political policy of community cohesion in the 2000s – witnessed a return to integration policy. As Meer and Modood (2013, pp. 82–84) imply, 'It can be argued that [the Equality Acts of 2006 and 2010] do add up to a *British* multiculturalism which although lacking an official "Multicultural Act" or "Charter" in the way of Australia or Canada has rejected the idea of integration based upon unity achieved through uncompromising cultural "assimilation".' It can be argued that in many countries a type of multiculturalism exists which is based on an official accommodation of diversity (Malik, 2010). However, as we will see in the next section of this chapter, integration is still visible, not only in political speeches, but also specifically in education policy in the 2000s (Race, 2011).

Within education, state policies control performance achievement in different ethnic groups. Archer and Francis (2007) show how different children from different minority ethnic groups (as well as their achievements or underachievement) can be influenced not only by their ethnic groups – be they White, Mixed, Asian, Black, Chinese or other categories – but they are also influenced by teachers' and parents' views of their aspirations (see Rhamie's chapter in this collection). There are, as

Gillborn (2008, pp. 146–161) describes, the creation and development of 'model minorities', for example, Indian and Chinese pupils who are achieving educationally, but these are political and social constructions and give us another application of Malik's (2010) notion of the official accommodation of diversity. There are winners and losers in these categories, and these generalisations and stereotypes are reinforced as students are defined within model minorities as 'hard working and successful [which] enables the education system to sustain its claim to fairness and impartiality' (Gillborn, 2008, p. 160).

Can multiculturalism offer anything in this debate when examining ethnicity? As mentioned in the Introduction to this edited collection, among the issues highlighted by several authors herein, and within the literature (Walters, 2011), are the limitations of statistical studies of students from underachieving ethnic minority communities. If we take Gillborn's construction of the 'model minority' and reverse it, we get a 'failing minorities' paradigm which, like the model minority communities, offers stereotypical and racist images of ethnic groups. What both Archer and Francis (2007) and Gillborn (2008) have done through their research is to provide us with greater understandings of how ethnic identities – be they performing or underperforming – are produced within education, but also how they are also reproduced and reinforced through education and achievement or underachievement discourses. The picture is even more complicated when we define our boundaries when focusing on one or two ethic groups, or it becomes even more complex when we focus on intersectionality, as Archer and Francis (2007) do when they examine race, gender and class alongside ethnic (under)achievement. The work of Stephen May (see the chapter in this collection) offers even more complexity when he analyses critical multiculturalism which, 'gives priority to structural analysis of unequal power relationships analysing the role of institutionalized inequities, including *but not necessarily limited to*[,] racism' (May and Sleeter, 2010, p. 10). CRT, intersectionality and critical multiculturalism all offer us, as Fass (2010, p. 222) argues, 'the need to rethink identities and in particular youth identities as well as political identities' when reflecting on how social constructions relating to education performance can do immense damage to ethnic minority individuals and communities.

This re-think needs to be carried out in both staffroom and classroom. Multiculturalism at the very least gives us a starting point to examine race and ethnicity issues. Murphy (2012, p. 5) reminds us that 'cultural minorities themselves are tremendously diverse in terms of their characteristics, the nature of their demands they make on the state, and the kinds of policies and institutions most appropriate to the satisfaction of those demands'. A solution for helping teachers increase understandings of cultural diversity in the classroom and avoid stereotypical perceptions raised by Archer and Francis (2007) has to come through more Continuing Professional Development (CPD) and lifelong learning for all professional practitioners within education. We need to move toward what Dolby (2012) has described as a new multicultural teacher education. This can theoretically improve existing teaching and learning but also encourage contemporary and relevant curriculum, for example, citizenship education before and after the 2010 General Election in England (Race, 2011; OFSTED, 2013).

Integration, race and ethnicity in education

There are ongoing complex debates in relation to the idea of integration and how the state politically manipulates the idea through policy. The continuing of integrationist-based social and education policy is visible in England (Race, 2012a). However, attempting to define integration seems to be problematic as we can see from the following examples. Saggar and Somerville (2012, p. 1) examine three main categories of integration: 'firstly; how measures are deployed concerning a perceived dilution of distinctive national identities; secondly; immigrant outcomes i.e. jobs (Hansen, 2012) and education attainment; and thirdly, successful communities or community cohesion whereby people coexist in harmony'. Uberoi and McGhee (2012, pp. 59–62) identify five ideal types to integration that they claim the British or any government might use: proceeduralism; assimilation; civic assimilation; pluralism; and radical pluralism. We have helpful categories and ideal types here concerning integration but no actual definition. This notion of no definition also applies to policy documents in England, for example, the Department of Communities and Local Government (DCLG, 2012), which underline five key factors that contribute to integration: tackling extremism and intolerance; common ground; responsibility; participation; and social mobility. Interestingly Joppke (2012, p. 1) when recommending three guiding principles and three policy stances for governments to improve cultural integration, argues that 'policy is not a cure all and how labour markets, education systems and other institutions not specific to immigrants' is as important. So, examining education systems as part of this need to increase understandings of integration and a significant literature from the United States shows perceived successes and failures in relation to the application of integration from desegregation to resegregation concerning different education systems (Cashin, 2004; Frankenberg and Orfield, 2007; Tyson, 2011; Freeman and Tendler, 2012).

The issue for integration in England is highlighted by Joppke (2012, p. 5) when he claims that the critical context to public opinion on integration is British hostility to immigration. It is interesting to compare Joppke (2012) with Williams (2013) which she describes within the notion of multicultural dilemma, the host population's hostility to immigrants. It would certainly not be politically prudent for the Secretary of State at the DCLG, Eric Pickles (2013), to be hostile towards immigrants when he talks about 'integration, integration, integration', but underlines immigration as a major policy theme, as well as a social issue. The objective here is to focus more specifically on how a working definition of integration can assist us when examining race and ethnicity within education rather than exclusively focusing on a more general debate on immigration. A change of focus is necessary, from immigration being perceived as the problem through politics and public opinion to the social and cultural consequences integration has had on policy, because the refocus here analyses both state policy and the available choices policy gives to everyone, that is, minority and majority communities. An education example of this is whether parents decide to send their children to school, or to what type of school, or whether they will be home educated (Forrester and Taylor, 2011). This is, I would suggest, a more productive direction for education policy debate and wider policy analysis. Thus, in relation to the nation state and education policymaking, the aim here is to continue to develop a working definition of integration (Race, 2011). I believe integration to be a conditional two-way relationship (Modood, 2013) whereby the state, through policy, creates the conditions in which individuals and communities either have the choice of totally conforming through assimilation or partly, through integration, or rejecting through separation (Merry, 2013). This partial acceptance allows people to keep part of their original identity as part of a wider cultural reality described as super-diversity (Vertovec, 2007). There are two main issues involved in this relationship. The first is state-focused. How does the nation state create policy within integrationist frameworks to preserve national identity (Saggar and Somerville, 2012)? Secondly, how do individuals and communities react to these policies? I would suggest that the multicultural dilemma shapes this reaction, that is, the reaction itself is necessarily or exclusively the hostility of the host population towards the immigrant. And as Anderson (2010, p. 183) warns: 'That integration in a world pervaded by segregation and stigmatization carries psychic costs, especially for the stigmatized, has important implications for integrationist ideals and policy.' The coping strategies of 'the stigmatized' have important consequences as it is, importantly, who is and who is not recognised within policy and who actually has the cultural capital to conform to, or resist, policy and its implementation (Race, 2013). One example of this social reaction and resistance is the increasing number of children in majority and minority communities who are being home educated, with the refusal of a significant percentage of the population in England not to have their children state educated within the integrationist national curriculum (Forrester and Taylor, 2011).

Katwala (2013) provides evidence from empirical research carried out in Eltham, South London, where Stephen Lawrence was murdered (Race, 2011, pp. 30–32). Half the sample data was collected from men around the age of 38, which is how old Stephen would have been if alive today. The respondents with children at different schools reported a general level of satisfaction with school quality. 'Despite the concerns about the pressures placed, particularly by increased diversity, immigration and children who begin without English as a first language, the schools most likely to face these challenges have thrived' (Katwala, 2013, p. 6). Local educational views highlighted a sense of confidence, and the essential foundations of integration are defined by the respondents of the research as: respect for the law, the ability to speak English, and the desire to contribute positively to society [and a] commitment to fair treatment (Katwala, 2013, p. 15). We can see here a locally focused movement towards what Katwala (2013) describes as an integrationist consensus, but it is people rather than politically focused – that is, the people in Eltham are choosing to uphold the integrationist consensus rather than it being forced on them by politicians within the state. The integrationist consensus is based on the cultural and social realities of life in Eltham, rather than media or political opinion focusing on immigration (DCLG, 2012; Pickles, 2013). However, integrationist realities concern the available choices of the individual, or the choice of the individual within a community, but their choices socially are at the very least influenced by the state through wider social policy and, in this case, more specific education policy. As Katwala (2013) highlights, individuals worked hard to improve education in Eltham, with the change to Academy status of the local secondary school, but expectations rather than academic performance remained a major issue. The integrationist consensus concerns people from all ethnicities applying their own conditions and values, in this case concerning education performance of children, but individual and communal choices continue to be influenced and shaped by state policies involving integration (Race, 2011 DCLG, 2012; Pickles, 2013).

Race and ethnicity within citizenship in education

It is worth revisiting the possibilities and potential of citizenship education in England during the 2000s and where issues concerning race and ethnicity could not only fit into the national curriculum but be taught by professional practitioners: for example, issues of racism and institutional racism when highlighting on-going cultural diversity and ethnic changes in society (Race, 2011). Race (2012b) argues that citizenship is in itself part of a wider integrationist discourse: for example, think of the conditional requirements set out by the [English] state within a citizenship test. Despite this, the original citizenship curriculum did offer, at the very least, a conditional examination of issues concerning race and ethnicity. The evidence set out in the 2000s by the Qualifications and Curriculum Development Agency (QCDA) for Key Stages 1 and 2 in England and Wales (non-statutory for children in primary schools aged between 5–11) and Key Stages 3 and 4 in England and Wales (statutory for children in secondary schools aged between 11–16) highlighted areas and subjects which teachers could theoretically teach within citizenship: for example, ethnicity and human rights. 'Theoretical' is an important term here because several respondents in the empirical data collected by Race (2011) argue: If you have not been trained to teach a diverse focused curriculum, how can you teach subjects like anti-racism and anti-discrimination?

There have been opportunities over the last four decades in England to not only develop, but allow, the concepts of race and ethnicity through citizenship focused education policymaking to evolve within professional practice. There is a comparative link between the Swann (DES, 1985) and the Ajegbo (DfES, 2007) reports in which both recommended greater diversity in relation to multiculturalism and citizenship was needed within English education. The Ajegbo Report (DfES, 2007) carried out a review of diversity and citizenship education within the National Curriculum in England. The review took place two years after the 7/7 London Bombings which refocused social and cultural debates on integration rather than multiculturalism in England (Eade et al., 2008; Osler, 2008). As Race (2011) highlights, the Ajegbo Report was published at a time when general policy in England was changing. One of Tony Blair's final speeches as prime minister, given in December 2006, focused on the importance of integrationist state policy. The

Ajegbo Report, published in January 2007, underlined an essential lack of culturally diverse content being taught in schools and, consequently, a lack of curricula focusing on race and ethnicity – which draws uncomfortable parallels with what Swann reported on in England and Wales, 22 years before. As Ajegbo (DfES, 2007, pp. 4–5), himself, wrote in the foreword to the Report: 'I believe issues around race, identity, citizenship and living together in the UK today are serious matters[.] ... I believe that schools, through their ethos, through their curriculum and through their work with their communities, can make a difference to those perceptions.' Citizenship, because of events like 7/7, had become more politically visible within education during the first decade of the twenty-first century and conceptually explains the policy shift in the 2000s from multiculturalism back to integration (Eade et al., 2008).

The first key finding of the Ajegbo Report (DfES, 2007, p. 6) was that, 'the quality and quantity of education for diversity are uneven across England'. Therefore, issues such as cultural diversity were not being taught universally in state-maintained schools across the country. In relation to citizenship, the report found:

- Many teachers are unsure of the standard expected in citizenship.
- Our research review found consensus among secondary head teachers and school staff that one of the biggest challenges to delivering citizenship education was being taught by non-specialists.
- Issues of identity and diversity are more often than not neglected in citizenship education.
- Much citizenship education in secondary schools is not sufficiently contextualised for pupils to become interested and engaged with the local, national and international questions of the day and how politicians deal with them.
- Currently, in citizenship, issues of identity and diversity do not tend to be linked explicitly enough to political understanding (of legal and political systems) and active participation.
- The term 'British' means different things to different people. In addition, identities are typically constructed as multiple and plural. Throughout our consultations, concerns were expressed, however, about defining 'Britishness', about the term's divisiveness and how it can be used to exclude others.

(DfES, 2007, pp. 7–8)

Analysing the above points, many pre-2002 (the year citizenship was introduced into the national curriculum for England and Wales) qualified teachers are 'unsure' of citizenship because they have not been taught how to teach the subject. That in itself is an important observation because with the non-statutory nature of citizenship education in English primary schools, the number of citizenship teachers who would have had the training or continuing professional development would have been minimal (Murphy and Hall, 2008; Galton and MacBeath, 2008). More teachers and specialists in citizenship are still required to teach subjects such as race and ethnicity. As the report acknowledges, coverage (meaning who teaches and how the subject is taught) not only lacks conceptual depth, but teachers and students need to be engaged with relevant subject material. This lack of coverage also relates to issues like racism, segregation and the need to understand the changing nature of cultural diversity. Recommendations from the Ajegbo Report (DfES, 2007) to address these issues are highlighted below:

- Pupils' Voices – All schools have mechanisms in place to ensure that the pupil voice is heard and acted upon. Schools should consider the use of forums, school councils, pupil questionnaires or other mechanisms for discussions around identity, values and belonging.
- Education for Diversity in the Curriculum – All schools should be encouraged to audit their curriculum to establish what they currently teach that is meaningful for all pupils in relation to diversity and multiple identities. The Qualifications and Curriculum Authority (QCA), 'Respect for all', is a useful audit tool. In the light of this audit, all schools should map provision across years and subjects and ensure that coverage is coherent.
- Harnessing Local Context – Schools should build active links between and across communities, with education for diversity as a focus:
  (a) This might range from electronic links (local, national and global) to relationships through other schools (for example as part of a federation), links with businesses, community groups and parents.
  (b) These links should be encouraged particularly between predominately monocultural and multicultural schools.
  (c) Such links need to be developed in such a way as to ensure they are sustainable.
  (d) Such work between schools must have significant curriculum objectives and be incorporated into courses that pupils are studying. This will help avoid stereotyping and tokenism.

(DfES, 2007, pp. 9–11)

Listening to what pupils and students have to say especially in relation to identity or identities in the classroom is important because it
raises the issue of relevant curricula in relation to cultural diversity
and multiculturalism. The issue of increasing student voice(s) is significant when considering promoting multicultural education, as it gives
education spaces for all students from different cultural backgrounds to
express themselves. Changing the curriculum to make it 'meaningful'
for all students highlights the previous point of promoting multicultural
education in the sense that what is taught has to have contemporary
relevance to the student. How citizenship is taught is also significant
because this relates to teaching method and learning, that is, pedagogy.
Links with the local community are significant and build on existing
legislation within the Education and Inspections Act (DfES, 2006) which
calls for more involvement by parents in schools and for the joining
of schools into federations. The introduction of Beacon schools, therefore, theoretically offered subject centres of excellence and expertise
in curriculum subjects. But there are more recent warnings about the
promotion and recent opening of Academy and Free Schools in England
with increased commercialisation and marketisation of primary and
secondary schooling (Gunter, 2011; Hoskins, 2012) which continues to
have detrimental consequences in relation to school choices for both
majority and minority communities in England (Gillborn, 2008, 2011).

However, even within Free and Academy Schools, subjects and debates
surrounding subjects like race and ethnicity 'should be encouraged' and
advanced because this implies that multicultural and citizenship education should be promoted within the classroom (Banks, 2009). Ajegbo
(DfES, 2007) called for an agenda for a revised citizenship education
which encompassed more diversity (Osler, 2009). However, with the
closing of the Qualifications and Curriculum Development Agency
(QCDA) in the Education Act of 2011 (DfE, 2011), the opportunities to
teach subjects relating to race and ethnicity have been reduced because
the syllabuses which were visible on the QCDA website on citizenship
have now disappeared. Despite this, the importance and potential of
citizenship education are highlighted by Hewitt:

> [C]itizenship education typically has a dual function – it promotes a
> national identity within each constituent national group, defined by a
> common language and history, but it also seeks to promote some sort
> of transnational identity which can bind together the various national
> groups within the state. Unfortunately, recent developments...in
> states[,] e.g. the breakdown of Yugoslavia and Czechoslovakia, the

constitutional crises in Belgium and Canada – suggest that is very difficult to construct and maintain this transnational identity.

(Hewitt, 2005, p. 214)

The promotion of a transnational identity, which Hewitt describes above as being difficult to teach, is in constant flux and continues to shift with every migratory movement; transnational identity still needs to be addressed to avoid what Hewitt (2005) describes in his research as a 'White backlash', that is, the hostility of the host population to the immigrant within the multicultural dilemma (Williams, 2013). At the very least, the Ajegbo Report (DfES, 2007) offered recommendations that attempted – through student voice, community involvement and continuing professional development – a culturally diverse agenda which theoretically can be addressed through citizenship, therefore potentially addressing issues of ethnic difference and racism within education. The closing of the QCDA in 2011 reduced a virtually visible opportunity for professional practitioners to develop citizenship education in schools. However, the OFSTED (2013) report into citizenship delivery in schools in England highlights positive practice in relation to diversity studies – underlined in the conclusions to this chapter – and provides, at least theoretically, continued opportunities to advance issues of race and ethnicity within citizenship and also other subjects within the curriculum.

Application of multiculturalism dilemmas and integrationist consensus to race and ethnicity in education

The application of either the notions of multiculturalist dilemma or integrationist consensus depends very much, in this chapter, on not only what was happening politically in the 2000s in countries such as England and Germany, but specifically on what was being taught in schools and universities in relation to subjects like citizenship. The idea of the multicultural dilemma is not so much about whether it exists, but how we apply and interpret the idea. For Williams (2013), the 'Dilemma' itself is how the host population sees the immigrant and, therefore, how the state creates policy to cope with immigrant issues. Thinking of multiculturalism, we can further increase our theoretical understanding of the term by looking at Erikson and Stjenfelt's (2012, p. 4) notions of 'soft' and 'hard' multiculturalism: 'The "soft" version of multiculturalism ... is perceived as a system where the individual can choose to live in whatever way she or he wishes ... [The "hard" version of multiculturalism is where] a community may legally and socially enforce its own mores and traditions, whatever it holds most sacred.' The 'hard' version of multiculturalism moves the focus away from the state towards communities and individuals and gives them more of a say beyond state policy, making the choice, for example, of home rather than school education. The 'soft' version of multiculturalism also gives the individual the choice to either accept state policy or decline or separate from national society. If, indeed, a movement is possible from the integrationist consensus in which a majority of people accept (education) policy towards 'soft' multiculturalism, the multicultural dilemma still needs to be overcome: that is, the hostility within the host population (Williams, 2013) to agreeing and accepting immigration and the state producing policy that integrates immigrants.

In relation to race and ethnicity, we also have to take into account the other side of the multicultural dilemma by considering what the immigrant thinks of the host population and whether there is hostility from this perspective. Ideally, one could argue we are looking for 'soft' multiculturalism, but a hostile or different response to state policy could lead to 'hard' multiculturalism within immigrant communities. This implies two perspectives within the multicultural dilemma whereby both host and immigrant populations need to be considered when examining notions of 'soft' and 'hard' multiculturalism. For Erikson and Stjenfelt (2012, p. 4), 'the question arises whether a variant somewhere between the two extremes could function as a political idea.'

This moves us to an integrationist consensus idea and how the state creates acceptable conditions within policy to theoretically accommodate the immigrant, that is, finding a compromise between 'soft' and 'hard' multiculturalism. The previous section examined how citizenship within English education has been created to reinforce this integrationist consensus. Citizenship is being used in the classroom today to consolidate notions of the nation and identities when we live in a more global, transnational world (Ong, 1999; Hewitt, 2005). Citizenship seems to be more fixed as a concept when thinking of integration, but Ong (1999) provides us with the notion of 'flexible citizenship', which gives us more insight and understanding of evolving cultural diversity (Deaux, 2006). However, this notion of flexibility is being marginalised by states to preserve nation and identity within integrationist policy rather than a wider promotion of the idea of transnational identities. However, it is worth examining Ong's (1999) notion of flexible citizenship in more depth. Flexible citizenship is applied to the practices of refugees and business migrants who work in one location while their families are lodged in 'safe havens' elsewhere. The art of flexibility, which is constrained by political and cultural boundaries, includes sending families and businesses abroad, as well as acquiring multiple passports, second homes, overseas bank accounts, and new habits. Here, I turn the question around and look at how the art of government which is strained by the condition of transnationality, has to further stretch the bounds of political economy and sovereignty.

(Ong, 1999, p. 214)

The art of government is crucial here because flexible citizenship has to be controlled, or at the very least influenced, by policy to produce an integrationist consensus (Katwala, 2013). We can analyse education performance of minority pupils (Archer and Francis, 2007) or how the market shapes education performativity (Ball, 2013) but it remains the state – through policymaking and the integrationist terms it uses, for example, responsibility, tolerance and citizenship – which helps us increase understandings of how individual choices (in relation to education) are influenced or controlled by the state (DCLG, 2012). Within the conditions set down in policymaking, for example within education, the national curriculum in England and Wales, ambiguities between ethnic difference and national identity are not easily resolved. Objective definitions and subjective understandings can be contradictory (Adonis, 2012; Baker, 2013). As Deaux (2006, p. 94) suggests within an American context, 'the identity hyphenation so common in the United States (for example, Korean-American) suggests a belief that one can simultaneously hold and blend together the ethnicity of origin and the nationality of current citizenship of residence'. This seems like a classic integrationist compromise with the condition of an individual being able to keep elements of a previous culture within an identity framework, but having to sign up to the new culture which is very much a conditioned and controlled process through, for example, education, a citizenship test and work. The debate becomes even more complicated when we think of the subject of *race*. As Mirza and Meetoo (2012, p. 4) argue: 'Race is therefore not about objective measurable physical and social characteristics, but about relationships of domination and subordination. Racism is expressed in different ways in particular historical times and within regional and national contexts. In other words, there are different racisms at any one time' (Mirza and Meetoo, 2012, p. 4). In other words, race, creates real effects. Race may be ideological, but it produces material consequences (Leonardo, 2009, p. 133). Domination and subordination through social and education policy seem to be influencing minority and majority social choices. The integrationist consensus and even assimilationist policy are leading to material, racist consequences for different communities. As Williams (2013) implies, the multicultural dilemma is not only how the host population sees the immigrant but how the immigrant sees the host population and decides on whether to integrate or separate from the majority community (Merry, 2013). In conceptual terms we are ideally looking, in education, for a move from an integrationist consensus to a more anti-racist, anti-discriminatory education based on human rights curricula (Race, 2012b). However, the idea and application of the integrationist consensus (Katwala, 2013) remains not only about individual and community choices, but how the state controls both perspectives (host population and immigrant) within the multicultural dilemma through general social and specific education policymaking.

Conclusions

What this chapter has highlighted is that ideas such as the multicultural dilemma and integrationist consensus are very useful when increasing understandings of issues concerning race and ethnicity. Multiculturalism provides us with a specific starting point when examining minority ethic issues and education, that is, (under)achievement in education (Archer and Francis, 2007). The multicultural dilemma idea provides a more general social viewpoint and is not exclusively about host population views on immigrants; it is also about how immigrants view the host population. Erikson and Stjenfelt's (2012) notions of 'soft' and 'hard' multiculturalism also shed light on the complexity of social and cultural choices for majority and minority populations. Multicultural education (Banks, 2012; Dolby, 2012; Howe and Lisi, 2014) provides us with a more specific focus when addressing social and cultural choices when relating to the multicultural dilemma to cultural diversity and how significantly it is addressed by professional practitioners in classrooms and lecture theatres. As Race (2011) suggests, teachers need to be continually trained throughout their careers to gain greater understandings of changing diversity. This leads us to citizenship education and its possibilities and potential in relation to teaching a more diverse curriculum which includes race and ethnicity issues, but a social and education realisation that integrationist terminology (Race, 2011; Katwala, 2013) has been in existence and has shaped policy for decades, for example, in England since 1988 through the national curriculum, which continues to evolve (Race, 2012a; DCLG, 2012; Pickles, 2013; DfE, 2013).

OFSTED (2013) provide a balanced account of how citizenship between 2009–2012 is being consolidated within English schools. Within primary schools where citizenship is non-statutory, the subject is 'thriving', but in the few weaker primary schools visited by the Inspectorate, 'poor curriculum planning means there were key gaps in pupils' knowledge and understanding'. Within secondary schools, citizenship education was 'stronger' than previous evidence collected by OFSTED in 2010. Provision in the weaker secondary schools was characterised by insufficient teaching time, teachers' lack of subject expertise and a lack of systems that could identity and address important weaknesses (OFSTED, 2013, p. 4). This concurs with the evidence collected by Race (2011) with the need for continuing professional development of, not only citizenship teachers, but all teachers in relation to race and ethnicity. As OFSTED continue:

> More schools were delivering citizenship through other subjects ... but with mixed results. Some schools used a cross-curricular approach, with carefully planned units of work that were taught by teachers who understood how to include citizenship dimensions in the host subject effectively.
>
> (ibid.).

We should be talking more about how advancing race and ethnicity issues are not only taught generally in England, and globally, through both cross-curricular practice and through the subject of citizenship. A major issue within multicultural and integrationist studies is highlighting the continuing positive influences of immigrants within changing cultural diversity. But this is one of many issues this book is attempting to address when advancing race and ethnicity within education. Education must continue to have a key role in the positive promotion of the value of immigrants within all cultures and societies through cross-curricula and citizenship studies. Teachers and lecturers need to have the training and the Continuing Professional Development to teach diversity so that issues concerning social equity and social justice can be addressed with confidence rather than fear (Race, 2012a, 2012b, 2013). However, the reforms to the national curriculum (DfE, 2013), which will be introduced in 2014, will be crucial in the short term when thinking of the notions of the multicultural dilemma (Williams, 2013) and integrationist consensus (Katwala, 2013). The major issue here is that it raises questions concerning *which subjects* – for example, anti-racism and anti-discrimination – can be taught cross-curricular in English schools within the new national curriculum in relation to race and ethnicity.

References

Adonis, A. (2012) *Education, Education, Education. Reforming England's Schools*, London, Biteback Publishing.
Anderson, E. (2010) *The Imperative of Integration*, Princeton, Princeton University Press.
Archer, L. and Francis, B. (2007) *Understanding Minority Ethnic Achievement. Race, gender, class and 'success'*, London, Routledge.
Baker, K. (2013) *14–18. A New Vision for Secondary Education*, London, Bloomsbury.
Banks, J.A. (ed.) (2009) *The Routledge International Companion to Multicultural Education*, Abingdon, Routledge.
Banks, J.A. (ed.) (2012) *Encyclopedia of Diversity in Education*, Thousand Oaks, Sage.
Cantle, T. (2008) *Community Cohesion: A New Framework for Race and Diversity*, 2nd edition, Houndsmills, Palgrave Macmillan.
Cantle, T. (2012) *Interculturalism: The New Era of Cohesion and Diversity*, Houndsmills, Palgrave Macmillan.
Cashin, S. (2004) *The Failures of Integration: How Race and Class are Undermining the American Dream*, New York, Public Affairs Publishing.
Collier, P. (2013) *Exodus. Immigration and Multiculturalism in the 21st Century*, London, Allen Lane.
Deaux, K. (2006) *To Be an Immigrant*, New York, Russell Sage Foundation.
Department for Communities and Local Government (DCLG) (2012) 'Creating the Conditions for Integration'. Available at https://www.gov.uk/government/publications/creating-the-conditions-for-a-more-integrated-society. [Accessed on 6 March 2013]
Department for Education (DfE) (2011) 'The Education Act 2011'. Available at http://www.legislation.gov.uk/ukpga/2011/21/contents/enacted. [Accessed on 28 October 2013]
Department for Education (DfE) (2013) 2014 National Curriculum. Available at http://www.education.gov.uk/schools/teachingandlearning/curriculum/nationalcurriculum2014/ [Accessed on 29 October 2013]
Department of Education and Science (DES) (1985) *Education for All*, Swann Report, London, HMSO.
Department for Education and Skills (DfES) (2006) *The Education and Inspections Act*, Chapter 40, London, HMSO, full text available at http://www.opsi.gov.uk/acts/acts2006/pdf/ukpga_20060040_en.pdf. [Accessed on 17 August 2009]
Department for Education and Skills (DfES) (2007) *Diversity and Citizenship Curriculum Review*, London, DfES. Full text available at http://publications.teachernet.gov.uk/eOrderingDownload/DfES_Diversity_&_Citizenship.pdf. [Accessed on 15 August 2009]
Dolby, N. (2012) *Rethinking Multicultural Education for the Next Generation: The New Empathy and Social Justice*, New York, Routledge.

Eade, J., Barrett, M., Flood, C. and Race, R. (eds) (2008) *Advancing Multiculturalism, Post 7/7*, Newcastle-Upon-Tyne, Cambridge Scholars Publishing.

Erikson, J.-M. and Stjernfelt, F. (2012) *The Democratic Contradictions of Multiculturalism*, New York, Telos Press Publishing.

Fass, D. (2010) *Negotiating Political Identities*, Farnham, Ashgate.

Forrester, G. and Taylor, E. (2011) 'Home Alone? Developments in the surveillance and monitoring of Home Education in England', paper presented to the British Education Research Association Conference, Institute of Education, London University, 7 September. Available at http://www.bera.ac.uk/bera2011/pdf/BERA2011_0703.pdf. [Accessed on 30 October 2013]

Frankenberg, E. and Orfield, G. (eds) (2007) *Lessons in Integration: Realising the Promise of Racial Diversity in American Schools*, Virginia, Charlottesville, Virginia University Press.

Freeman, G.P., Tendler, S.M. (2012) 'United States of America', in Joppke, C. and Leslie Seidle, F. (eds), *Immigrant Integration in Federal Countries*, Montreal, McGill-Queen's University Press, 192–220.

Galton, M. and MacBeath, J. (2008) *Teachers Under Pressure*, London, National Union of Teachers and Sage.

Garratt, D. and Forrester, G. (2012) *Education Policy Unravelled*, London, Continuum.

Gillborn, D. (2008) *Racism and Education: Coincidence or Conspiracy?* London, Routledge.

Gillborn, D. (2011) 'Fine Words and Foul Deeds: why coalition education policy will make things worse for Black students and the White working class', *Race Equality Teaching*, 29 (2), 9–14.

Gunter, H. (ed.) (2011) *The State and Education Policy: The Academies Programme*, London, Continuum.

Hansen, R. (2012) *The Centrality of Employment in Immigrant Integration in Europe*, Washington, D.C., Migration Policy Institute.

Hewitt, R. (2005) *White Backlash and the Politics of Multiculturalism*, Cambridge, Cambridge University Press.

Hoskins, K. (2012) 'Raising Standards 1988 to the present: a new performance policy era?' *Journal of Educational Administration and History*, 44 (1), 5–20.

Joppke, C. (2012) *The Role of the State in Cultural Integration: Trends, Challenges, Ways Ahead*, Washington, D.C., Migration Policy Institute.

Katwala, S. (2013) *The Integration Consensus, 1993–2013: How Britain Changed since Stephen Lawrence*, London, British Future.

Leonardo, Z. (2009) *Race, Whiteness, and Education*, London, Routledge.

Mahamdallie, H. (ed.) (2011) *Defending Multiculturalism*, London, Bookmarks Publications.

Malik, M. (2010) 'Progressive multiculturalism: the British experience', in Silj, A. (ed.), *European Multiculturalism Revisited*, London, Zed Books, 11–64.

May, S. and Sleeter, C.E. (2010) 'Introduction: critical multiculturalism: theory and praxis', in May, S. and Sleeter, C.E. (eds), *Critical Multiculturalism: Theory and Praxis*, New York, Routledge, 1–18.

May, S. and Westendorf, S. (2010) *The Multicultural Backlash: European Discourses, Policies and Practices*, New York, Routledge.

Mirza, H.S. and Meetoo, V. (2012) *Respecting Difference: Racism, Faith and Culture for Teacher Educators*, London, Institute of Education, London University.

Meer, N. and Modood, T. (2013) 'The "Civic Re-balancing" of British multiculturalism, and beyond', in Taras, R. (ed.), *Challenging Multiculturalism. European
Models of Diversity*, Edinburgh, Edinburgh University Press, 75–96.

Merry, M.S. (2013) *Equality, Citizenship and Segregation: A Defence of Separation*,
Houndsmills, Palgrave Macmillan.

Modood, T. (2013) *Multiculturalism*, 2nd ed., Cambridge, Polity Press.

Murphy, M. (2012) *Multiculturalism: A Critical Introduction*, London, Routledge.

Murphy, P. and Hall, K. (2008) *Learning and Practice: Agency and Identities*, London,
The Open University and Sage.

Office for Standards in Education (OFSTED) (2013) 'Citizenship consolidated? A
survey of citizenship in schools between 2009 and 2012'. Available at http://
www.ofsted.gov.uk/resources/citizenship-consolidated-survey-of-citizenship-
schools-between-2009-and-2012. [Accessed on 28 October 2013]

Ong, A. (1999) *Flexible Citizenship: The Cultural Logics of Transnationality*, London,
Duke University Press.

Osler, A. (2008) 'Citizenship education and the Ajegbo Report: re-imaging a
cosmopolitan nation', *London Review of Education*, 6 (1), 11–25.

Osler, A. (2009) 'Patriotism, multiculturalism and belonging: political discourse
and the teaching of history', *Educational Review*, 61 (1), 85–100.

Pickles, E. (2013) 'Uniting our Communities. Integration in 2013'. Speech given
by Secretary of State Eric Pickles at an event hosted by Policy Exchange and
British Future. Originally given at the Institution of Civil Engineers, London,
15 January 2013. Available at https://www.gov.uk/government/speeches/unit-
ing-our-communities-integration-in-2013. [Accessed on 6 April 2013]

Race, R. (2008) 'Introduction', in Eade, J., Barrett, M., Flood, C. and Race, R.
(eds), *Advancing Multiculturalism, Post 7/7*, Newcastle-Upon-Tyne, Cambridge
Scholars Press, 1–7.

Race, R. (2011) *Multiculturalism and Education*, London, Continuum.

Race, R. (2012a) 'Multiculturalism and the Impacts in Education Policy in
England', in Garner, S. and Kavak, S. (eds), *Debating Multiculturalism 2*, London,
The Dialogue Society, 243–258.

Race, R. (2012b) 'Integrationist to Citizenship Education Policy within England:
a forward movement or a backward step?', in Eade, J., Barrett, M. and Flood, C.
(eds), *Nationalism, Ethnicity, Citizenship: Multidisciplinary perspectives*, Newcastle-
Upon-Tyne, Cambridge Scholars Publishing, 181–194.

Race, R. (2013) 'Reflections on multiculturalism and education', *Contemporary
Issues in Education*, 3, 1, 7–22.

Saggar, S. and Somerville, W. (2012) *Building A British Model of Integration in an
Era of Immigration: Policy Lessons for Government*, Washington, D.C., Migration
Policy Institute.

Triandafyllidou, A., Modood, T. and Meer, T. (2012) 'Introduction: Diversity.
Integration, Secularism and Multiculturalism', in Traindafyllidou, A., Modood,
T. and Meer, N. (eds), *European Multiculturalisms: Cultural, Religious and Ethnic
Challenges*, Edinburgh, Edinburgh University Press, 1–32.

Tyson, K. (2011) *Integration Interrupted. Tracking, Black Students, and Acting White
after Brown*, Oxford, Oxford University Press.

Uberoi, V. and McGhee, D. (2012) 'Integrating Britain's culturally diverse citizens', in Friders, J. and Biles, J. (eds), *International Perspectives. Integration and
Inclusion*, Montreal, McGill-Queen's University Press, 59–78.

Vertovec, S. (2007) 'Super-Diversity and its implications', *Ethnic and Racial Studies,* 30 (6), 1024–1054.

Vertovec, S. and Wessendorf, S. (2010) 'Introduction: assessing the backlash against multiculturalism', in Vertovec, S. and Wessendorf, S. (eds), *The Multiculturalism Backlash. European Discourses, Policies and Practices,* New York, Routledge, 1–31.

Walters, S. (2011) *Ethnicity, Race and Education: An Introduction,* London, Continuum.

Williams, M.H. (2013) 'Introduction: the multicultural dilemma', in Williams, M.H. (ed.), *The Multicultural Dilemma,* Abingdon, Routledge, 1–11.

14
Resilience, the Black Child and the Coalition Government

Jasmine Rhamie

In a climate of austerity and radical change in education, this chapter considers the challenges faced by Black parents to find ways to achieve the best educational outcomes for their children in an ever selective and competitive educational environment. It examines the current educational climate and some recent policy directions and legislation, and it demonstrates the need for Black pupils to develop greater resilience in order to succeed in an education system set up to increase the purchasing power of the White middle class to the disadvantage of Black pupils. The impact of these changes will be considered in relation to Black pupils, particularly as they often come from the most disadvantaged communities. For the purpose of this chapter Black predominately refers to Black African, Black Caribbean and Black other groups, but does not exclude other minority groups who also experience inequality as a result of government policy. The chapter will discuss resilience and how it impacts and enables Black children to achieve against the odds. It highlights a greater need within the current educational climate for parents and communities to work harder to ensure the academic success of their children.

It is important here to provide some theoretical background to the discussions. The recent focus on Whiteness studies and Critical Race Theory is important in supporting a deeper analysis and recognition of the underlying forces at play in policy development. Gillborn (2005) suggests that White supremacy lies at the heart of policy direction and decisions. He describes Hooks's notion of White supremacy (Hooks, 1989, p. 492) as being 'a deeply rooted exercise of power that remains untouched by moves to address the obvious forms of more overt racial discrimination'. Ladson-Billings (2004, p. 51) notes that the use of conceptual categories such as Whiteness does not refer to White

people, per se, but indicates the positioning of Whiteness as normative, whereas all others are 'ranked and categorised' in relation to this
norm. Furthermore, Leonardo (2004) asserts that the diversity of White
ethnic groups are homogenised under the term Whiteness as a means of
asserting power and maintaining White racial dominance. It is important, then, to recognise the structural racisms that are constantly at play
within education policy, and that the changes currently being undertaken by the coalition government serve to further establish White
supremacy and reinforce Black subordination and powerlessness. In any
consideration of policy, Gillborn (2005, p. 492) suggests an approach
which addresses the following fundamental questions: Who or what is
driving education policy? Who wins or loses as a result of these priorities? What is the impact of these policies? It is intended that this chapter
address these questions and enable a more critical consideration of the
coalition's education policy.

In a period of austerity, the coalition government has sought to suggest
that their cuts in budget funding will impact the rich rather than the
poor (Wintour, 2012). However, research undertaken by the Institute for
Fiscal Studies suggested that when considering the cuts overall, which
include those to housing benefit, the poor will be disproportionately
disadvantaged (Brown and Levell, 2010). Furthermore, recent financial
policies have led to headlines charging the government with robbing
the old to fund tax cuts for the rich (BBC News, 2012). The disadvantages to the poor, including ethnic minorities, within fiscal policy are
also echoed in the way in which educational policy is developing.

The former Labour government promoted and encouraged the recognition of pupil identities through an emphasis on inclusive education.
This was supported by the introduction of the 'Every Child Matters'
agenda (DfES, 2004) and *The Children's Act* (2004). Funding was provided
to implement a range of initiatives to support an inclusive agenda and
raise the achievement of vulnerable and disadvantaged groups. This is
not to suggest that Labour was the champion of equality and inclusion.
Furthermore, education policy under Labour was responsible for contributing to the extension of market forces within education, increasing
parent choice and leading to those with the necessary social and educational capital being able to take advantage of the education system to the
detriment of those without. Research found that under Labour, despite
significant accounts of racism or racist incidents taking place, schools
failed to record these incidents in their reports to the local authority
(Parsons, 2010). Parsons stated that Labour achieved 'rhetorical success
but practical failure' (Parsons, 2009, p. 253). Tomlinson (2008, p. 151)

suggested that Labour implemented contradictory policies by utilising 'crude anti-immigration rhetoric' and working towards introducing harsher immigration legislation while at the same time promoting race equality and community cohesion. Despite these criticisms, Labour attempted, with varying success, to provide funding to support raising the achievement of those from BME and poorer backgrounds.

Within the coalition government's education policies there has been a definite shift away from this agenda. This shift moves away from an inclusive agenda to one in which individuality and parental choice are aggressively promoted – however, those with the appropriate capital to take advantage of the freedom to make a 'choice' tend to be White and middle class, leaving behind the vulnerable, disadvantaged and those from ethnic minority groups.

Recent policy decisions, such as the Education Act 2011 (DfE, 2011a) and the change in the OFSTED inspection framework, have raised concerns about the commitment of the government to inclusion and to challenging racism (OFSTED, 2012). The Education Act 2011 has taken power away from local authorities and parents, placing greater power in the hands of the government and, more specifically, conferring greater autonomy to the Secretary of State for Education and power to new academies and free schools. Further, it gives schools new powers to search pupils and takes away the requirement for schools to give 24 hours' notice to parents prior to issuing a detention (DfE, 2011a). This reduction in localised power has a number of specific implications for Black pupils. The act makes it easier for schools to exclude pupils, and it has removed the independent appeal panels convened in the case of exclusions, replacing them with review panels which can only reinstate a pupil in cases in which Head Teachers' actions were deemed unlawful. Given the disproportionate number of Black young people being excluded from school for trivial reasons, this raises real concerns about the level of protection in place for at-risk pupils (Younge, 1997; OCC, 2012).

In 2009–2010, pupils with a statement of SEN were eight times more likely to be permanently excluded than those without a statement. Amongst ethnic minority groups, Black Caribbean pupils continue to be nearly four times more likely to be permanently excluded from school. Only Traveller children of Irish heritage experienced more permanent exclusions (DfE, 2011b). In an inquiry into school exclusions, the Office for the Children's Commissioner found that a Black Caribbean boy with SEN and receiving free school meals in 2009–2010 was 168 times more likely to be excluded from school than a White female who is from a wealthy home and does not have special needs (OCC, 2012). The continuing trend for both Black Caribbean boys and girls and Mixed White and Black Caribbean pupils to be excluded more than other groups is troubling in light of the changes introduced in the recent Education Act (Parsons et al., 2005; DFE, 2011a). Moreover, since 2000, the proportion of excluded Black pupils has increased at a greater rate and number than other groups (DfES, 2006), suggesting that it is these pupils who will be disproportionally disadvantaged by these changes.

In response to the Macpherson Report after the death of Stephen Lawrence, OFSTED were required to inspect schools for race equality, examining how strategies to prevent and combat racism in schools were implemented. A number of useful publications and reports have been produced as a result of OSTED's work in this area: Raising the Attainment of Minority Ethnic Pupils: Schools and LEA responses (OFSTED, 1999); Achievement of Black Pupils: Three successful primary schools (OFSTED, 2002a) and achievement of Black pupils: Good practice in Secondary schools (OFSTED, 2002b); Race Equality in Education: Good practice in schools and local authorities (OFSTED, 2005), to name a few. These documents have been useful in providing evidence-based recommendations for raising the attainment of these groups. Coalition government changes in OFSTED inspection criteria have resulted in inspection for race equality, and in the duty to promote community cohesion no longer being a requirement. This is a strong indication of the lack of recognition and concern for matters relating to race and ethnicity, particularly given the research evidence of real challenges within schools in this area.

There is a wealth of research evidence of the disadvantages already faced by ethnic minorities in schools, with some groups being largely overrepresented in particular negative statistics. The depth and nature of the problem is highlighted through the over-representation of African Caribbean children in the figures for school exclusion, poor exam results, having emotional and behavioural difficulties, and receiving statements of Special Educational Need (Gillborn and Mirza, 2000; Osler et al., 2001; Parsons et al., 2005; Bhattacharyya et al., 2003; Strand, 2012). Researchers have identified structural factors leading to racism and differential outcomes for ethnic minority children and other vulnerable groups.

This is against the background of a recent *Times Educational Supplement* (TES) survey which found that 83 per cent of teachers reported they had witnessed racism taking place in schools and felt ill-equipped to deal with these incidents (Maddern, 2011). A Teacher's TV survey found similar results, with 48 per cent of teachers indicating that they were aware of racist bullying taking place in school, but 68 per cent felt that their schools did not have an effective strategy for addressing it (Teacher's TV, 2009). Research conducted by Show Racism the Red Card found that racism is still a significant issue amongst pupils and some teachers in England's schools (Show Racism the Red Card, 2011).

Performance tables will no longer collect data on pupil race and ethnicity, which results in a crucial aspect of a child's identity being ignored. Without this information, it will be difficult to determine the impact, on pupils, of institutional racism and policy decisions. Lacking this information will also make it difficult to monitor differential outcomes for pupils and identify good and poor practice in relation to vulnerable groups of pupils who experience multiple discriminations due to the intersections of particular characteristics, such as race, ethnicity, social class, gender and SEN, for example. To seek to provide data only on gender and those eligible for FSM portrays a deep ignorance of the complex and multiple challenges faced by disadvantaged and underachieving pupils.

Given the importance of statistical data and monitoring that is essential in highlighting the disproportionate disadvantages faced by specific ethnic minority groups, this move away from an emphasis on, or specificity of, race and ethnicity is worrying. The decision to end ethnic monitoring in education has been reflected in reports of particular police forces deciding not to keep records of the ethnicity of individuals who are subjected to stop-and-search activities. What is interesting is that the forces that have indicated a move in this direction are those with, historically, the highest number of stop-and-search occurrences on BME people (Dodd, 2011). These actions will result in a reduction in protection for Black groups and remove the need for public services such as the schools and the police to be accountable for their actions and for the impact of those actions on vulnerable groups. The increasingly consistent absence of 'race' in Coalition policy discourse has been noted by Tomlinson (2011), who describes a return to a colour-blind agenda.

Other coalition policies, such as free schools and academies (which have been promoted as bringing about better quality education for the poorest of society) have so far failed to achieve this purported ambition. Reporters found that the first 24 free schools were, in fact located within wealthier, middle class areas (Vassagar and Shepherd, 2011). Furthermore, Race on the Agenda (ROTA, 2011) suggests that local communities already facing educational disadvantage are losing out to free schools. ROTA raised concerns about the ways in which free schools can draw boundaries for their catchment area, leaving out primary schools serving more deprived areas of the borough (ROTA, 2011).

The government have indicated that academies will not need to employ qualified teachers but can recruit staff who are experts in their fields. This has resulted in condemnation, as these schools are publicly funded and, according to Husbands (2012), this goes against both national and international research evidence which suggests that lowering the qualifications of those entering teaching lowers standards. Furthermore, the removal of these schools from local authority control mean that they are not required to adhere to the statutory admissions code. This has the potential to result in a situation in which these schools can exclude or include whomever they want without parents having recourse to challenge decisions. Groups of pupils deemed to be at risk or underachieving or requiring too much effort could be excluded from these schools, which now have the power to become elitist.

In 2012, the government introduced its revised Qualified Teachers' Standards (QTS), which sought to simplify the previous 33 standards (DfE, 2012). These revised standards failed to include equality and inclusion as key themes. In the previous standards Q18 made specific references to equality and inclusion and to the importance of having an awareness of the range of cultural, social, ethnic, religious and linguistic factors that impact children's learning. Teachers were also required to take 'practical account of diversity and promoting equality and inclusion' when planning teaching strategies and resources for lessons (Q19, Q25a) (TDA, 2007).

However, the revised standards state that teachers should 'set goals that stretch and challenge pupils of all backgrounds, abilities and dispositions' in Standard 1 and 'have a clear understanding of the needs of all pupils, including those with special educational needs; those of high ability; those with English as an additional language; those with disabilities; and be able to use and evaluate distinctive teaching approaches to engage and support them' in Standard 5, which dilutes the specific focus on key aspects of inclusion and equality such as race and ethnicity, religion and social class factors, which are known to impact achievement (DfE, 2012). Furthermore, the second part of the QTS standards refers to personal and professional conduct. In this section, teachers are required 'not to undermine fundamental British values' (DfE, 2012). There is, however, no guidance as to what those British values are. Academics do not agree on what they are and suggest that 'Britishness' and its values is too vague a concept. Instead, they say that a focus on citizenship and equal rights would be preferable (Khan, 2007; Parekh, 2007).

Furthermore, Rhamie et al. (2012) found that pupils' own understandings of Britishness were complex and diverse. They concluded that the normalisation of Whiteness and its associations with Britishness and power contributed to the schoolboys in their study struggling with their own identities and connectedness to Britishness and schooling. Given that academics and pupils struggle with defining and understanding what Britishness and its associated values are, it would be difficult for teachers and student teachers to understand exactly what they are and how to comply with this requirement.

The lack of explicit statements about the need to ensure equality and inclusion in the new Teacher Standards, and the lack of guidance on what British values are coupled with the potential impact of this on the training and preparation of student teachers for a diverse pupil population, raise further concerns. In recent research, Hick et al. (2011) found that many teacher educators lacked confidence in discussing issues relating to race and race equality with their students and required these issues to be embedded within Initial Teacher Education (ITE). Lander's research (2011) found that many student teachers feel unprepared to deal with issues having to do with 'race', particularly if students reside in predominantly White areas where there is little or no perceived diversity.

Many ITE students have acknowledged the importance of these issues, but they have been unsure how to approach them in the classroom, particularly in relation to how these issues would be taught. ITE students have also reported that they feel ill equipped when thinking about how they would deal with racist incidents in the classroom (Bhopal and Rhamie, forthcoming). An international study also suggests that there is an ever-greater need to ensure that teachers are prepared for teaching a diverse student population in an increasingly diverse society. OECD (2010) suggests that successful schools treat diversity as a valuable resource that provides an opportunity for mutual, and reciprocal, learning.

It is difficult to refute the evidence of a return to the marginalisation of matters relating to race and equality in current government policy directions. These changes will have a greater impact on vulnerable groups within the education system than presently acknowledged. In a priority review of exclusions amongst Black pupils, the DfES suggested that the range of responses to race equality legislation has ranged from 'grudging compliance to outright hostility' (DfES, 2006). Law et al. (2012) describes the new political climate as 'muscular majoritarianism', where increases in racial and ethnic inequalities are acceptable, the 'racialisation of education' is ignored and the government is hostile to specific programmes and initiatives designed to support and develop ethnic minority groups (2012, p. 2). These changes in education policy serve to disadvantage the most vulnerable pupils, many of whom belong to ethnic minority communities.

The rapid changes within education and the move towards the invisibility of race lead me to consider the impact of these policies on one of the ethnic minority groups that features highly in most of the negative education statistics – African Caribbeans. In previous research (Rhamie, 2007), I identified the importance of resilience in explaining how some African Caribbean pupils defied the odds and succeeded at school, achieving above expectations in academic results. Resilience has been defined as the ability to recover from hardship due to protective factors. Resilience is a process by which individuals are able to adapt and change when faced with adverse situations, resulting in positive outcomes. The two dimensions to resilience are the experience of hardship, or adversity, and the capacity for successful adaptive functioning (Schoon, 2006). Resilience is not a static characteristic, but is dynamic, and is dependent upon the individual and the particular risks being faced (Rutter, 1987, p. 317). Thus, one may be resilient at school and achieve success, but the protective factors that ensure success at school may not be as effective in another adverse situation.

The concept of resilience originates in the field of psychiatric risk research and considers risk and protective factors which can assist in understanding how individuals are able to achieve despite adversity (Rutter, 1987; Crosnoe and Elder, 2004). Risk factors would be anything that results in deterioration (or digression) towards a worsened state or a situation that leads to the continuance of a problem situation (Kirby and Fraser, 1997). Risk factors in the context of education would be: negative school experiences, the low educational attainment of parents and their employment in low-level occupations. Historically, there has been a focus on risk factors, which has resulted in a deficit model approach to families. This has led to a perception that disadvantaged families and their problems are the responsibility of families themselves. For families experiencing multiple risk factors that, within education, are deemed to place pupils at risk of underachievement and academic failure, the responsibility for addressing these factors is seen to lie with the family – therefore, the expectation that these children will achieve is limited. Furthermore, the risk of underachievement and academic failure is then perceived to be inevitable. More recently, there has been a move away from risk perspectives (which imply that there are deficiencies, weaknesses or disadvantages) to a greater consideration of the strengths and positive attributes: in short, to the protective factors that contribute to resilience (Cefai, 2008).

There is no consistent definition of protective factors; however, Kirkby and Fraser (1997) define them as the 'internal and external forces that help children resist or ameliorate risk' (p. 16). Protective factors promote resilience in children. Protective factors have been categorised into three groups: within child factors, such as personality, sociability, coping skills and cognitive abilities; within family factors, such as a positive relationship with at least one parent, family warmth and care; and external protective factors, such as social support and access to, and availability of, external resources (Garmezy, 1985). Other researchers similarly describe protective factors as positive interactions with parents as well as support in the home, high expectations, positive and constructive interactions, and consistent, positive, activities within the community (Richman and Bowen, 1997).

Research evidence has found that, despite experiencing highly stressful, high-risk situations – such as growing up in families where there is drug/alcohol abuse or mental illness, physical, sexual or emotional abuse or high levels of deprivation – for some children these factors have not had a detrimental effect on their emotional well-being, and they have 'fared well in life' through being successful in school and/or developing positive relationships with others (Kirby and Fraser, 1997, p. 13).

The nature of risk and protective factors has been found to be dependent upon the socio-cultural context of development. Haight (2002) examined how, within her sample community, the Black church played a significant role in building resilience. She found that the religious practices of African American children, such as their spiritual belief systems, socialisation and participation through the child-centred activities of the church, promoted the development of protective factors in children who face the harsh reality of racism, poverty and disadvantage (p. 8). This positive experience inevitably had a positive impact on their educations. This is in line with my own research, which found that the development of resiliency occurred as a result of positive relationships with adults and consistent, constructive, supportive interactions at home and in the community which, in some cases, included religious practices such as church attendance and active involvement (Rhamie, 2007). Other researchers have described protective factors in terms of providing a buffer against adverse stresses encountered and suggest that it is the individual, and factors within families and communities, which mediate against adverse circumstances (Pollard, 1989).

For the academically successful African Caribbean respondents in my study, protective factors came as a result of the wide range of support they received in their homes and communities. There was access to a range of family members and friends who provided help with homework, study resources and verbal and practical help, support and encouragement. The high value that parents placed on education was transmitted to their children who, in turn, had high expectations and a determination to set and achieve clear academic goals (Rhamie, 2007). Rhamie and Hallam (2002) also found that parental support was an important factor. This positive support engendered resilience in children, which helped to counteract the negative impact of their school experiences. It was the interaction between the home and community which provided children with what they needed to succeed in school. If the school also provides a strong and supportive achievement-oriented environment, success is even more likely (Rhamie and Hallam, 2002). Despite the value and significance of parental support, it is important to recognise that, despite possessing the appropriate cultural, economic and social capitals, middle-class Black parents have to work much harder in order to ensure equal opportunities for their children in school (Vincent and Ball, 2013). For Black parents who are coming from more deprived backgrounds, this reality presents a greater challenge to achievement by Black children.

Law et al. (2012) identified a strong sense of resilience amongst a sample of ten Black boys. Here, the boys' high aspirations were a driving force supported by family members, which fostered resilience despite experiencing overt racism and barriers to fully accessing education. They refused to allow their focus on their goals to be deterred by these negative experiences. Ploner (2011) also identified resilience in ethnic minority university students as developing from community cultural capital, which enabled what he referred to as 'resilient thinking' in his sample. For example, students utilised a range of strategies, including seeing the positives in negative situations, having a sense of humour, adopting a 'don't care' attitude, maintaining perspective, working harder and drawing on religion/spirituality and/or family/community, all of which develop resilient thinking. Other research has identified the range of ecosystems such as the home, community and schools, which can provide and enhance the development of protective factors for young people (Pianta and Walsh, 1998; Crosnoe and Elder, 2004; Rhamie and Hallam, 2002; Rhamie, 2007).

Some of the factors shown to be beneficial are positive relation-ships with family members, positive social-support networks, a sense of agency, individual coping skills and personal factors (Sawyer, 2009). Social-life rituals and routines were also identified, mirroring my own research findings. It is important to highlight here that the responsi-bility for educating children lies within schools, particularly as many parents do not have the skills or resources to educate their children at home, given the pressures and stresses associated with families expe-riencing high levels of deprivation. Therefore, given that vulnerable groups were successful due to outside school factors, it is important that schools consider how they might support the development of resilience to enhance children's achievements.

The recent shift to a focus on resilience and protective factors has led to attention being given to understanding the factors that support children's academic success, and how schools might begin to support children through fostering and promoting resilience. In the descrip-tions cited above of protective factors and resilience developers, school factors are often included. These include teachers and relationships at school as well school culture and classroom environment. Where these relationships and experiences are positive they are described as supportive environments which provide encouragement and build confidence in pupils' abilities (Sawyer, 2009; Schoon and Bartley, 2008). Furthermore, they are identified as being important in supporting the development of resilience. Cefai (2008) highlighted the significance of caring and nurturing relationships between pupils and teachers in schools as a critical protective factor. These relationships are critical in promoting learning and social competence. Adopting a personal-ised approach to classroom learning and strengthening the teaching of PSHE has also been shown to be beneficial in building resilience at school (Cassen et al., 2008).

Indeed, some progress has been made towards highlighting the value of these matters in school through the introduction of the Social and Emotional Aspects of Learning (SEAL) materials, which were designed to develop children's emotional intelligence and support their mental health and well-being. The term emotional intelligence was introduced by Salovey and Mayer in 1990. Their definition related to understanding how to manage relationships, how to be self-motivating and knowing how to manage one's own emotions, as well as being able to recognise emotions in others. The idea of emotional intelligence was further developed by Bar-On (1997) with the addition of intra-personal and inter-personal skills and adaptability, and being able to manage stress effectively. These aspects have been incorporated into the SEAL materials and contribute to the development of resilience in school.

The evaluation of the SEAL materials found they were successful in helping staff to understand their pupils better, which resulted in teachers' changing their behaviour and interactions with pupils. Furthermore, teachers reported that children were more confident, which had a positive impact on their social, communication and negotiation skills (Hallam et al., 2006). All staff perceived a positive impact on the children's behaviour and well-being. Classrooms and playgrounds were calmer. Children's confidence, social, communication and negotiating skills and attitudes were reported to have improved. The majority of the teachers in the study stated that the programme was successful (ibid., 2006).

The development of resilience amongst the sample in my research was largely due to out-of-school factors, as all participants (regardless of their educational success) experienced negative encounters within school with teachers and/or other pupils. At home, and within the community, the successful participants experienced a sense of belonging that supported their educational endeavours. However, what was unfortunate for my sample was the lack of a sense of belonging and support experienced within the school environment (Rhamie, 2007).

The significance of resilience in the classroom has been highlighted in a number of research studies recognising the importance of a caring classroom environment on the self-esteem, learning and behaviour of children (Cefai, 2008; Reese and Bailey, 2003; Schoon, 2006). Classrooms where teachers set high expectations for all the pupils in their class and are aware of the challenges faced by vulnerable, at-risk pupils with SEN, or with ethnic or cultural differences, are necessary for schools to support and promote resilience. Teachers promote resilience when they value each pupil as an individual and seek to ensure that the variety of cultural, religious and ethnic communities are welcomed, embraced and valued within the classroom and that this approach is embedded within everything the teacher does.

Unfortunately, qualitative research has often found that many Black pupils do not report having these experiences in school. For many, their school experiences are characterised by: being treated differently compared to their White peers (Maylor et al., 2009); being subject to greater surveillance and discipline (Youdell, 2003); facing low teacher expectations (DCSF, 2008; Tickly et al., 2006; Strand, 2008) and experiencing institutional racism (Graham and Robinson, 2004; DfES, 2006). There is acknowledgement within Western society of the value and importance of academic achievement. The level of education attained and academic qualifications achieved have long-term implications for life chances in terms of social, economic and employment security and emotional health and well-being (Schoon, 2006). Academic achievement is recognised as being critical in British culture yet, too many schools continue to fail significant numbers of pupils, thereby preventing them from reaching their full potential.

I believe that, within the new direction of government policy (DfE, 2011a), there are serious implications for vulnerable families, particularly Black families. It seems to me that the changes taking place will reduce schools' ability, willingness and need to ensure that their classrooms are places that ensure sensitivity and that the needs of Black pupils are taken into account. The lack of specific requirements to ensure that cultural, ethnic and religious needs are considered and met leaves Black children in a more vulnerable position in the classroom and parents with less power to challenge unacceptable practices. Furthermore, as Archer (2008) suggests, the dominant discourse within UK education implies that the concept of an 'ideal student' excludes ethnic minority pupils. She suggests that the 'othering' of Black pupils results in their marginalisation in the classroom.

Youdell (2006, p. 33) suggested that school processes effectively maintain the exclusion of certain groups of pupils perceived as 'impossible learners'. She recognised the ways in which Black pupils experience daily micro exclusions in classrooms and how these micro exclusions need to be understood in terms of what actually constitutes who can be a student. She suggests that it is the identity of those who are excluded that is essential to their exclusion (Youdell, 2006, p. 13). The embodiment of different types of learners associated with particular ethnic and gendered identities is demonstrated in the ways in which school discourses constitute African Caribbean pupils as 'unacceptable learners' (Youdell, 2003, p. 21). These negative constructions of Black learners serve to impact their school interactions and responses, thus leading to their inevitable failure.

Stereotyped perceptions of African Caribbean parents remain, and research identifies the continual marginalisation of Black parents, which renders them powerless to engage fully in their children's education (Crozier, 2001). Furthermore, the myth of parents' lack of interest in Black children's education has been challenged. A number of studies have highlighted Black parents seeking additional educational support for their children through supplementary schooling (Crozier, 2001; Reay and Mirza, 2005) or providing private tuition or additional help with homework (Rhamie, 2007). Black families too often continue to be regarded by schools as contributing to their children's difficulties (Gazeley, 2010).

Research undertaken on Black middle class parents found that despite parents possessing the social, economic and cultural capital – thereby fitting within what would be described as the middle classes – they felt that their ethnicity prevented them from identifying with the middle class due to its strong association with Whiteness (Archer, 2011). This experience has been echoed in Vincent and colleagues' (n.d.) larger research project on the educational strategies utilised by Black middle-class parents. Bourdieu described the concept of *habitus* as being the subjective ways in which different classes, and groups within those classes, understand and perceive themselves and how they are perceived by others (Bourdieu, 1984). Taking habitus into account it is evident that Black groups struggle to have their culture accepted as legitimate. However, dominant White groups maintain the status of middle-class groups, making it difficult for even those Black groups with the necessary cultures (middle class cultures) to attain or develop the habitus that would enable them to access the power held by the middle classes to access and engage fully in education or to be perceived or regarded as equally entitled.

If we accept, as Bourdieu suggests, that habitus is constructed by powerful establishments, such as educational institutions, it is clear to see how the habitus of African Caribbeans could then be perceived to be associated with academic failure and parental unwillingness either to support their children's education or to engage positively with schools (Bourdieu, 1984). Reay and colleagues (2005) found that the habitus associated with Black families was related to school underachievement. In separate research, Reay (1995) found that schools influenced and informed the habitus of Black pupils and that this habitus was embodied within those pupils. Carlile (2012) found that institutionalised racism was at play in the exclusion decisions of minority ethnic children and recommended the need for schools to acknowledge the continued active presence of their own institutional racism. Parsons (2009) substantiates this with his discussion on the operation of passive racism which serves to perpetuate the disproportionate level of Black exclusions. Racism was highlighted in research on the Black middle classes which, despite possessing the middle class capitals, recognised that racism and discrimination continued to be a real threat to their children's educational success (Vincent et al., n.d.). The enduring nature and impact of racism in whatever form has to be confronted and addressed if the practices of school staff, as described in this paper, are to change and be fully eliminated.

When reflecting on the part that racism plays in many of the disadvantages experienced by ethnic minority groups, it is important to acknowledge the role played by those who have power over the major structures within society. These economic, political and social structures are controlled by the White majority, which exerts power over how the available resources within these structures are distributed and who is entitled to access them (Baker, 1983, p. 138). This results in structural inequalities in accessing good quality education and how Black pupils are perceived, resulting in persistent barriers to equal opportunity in education (Darling-Hammond, 2004). Baker (1983) suggests that, through their underlying structural and cultural systems, policy decisions have the effect of excluding Black groups and impacting the extent to which those groups are able to access, and have power over, critical resources. There needs to be an acknowledgement of Whiteness and White privilege which, through their operation, serve to subordinate minority groups that are deemed to be 'other' or on the outside of the dominant group. However, individual White groups are not conscious or aware of the power they have and how this dominates and subordinates certain groups. Neither are they cognisant of the inequalities faced by minority groups because they, themselves, have not faced such barriers or experienced them. The only way to highlight the inequalities is through careful monitoring and consistent review, and drawing on the research literature to ensure that particular groups are not disadvantaged as a result of the implementation of new policies. My concern is that the move towards the invisibility of race within current educational policy will result in the inequalities becoming invisible and, thereby, no longer being acknowledged, recorded or addressed, resulting thereby in continued disadvantage and underachievement by Black Caribbeans, particularly. What is needed is a comprehensive equality impact assessment to be undertaken to determine the effect of government policies on vulnerable and minority groups.

Within the current educational policy climate, I believe that Black families will find diminishing interest from schools in the progress, welfare and academic success of their children. The slow progress in improving the attainment and achievement of Black pupils over numerous decades leaves little hope for Black parents that relying on the education system or improvements in teacher education will change the situation. As such, it is my belief that Black parents need to become more aware of how the system is changing and seek to find ways to identify individuals or groups with the necessary social, cultural and educational capital to seek alternative ways to enable their children to achieve educational success – with their self esteem, identity and self confidence intact. It seems to me that, despite successive government policies, Black parents can no longer rely on the education system to educate their children.

At the start of this chapter I suggested that it is useful to consider Gillborn's key questions of who or what is driving education policy. Who wins or loses as a result of these priorities? What is the impact of these policies? It is hoped that this chapter has addressed some of these questions and helped to identify the key concerns with government policies. The current direction of government education policy should be challenged, as it serves to further disadvantage vulnerable groups, particularly Black groups. There is a need for additional support to be provided for Black families. It is hoped that this will be achieved through ensuring a greater understanding of the impact of government changes on Black families and will encourage Black parents to recognise that it is imperative that they actively build resilience in their children and recognise that, without it, their children are at risk of failing. Black parents now need to become more informed about the impact of current policies' decisions and be empowered to examine new ways of ensuring their children achieve educational success.

References

Archer, L. (2008) 'The impossibility of minority ethnic educational "success?" an examination of the discourses of teachers and pupils in British secondary schools', *European Educational Research Journal*, 7 (1), 89–107.

Archer, L. (2011) 'Constructing minority ethnic middle class identity: An exploratory study with parents, pupils, and young professionals', *Sociology*, 45 (1), 134–151.

Baker, D. (1983) 'Race, ethnicity and power: a comparative study', Henley on Thames, Routledge, Keegan Paul.

Bar-On, R. (1997) *The Emotional Intelligence Inventory, (EQ-i)*, Technical Manual, Toronto, Multi-Health Systems.

BBC News (2012) 'Bakewell: granny tax funding tax cuts for rich', 19 April. Available at http://www.bbc.co.uk/news/uk-politics-177772631. [Accessed on 27 August 2012]

Bhattacharyya, G., Ison, L. and Blair, M. (2003) *Minority Ethnic Attainment and Participation in Education and Training: The Evidence.* DfES RTP01–03.

Bhopal, K. and Rhamie, J. (forthcoming) 'Initial Teacher Training: understanding 'race', diversity and inclusion', *Race Ethnicity and Education Special Issue*.

Bourdieu, P. (1984) *Distinction: A Social Critique of the Judgement of Taste,* London, Routledge, Keegan and Paul.

Brown, J. and Levell, P. (2010) 'New IFS research challenges Chancellor's "progressive Budget" claim', Press release Institute for Fiscal Studies.

Carlile, A. (2012) 'An ethnography of permanent exclusion from school: revealing and untangling the threads of institutionalised racism', *Race Ethnicity and Education*, 15 (2), 175–194.

Cassen, R., Feinstein, L. and Graham, P. (2008) 'Educational outcomes: adversity and resilience', *Social Policy and Society*, 8 (1), 73–85.

Cefai, C. (2008) *Promoting Resilience in the Classroom: A Guide to Developing Pupils' Emotional and Cognitive Skills,* London, Jessica Kingsley Publishers.

Crosnoe, R. and Elder, G. (2004) 'Family dynamics: supportive relationships and educational resilience during adolescence', *Journal of Family Issues,* 25 (5), 571–602.

Crozier, G. (2001) 'Excluded parents: the de-racialisation of parental involvement [1]', *Race Ethnicity and Education,* 4 (4), 329–341.

Darling-Hammond, L. (2004) 'What happens to a dream deferred? The continuing quest for equal educational opportunity', in Banks, J. and McGee-Banks, C. (eds), *Handbook of Research on Multicultural Education,* San Francisco, Jossey Banks, 607–630.

Department for Children, Schools and Families (DCSF) (2008) *Excellence and Enjoyment: Learning and Teaching for Black Children in the Primary Years,* Nottingham, DCSF.

Department for Education (DfE) website (2011a) *The Education Act 2011.* Available at http://www.education.gov.uk/aboutdfe/departmentalinformation/educationbill/a0073748/education-bill. [Accessed on 27 August 2012]

Department for Education (DfE) (2011b) *First Statistical Report: Permanent and Fixed Period Exclusions from Schools and Exclusion Appeals in England,* 2009–2010.

Department for Education (DfE) (2012) *Teachers' Standards,* London, DFE.

Department for Education and Skills (DfES) (2004) *Every Child Matters: Change for Children,* London, DfES.

Department for Education and Skills (DfES) (2006) *Exclusion of Black Pupils Priority Review. Getting It. Getting It Right,* London, DfES.

Dodd, V. (2011) 'Police forces stop recording race of people they stop', *The Guardian.* Available at http://www.guardian.co.uk/uk/2011/sep/22/police-record-race-stop. [Accessed on 10 September 12]

Gazeley, L. (2010) 'The role of school exclusion in processes in the re-production of social and educational disadvantage', *British Journal of Educational Studies,* 58 (3), 293–309.

Graham, M. and Robinson, G. (2004) 'The silent catastrophe: institutional racism in the British educational system and the underachievement of Black boys', *Journal of Black Studies,* 34 (5), 653–671.

Gillborn, D. (2005) 'Education policy as an act of White supremacy: Whiteness, critical race theory and educational reform', *Journal of Education Policy,* 20 (4), 485–505.

Gillborn, D. and Mirza, H.S. (2000) *Educational Inequality: Mapping Race, Class and Gender: A Synthesis of Research Evidence,* London, OFSTED.

Garmezy, N. (1985) 'Stress resistant children: the search for protective factors', in Stephonson, J.E. (ed.), *Recent Research in Developmental Psychopathology,* New York, Pergamon Press, 213–233.

Haight, W.L. (2002) *African-American Children at Church: A Socio-cultural Perspective,* Cambridge, Cambridge University Press.

Hallam, S., Rhamie, J. and Shaw, J. (2006) *Primary Behaviour and Attendance Pilot Evaluation,* London, DFES.

Hick, P., Arshad, R., Mitchell, L., Watt, D. and Roberts, L. (2011) *Promoting Cohesion, Challenging Expectations: Education the Teachers of Tomorrow for Race Equality and Diversity in 21st Century Schools,* Manchester, Manchester Metropolitan University.

Hooks, B. (1989) *Talking Back: Thinking feminist. Thinking black,* Boston, South End Press.

Husbands, C. (2012) 'Government's decision on unqualified teachers "contradicts its own White Paper"', www.ioe.ac.uk/65693.html. [Accessed on 10 September 2012]

Khan, O. (2007) 'Policy, identity and community cohesion: how race equality fits', in Wetherell, M., Lafleche, M. and Berkeley, R. (eds), *Identity, Ethnic Diversity and Community Cohesion,* London, Sage, 40–58.

Kirby, L. and Fraser, M. (1997) 'Risk and resilience in childhood', in Fraser, M. (ed.), *Risk and Resilience in Childhood: An Ecological Perspective,* Washington, D.C., NASW Press, 10–33.

Ladson-Billings, G. (2004) 'Just what is critical race theory and what's it doing in a *nice* field like education?' In Ladson-Billings, G. and Gillborn, D. (eds), *The RoutledgeFalmer Reader in Multicultural Education,* London, Routledge, 49–68.

Lander, V. (2011) 'Race, culture and all that: an exploration of the perspectives of White secondary student teachers about race equality issues in their initial teacher education', *Race, Ethnicity and Education,* 14 (3), 351–364.

Law, I., Finney, S. and Swann, S.J. (2012) 'Searching for autonomy: young Black men, schooling and aspirations', *Race and Ethnicity and Education,* iFirst article, 1–22.

Leonardo, Z. (2004) 'The souls of White Folk: Critical pedagogy, Whiteness studies and globalisation discourse', in Ladson-Billings, G. and Gillborn, D. (eds), *The RoutledgeFalmer Reader in Multicultural Education,* London, Routledge, 117–136.

Maddern, K. (2011) 'Racism a "very real issue" in English schools, Times Education Supplement, Available at http://www.TES.co.uk/article.aspx?storycode=6099476. [Accessed on 20 July 2012]

Maylor, U., Smart, S., Abol Kuyok, K. and Ross, A. (2009) *The Black Child Achievement Programme Evaluation,* London, DCSF RR177.

Office for Economic Co-operation and Development (OECD) (2010) *Educating Teachers for Diversity: Meeting the Challenge,* Paris, Educational Research and Innovation, OECD Publishing.

Office for the Children's Commissioner (OCC) (2012) *They Never Give Up on You: Office of the Children's Commissioners School Exclusions Inquiry,* London, OCC.

Office for Standards in Education (OFSTED) (2002a) *Achievement of Black Pupils: Three Successful Primary Schools,* London, OFSTED.

Office for Standards in Education (OFSTED) (2002b) *Achievement of Black Pupils: Good Practice in Secondary Schools,* London, OFSTED.

Office for Standards in Education (OFSTED) (1999) *Raising the Attainment of Minority Ethnic Pupils,* London, OFSTED.

Office for Standards in Education (OFSTED) (2012) *The Framework for School Inspection,* London, OFSTED.

Office for Standards in Education (OFSTED) (2005) *Race Equality in Education: Good Practice in Schools and Local Authorities,* London, OFSTED.

Osler, A., Watling, R., Busher, H., Cole, T. and White, A. (2001) *Reasons for Exclusion from School,* London, DfEE.

Parekh, B. (2007) 'Reasoned identities: a committed relationship', in Wetherell, M., Lafleche, M. and Berkeley, R. (eds), *Identity, Ethnic Diversity and Community Cohesion,* London, Sage, 130–135.

Parsons, C., Godfrey, R., Annan, G., Cornwall, J., Dussart, M., Hepburn, S., Howlett, K. and Wennerstrom, V. (2005) *Minority Exclusions and the Race Relations (Amendment) Act 2000,* Nottingham, DfES Research Brief 616.

Parsons, C. (2009) 'Explaining sustained inequalities in ethnic minority school exclusions in England – passive racism in a neoliberal grip', *Oxford Review of Education,* 35 (2), 249–265.

Parsons, C. (2010) 'Achieving zero permanent exclusions from school, social justice and economy', *Forum,* 52 (3), 395–404.

Pianta, R. and Walsh, D. (1998) 'Applying the construct of resilience in schools: cautions from a developmental systems perspective', *School Psychology Review,* 27 (3), 407–417.

Ploner, J. (2011) 'Promoting students' resilience thinking in higher education and beyond. Paper presented at HEA Seminar Series Improving the degree attainment of black and minority ethnic students', Leeds Metropolitan University, 6 June 2011.

Pollard, D.S. (1989) 'Against the odds: a profile of academic achievers from the urban underclass', *Journal of Negro Education,* 58, 297–308.

Race on the Agenda (ROTA) (2011) *Coalition's Free Schools Project Spells Disaster for Many Already Facing Acute Educational Disadvantage.* Available at sw http://www.rota.org.uk/content/coalition%E2%80%99s-free-schools-project-spells-disaster-many-already-facing-acute-educational-dis-0. [Accessed on 13 August 2012]

Reay, D. (1995) 'Using habitus to look at 'race' and class in primary school classrooms', in Griffiths, M. and Troyna, B. (eds), *Anti-racism Culture and Social Justice in Education,* Stoke on Trent: Trentham Books, 115–132.

Reay, D. and Mirza, H.S. (2005) 'Doing parental involvement differently: Black women's participation as educators and mothers in Black supplementary schooling', in Crozier, G. and Reay, D. (eds) *Activating Participation: Parents and Teachers Working towards Partnership.* Stoke-on-Trent, UK: Trentham Books, pp. 137–154.

Reay, D., David, M. and Ball, S. (2005) *Degrees of Choice: Social Class, Race and Gender in Higher Education,* Stoke on Trent, Trentham Books.

Rees, P. and Bailey, K. (2003) 'Positive exceptions: learning from students who "beat the odds"'. *Educational and Child Psychology,* 20 (4), 41–59.

Rhamie, J. (2007) *Eagles who Soar: How Black Learners Find Paths to Success,* Stoke on Trent, Trentham Books.

Rhamie, J., Bhophal, K. and Bhatti, G. (2012) 'Stick to your own kind: Secondary pupils' experiences of ethnicity, identity and diversity in secondary schools', *British Journal of Educational Studies,* 60 (2), 171–191.

Rhamie, J. and Hallam, S. (2002) 'An investigation into African Caribbean Academic Success in the United Kingdom', *Race, Ethnicity and Education,* 5 (2), 151–170.

Richman, J.M. and Bowen, G.L. (1997) 'School failure: an ecological-interactional-development perspective', in Fraser, M.R. (ed.), *Risk and Resilience in Childhood: An Ecological Perspective,* Washington, D.C., NASW Press, 95–116.

Rutter, M. (1987) 'Psychosocial resilience and protective mechanisms', *American Journal of Orthopsychiatry,* 53 (3), 316–331.

Salovey, P. and Mayer, J.D. (1990) 'Emotional intelligence', *Imagination, Cognition and Personality,* 9, 185–211.

Sawyer, E. (2009) *Building Resilience in Families Under Stress*, London, National Children's Bureau.

Schoon, I. (2006) *Risk and Resilience: Adaptations in Changing Times*, Cambridge, Cambridge University Press.

Schoon, I. and Bartley, M. (2008) 'The role of human capability and resilience', *The Psychologist*, 21 (1), 24–27.

Show Racism the Red Card (2011) 'The barriers to challenging racism and promoting race equality in England's schools'. Available at http://www.srtrc.org/uploaded/SRTRC%20BARRIERS.pdf. [Accessed on 13 August 12]

Strand, S. (2008) *Minority Ethnic Pupils in the Longitudinal Study of Young People in England Extension Report in Performance in Public Examinations at Age 16*, Nottingham, DCSF.

Strand, S. (2012) 'Disproportionate identification of ethnic minority students with SEN: recent national data from England', paper presented at BERA conference, University of Manchester, 4–6 September.

Teacher Development Agency (TDA) (2007) *Qualified Standards for Qualified Teacher Status and Requirements for Initial Teacher Training*, London, TDA.

Teacher's TV (2009) *Racism Significant Issue in our Schools Say Teachers*. Available at http://www.teacherstv.co.uk/pressreleases/33771. [Accessed on 20 January 2012]

The Children's Act. Elizabeth II (2004) Chapter 31, London, The Stationery Office.

Tickly, L., Haynes, J., Callabero, C., Hill, J. and Gillborn, D. (2006) *Evaluation of Aiming High: African Caribbean Achievement Project*, Nottingham, DCFS.

Tomlinson, S. (2008) *Race and Education: Policy and Politics in Britain*, Milton Keynes, Open University Press.

Tomlinson, S. (2011) 'More radical reform (but don't mention race) gaps and silences in the government's discourse', *Race Equality Teaching*, 29 (2), 25–29.

Vassagar, J. and Shepherd, J. (2011) 'Free schools built in mainly middle-class and wealthy areas', *The Guardian*. Available at http://www.guardian.co.uk/education/2011/aug/31/free-schools-middle-class-areas. [Accessed on 17 January 2012]

Vincent, C. and Ball, S. (2013) 'The educational strategies of the Black middle classes', paper presented at University of Roehampton, London, 21 March 2013.

Vincent, C., Rollock, N., Ball, S. and Gillborn, D. (n.d.) 'The Educational Strategies of the Black Middle Classes: Project Summary'. Available at http://www.ioe.ac.uk/Study_Departments/CeCeps_The_Education_Strategies_Summary.pdf. [Accessed on 17 April 2013]

Wintour, P. (2012) 'Budget cuts will hit rich insist coalition'. *The Guardian*. Available at http://www.guardian.co.uk/uk/2012/mar/19/budget-rich-coalition-50p-tax-cut. [Accessed on 20 June 2012]

Youdell, D. (2003) 'Identity traps, or how Black students fail: the interactions between biographical, sub-cultural and learn identities', *British Journal of Sociology of Education*, 24 (1), 3–20.

Youdell, D. (2006) *Impossible Bodies, Impossible Selves: Exclusions and Student Subjectivities*, Dortrecht, Springer.

Younge, P. (1997) 'Lost Boys', in Martin, C. and Hayman, S. (eds), *Absent From School: Truancy and Exclusion*, London, ISTD Publications.

Index

multicultural education, 97, 162, 163–164, 166, 173–175
multiculturalism, 145, 149, 153–156, 158, 162, 168, 171, 210–211, 213, 220, 223–224
Multiverse, 98
Muslim communities, 45
Muslim families, 40
Muslim schools, 32, 35, 37, 38, 42
Muslim student, 106
Muslim, 32, 42, 45, 152, 157

No Child Left Behind (2001), 117
Noble, Greg, xvii, 11, 162, 167, 169
Northern Ireland, 178, 182, 185, 188

Oscar, Odena, xvii, 11, 178, 187, 188

Parekh, Bhikhu, 149, 204
Peat, Jo, xvii, 7, 82
performance theory, 25
Pilkington, Andrew, xviii, 12,193, 202, 204
Plowden Report (1967), 50
Preston, John, 1, 4, 112

Qualified Teacher Status (QTS), 36

race, viii, 1, 2, 64, 70–74, 79, 165, 222–223, 234
Race, Richard, xviii, 1, 13, 97, 141, 210, 211, 212, 214, 215, 216
racism, viii, 18, 57, 59, 223
racist, 23

recognition, xii, 153
Rhamie, Jasmine, xviii, 4, 14, 212, 230, 236, 238, 239, 242
Rollock, Nicola, 4
Roma, x, 52

Show Racism the Red Card, 234
structural racism, 101
Swann Report (1985), 50, 97, 212

teacher education, 94–95, 184
teacher educators, 72, 78–79, 104, 107
teachers in the United States, 68–69
teachers of colour, 73
teachers standards, 96–99, 100, 235
teaching and learning, 70, 86
traveller culture, 56–57
travellers and education, 49–51
travellers children, 50, 51, 55, 232
travellers, x, 47–48, 53, 57

United States education, 63, 101
university curriculum, 88

voluntary aided schools, 38
voluntary aided sector, 40
voluntary aided status, 32, 42

Walters, Sue, 2, 3
Watkins, Megan, xix, 11, 162, 167, 169, 213
whiteness, 93, 100–101, 104, 106–107, 193, 243

Printed and bound by CPI Group (UK) Ltd, Croydon, CR0 4YY